Knish

Knish

IN SEARCH OF THE
Jewish Soul Food

⊚ ⊚ ⊚ ⊚ ⊚ ⊚ ⊚ ⊚ ⊚ ⊚ LAURA SILVER

Brandeis University Press
Waltham, Massachusetts

Brandeis University Press
An imprint of University Press of New England
www.upne.com
© 2014 Laura Silver
All rights reserved
Manufactured in the United States of America
Designed and typeset in Skolar and Thirsty Rough
by Eric M. Brooks

University Press of New England is a member of the
Green Press Initiative. The paper used in this book meets
their minimum requirement for recycled paper.

The author gratefully acknowledges permission to reproduce
the following: Five lines from "In the City of Slaughter" from
Selected Poems by C. N. Bialik, translated by David Aberbach.
Translation copyright © 2004 by David Aberbach. Published
in 2004 by the Overlook Press, Peter Mayer Publishers, Inc.,
www.overlookpress.com. All rights reserved.

Library of Congress Cataloging-in-Publication Data
Silver, Laura.
Knish: in search of the Jewish soul food / Laura Silver.
    pages   cm. — (HBI series on Jewish women)
Includes bibliographical references and index.
ISBN 978-1-61168-312-7 (cloth : alk. paper) —
ISBN 978-1-61168-545-9 (ebook)
1. Jewish cooking — History. 2. Jews — Food — History. I. Title.
TX724.S539   2014
641.5'676 — dc23   2013040545

5 4 3 2

To my parents

BARBARA & MICHAEL SILVER

with love

Who will last? And what? The wind will stay,

And the blind man's blindness when he's gone away,

And a thread of foam—a sign of the sea—

And a bit of cloud snarled in a tree.

⊛ "Ver Vet Blaybn?" from *Poems from a Diary* (1974),
   by Abraham Sutzkever
   Courtesy of Rina Sutzkever Kalderon

The receding world of our ancestors continues to shine

because we are all from there.

⊛ Knyszyn town historian Henryk Stasiewicz

Who doesn't love a knish?

⊛ Joan Rivers

Contents

xi   Preface

1   *Au Revoir,* Mrs. Stahl's
     Brighton Beach to the Lower East Side

73   In Search of the First Knish
     From the Holy Land to the Old Country

137   Mrs. Goldberg to Gangsta Rap
     The Knish in Culture

165   A Brief History of Competitive Knish Eating

175   The Fine Art of Knish Making

209   Epilogue

223   Recipe: Mrs. Stahl's Potato Knishes

225   Where to Get a Good Knish

227   Acknowledgments

235   Notes

253   Selected Bibliography

269   Illustration Credits

271   Index

Preface

The clouds came at me.

What are you doing here? What took you so long? Where's everyone else?

Not cumulus, not nimbus, and not cumulonimbus, those clouds hovered, strange but familiar. They sat low in the sky, stalwart, distant, and firm. I, too, had questions, but no chance to ask.

Downtown Knyszyn occurs at the intersection of Tykocka and Szkolna streets, named for the town of Tykocin, with its square, empty brick synagogue cum museum, and for the Jewish school that once stood down the block. Soon after the Jewish community of Knyszyn took root in 1705, there came to be a synagogue at that crossroads.[1]

Wrapped in countryside, Knyszyn was once the seat of Polish kings. Zygmunt August (in English, Sigismund II Augustus), known for saying "I am not the king of your conscience," came to Knyszyn for relaxation and game hunting, and in 1572, died there. The king (a statue of him stands near Town Hall) spent a total of five hundred days in Knyszyn.[2]

I had one. And my own hunt: a quest for the origins of the knish.

Knish

Au Revoir, Mrs. Stahl's

Brighton Beach to the Lower East Side

The knish situation in Brooklyn is not what it once was. I can say that because I'm third-generation Brooklyn, once removed. Queens, where I was born, had knishes, too, tons of them. I took them for granted, then they were gone.

More than latkes, matzoh, or the apple-and-walnut charoset that crowned the seder plate, knishes were my family's religion. For knishes, we went on pilgrimages. For knishes, we traversed

Long Island, top to bottom, from northern Queens to southern Brooklyn. For knishes, we drove Northern Boulevard to the Grand Central, past LaGuardia to the BQE, through to the Prospect Expressway, which deposited us on Ocean Parkway amid old trees and religious Jews, a straight shot to Mrs. Stahl's.

A knish is a pillow of filling tucked into a skin of dough. The ones at Mrs. Stahl's were baked round mounds, each plump with a stuffing, savory or sweet. Each piece — the size of a fist or just bigger — revealed a hint of filling on the top, a bald spot, as if for a yarmulke. But the real secret to the construction of a Mrs. Stahl's knish remained hidden: Yet if you cut the knish in half, the cross-section revealed a membrane of dough that split the innards into chambers, like those of the human heart.

We harbored them in our freezer. We ushered them to the toaster oven and moved magazines and newspapers to welcome them to the Saturday afternoon table. In the 1980s, my native Flushing, Queens, was a haven for grandmother- and grandfather-types who had survived pogroms or the Holocaust. Like them, we frequented bakeries and delis of the Jewish persuasion. But to visit our own forebears, we had to go elsewhere.

Brooklyn was the Old Country, where kids once played in the street, flicked nickels onto corner-store counters, and maintained an allegiance to "the block." To hear my father, a native of Flatbush, tell it, in those days five cents could get you a hollow pink rubber ball called a Spaldeen — or a knish thick with liver.

When there was traffic, we abandoned the highway in favor of so-called shortcuts. We locked every door, turned up the jazz on

the car radio, and zigzagged through hollowed-out neighborhoods that made his old neighborhood look luxurious.

After decades in a dark apartment on Rugby Road, my grandmother landed a spot in senior housing, left Flatbush, and moved to Brighton Beach. As a young woman she'd had a bungalow there, but this was better. Her place overlooked the ocean and sunsets and provided incredible proximity to Mrs. Stahl's. The mythic knish maker and Gramma Fritzie were nearly synonymous. After college, I moved to Brooklyn, five miles from both of them. Every other week I delivered: a piping-hot kasha and a half-dozen frozens. Anyone who entered apartment 12A — visitors, and, eventually, home health aides — was offered a knish, split, heated, and served with extra grainy mustard, homemade by my dad.

The day she died, we didn't eat knishes — or anything. It was the tenth of Tishrei in the year 5758 on the Hebrew calendar, in other words, October 11, 1997, which coincided with Yom Kippur, the Day of Atonement and fasting. Her body was still in the bedroom. As per New York City protocol, a cop came to the house.

"Yes, of course I was here at the time of death," I lied, to appease the policeman — and myself — and avoid further inquiry. It never occurred to me that my grandmother could die without me. Angie, the home health aide, had summoned us in the morning. But since — *wink, wink* — a family member had been on the premises, there was no need to invite further investigation.

We divvied up adult diapers, sorted books, and used newspaper to cradle dishes. I'd like to say knishes were stashed in her freezer, but the truth is, I can't remember.

After that, I swore off the neighborhood.

On the first anniversary of my grandmother's death, we drove east, an hour to the cemetery, for the unveiling. This custom, prominent even among the nonobservant, concludes a year of mourning. We draped a piece of muslin on the gravestone, taped it in place, and ripped it off in one fell swoop. From a page that the rabbi sent, we recited *El Maleh Rachamim,* a prayer for the departed whose title addresses the "exalted compassionate Almighty." Uncle Mitch, who, technically, is not my uncle, chanted the prayer in Hebrew, which made it legitimate.

O, God, full of compassion, Thou who dwellest on high,
grant perfect rest beneath the shelter of Thy divine presence
among the holy and pure who shine bright as the firmament
to the soul of our beloved Fritzie Silver who has gone to her
eternal home.

If my grandmother's soul had indeed journeyed to its eternal resting place, I was fairly certain it was not the manicured lawns of Beth Israel Cemetery in Farmingdale, Long Island. Her spirit remained embedded in the boardwalk at Brighton with its creaky slats, cloaked Russians, and diehard aficionados of the knish. Waves hummed with nothingness; the sky languished and the whine of seagulls turned incessant. No savory pastry could console me. I kept my distance.

Two years after my grandmother's death, I felt the pull of Mrs. Stahl's. October 5760 came thick with wistfulness, downed leaves, and heaving winds. The High Holidays smudged the landscape with reminders to take stock, attempt atonement, and make friends with mortality. The Days of Awe, as they are also called, nudged me toward the beach. The sky reigned blue upon blue.

Beneath the elevated train at Coney Island and Brighton Beach avenues, the windows of Mrs. Stahl's remained opaque with steam. Like my grandmother in her last months, the shop showed evidence of decline. The counter that once dispensed cherry lime rickeys had morphed into a steam table bogged down with stews and purées. The place blanketed itself in a meat smell. Behind the counter, a cone of lamb lurked on a vertical pole. I wanted a hug. In the far corner, a woman with short dark hair attended to customers and knishes. Beige cap, thick glasses, and matter-of-fact manner, she was the only version of Mrs. Stahl I had ever known. I recognized her, of course, and hoped she would welcome me back, ask after my family, or remember my grandmother. (She was sustained on Mrs. Stahl's but rarely crossed its threshold.) The woman behind the counter — I never knew her name — didn't realize she had become a stand-in, first for Mrs. Stahl and then for my grandmother, who was similar in height and build. Gramma was not a baker or a maker of knishes, but she was a discerning connoisseur who knew better than to place a knish in a microwave.

The Incarnation of Mrs. Stahl shuffled behind the counter. She plucked knishes from the freezer, stationed them in the warming drawer, and bagged them for orders. She rang them up, took cash, and made change, all without small talk. I stood hollow and conspicuous, like a bright yellow squirt bottle with one last dollop of mustard lodged in its entrails. I had anticipated a momentous return to Mrs. Stahl's, but on that visit I lingered in anonymity. I was just another customer. And, as I discovered after I placed my order, a customer who had forgotten her wallet.

Probably it was just as well that the Incarnation of Mrs. Stahl did not remember me. She prepared my order — grabbed it, bagged it, and put a lid on the tea. I left to scrounge for change in the car. The ancient Volvo sunned itself, nose-in, in a parking spot

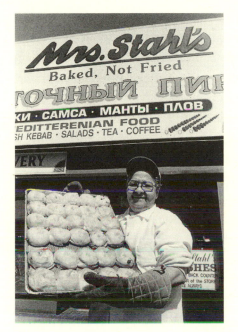

alongside the former site of the Brighton Beach Baths (where, as a kid, my dad had a locker). By then, the urban country club of the middle class was on the verge of its own transition: condos. I would never look down on the tidy brick-balconied buildings from my grandmother's apartment, and I was glad she wouldn't either.

The glove compartment disgorged three dollars in quarters, just enough, in 1999, for one kasha knish and one tea with milk.

Judaism is big on intuition passed down through the ages. It's stuffed with guidelines and injunctions and rules, relayed, at least originally, in Hebrew and Aramaic. I knew a few from Hebrew school — honor your parents, keep the Sabbath, don't eat McDonald's — but found them cryptic and tricky. A knish required no interpretation or unfurling. I could embrace it with hands, lips, fingers, and though I never noticed, heart. I understood its age-old secrets and sacred traditions. In the presence of a knish, all that was awkward dissipated.

The Torah, holy book of the Jews, is stored in a holy ark — not like the boat Noah used to rescue animals, but more like an armoire.[1] On holidays and the Sabbath, the ark is opened, the Torah is cradled and paraded through synagogue aisles. We kiss it. On Yom Kippur, when the doors of the divine armoire are opened, it is said that human prayers get a straight shot to the Almighty. Twice I have paid dues to a synagogue, but never really felt I belonged. Once, in the basement room of a place that welcomed nonmembers for free on the High Holidays, I lined up to pray before the ark. The anticipation held holiness and awe, but when I came breast-to-breast with the Torah, I stood clueless and mute.

In front of the open drawer of a knish warmer, however, I knew exactly how to proceed:

"One kasha, please. Hot."

My grandmother, who had been to synagogue as a young woman, encouraged me to drop in now and then, mostly for the social aspects. With the exception of a Hebrew naming (my mother's mother, Nana, had whisked me to her rabbi, down the block, in the Bronx) and a bat mitzvah (which I initiated), I grew up on the outskirts of Jewish life. I was largely unschooled, but curious enough to migrate to *shul* when it suited me. The night my grandmother died, I stood five miles from her bedside, in synagogue, fist to chest in confession, with a collective of strangers.[2]

Forgive us for we have (to summarize):
Transgressed
Robbed
Slandered
Scoffed
Rebelled
Provoked
Oppressed others
Been obstinate

Two years later, I had not forgiven my grandmother for:

Dying
Not waiting for me to arrive
Not telling me beforehand

And I had not forgiven myself for:

Not being there.

But when the Incarnation of Mrs. Stahl pulled one kasha from the warming drawer, the smell enveloped me. Nose-to-nose with the inner knish sanctum, I exhaled, as if sitting on the Jennifer Convertibles sofa bed at my grandma's house. I exhaled and drew comfort from the list of knishes suspended from the ceiling.

Kasha

Potato

Mushroom

Spinach

Cheese

Cherry Cheese

Blueberry Cheese

Vegetable

We — my grandmother, my father, my mother, all of us — preferred kasha. It means buckwheat groats, but there was no need to translate. Kasha was simply kasha: beige, fluffy, earth-smelling kernels destined to fill knishes, plates, and stomachs. We deigned to nosh other savory flavors: potato (our collective second choice) and things mixed with potato. Sweet cheese knishes sat flatter and rectangular, easy to mistake for wide-load blintzes plumped with fruit fillings — strawberry, blueberry, or cherry — that mingled with farmer cheese.

⊛ ⊛ ⊛ *My knish grandmother was born* Freyda Rifke Redalje in Riga (then Russia, now Latvia) and arrived at Ellis Island in 1906 with her mother and three brothers. They joined their father and lived in the cold-water flats of Brooklyn neighborhoods where Yiddish swaddled streets and bathrooms stayed in the hall. When her mother, Frume (the name means "religious one"), died, my grandmother quit school to care for her father.

When he died, my grandmother, at eighteen, went to work at Macy's, Herald Square. She changed her name to Fritzie Reidell and spritzed her customers with perfume, wordplay, and charm. The other spritzers became her friends and, by association, family. I learned to allocate a dedicated honorific to each one: Aunt Sallye, Aunt Ottlie, and Aunt Anne. Aunt Rose and Aunt Syd were sisters who shared an apartment off Avenue M, which must have stood for matzoh, because along with furniture of the deceased, they stockpiled boxes of the stuff. At Passover and in every season, they offered it to my grandmother.

Freyda Rifke Redalje (front), the author's grandmother, arrived in New York in 1906.

Fritzie spoke fluent English and waxed adamant about grammar, but never attempted citizenship. As a young woman, she saved her earnings and rented a one-room bungalow on Bay Tenth Street, ten minutes from the expanse of sand, insistent breezes, and wide skies of Brighton. Each morning she flitted to the beach for calisthenics with her friends.

When I knew them, they were older women laden with stories and stiffened by time, retired ladies who stuffed bills beneath seat cushions, carried rain hats, and upholstered their couches in stick-to-your-thighs plastic slipcovers. But back when they were nimble, when Fritzie and her Macy's sisters welcomed the tide with waist-bends and toe-touches, Mrs. Stahl baked knishes in her kitchen and sold them on the beach. Perhaps the women crossed paths.

Sixty years after that, when my grandmother got a spot at senior housing at JASA (the Jewish Association for Services to the Aged) in Brighton, she stationed herself at the window, in view of sky and sea. Fritzie Silver had been widowed at least as long as she had been married. In apartment 12A, she regaled me (the only grandchild) with an assortment of treats: lemon candies (sugar-free), popcorn from the air popper, and, our fallback, a kasha knish (half each), hot from the toaster oven. We stared at the ocean, sat on the couch, and watched game shows.

Two years after she died, I strolled the boardwalk, accompanied by a straight-out-of-the-oven, mustard-smeared knish (kasha), and stationed myself in view of the window where my grandmother used to sit. I was convinced she abided there and could look down on me. I consumed the knish, sat on a jetty, took in the sunset, and snuck away under the cover of dusk.

I would like to say I sensed her in the puddle of a receding wave, caught her laugh in a glint on the horizon, that she followed me home, or that I summoned her in a dream. But all that remained was the knish. Still, I believed solo pilgrimages of this sort could help manifest my grandmother. Every other week, I biked to the beach, grabbed a knish, nodded at her window, and communed with the waves.

They never had much to say.

Just before Thanksgiving, my knish supply had dwindled. That was 2005, a Saturday. The weather shone clear and crisp; I took Ocean Parkway to Mrs. Stahl's. Families strolled the boulevard in their finery; I pedaled in ripped jeans. At Brighton, women with stand-up shopping carts bargained in Russian. "No Parking" signs tilted slightly. I listened for Russian expressions I could decipher: *Da. Nyet. Pajalsta. Priviet. Khorosho.* Then I noticed: Mrs. Stahl's storefront was adorned in plastic flags — a grand opening.

Opening, *schmopening.*

This was a closing of the highest order. After seventy years beneath the elevated subway, Mrs. Stahl's knish shop had *become* a Subway.

A long breath came out of me. I whimpered and clung to the stalk of a parking meter. Overhead, the Q train lurched and groaned; ditto my stomach. The Subway was alive with customers and counter girls who converted sandwiches into "meals" with the simple addition of chips and a soft drink.

I had to act quickly. I wanted to tear my sweatshirt in grief, sit shiva, and notify the survivors.[3] I needed to mourn with the greater knish community, but had no idea how to identify them. How would I ever find the next of kin of the knish?

⬤ ⬤ ⬤ **When Gramma and I would sit** overlooking the ocean, she would point at the horizon and bellow, "To Riga!" None of the other terrace sitters noticed (or if they did, they didn't let on), but nonetheless her gesticulation embarrassed me. Why call attention to such a foreign place? And why in public? We had no family in Riga, no link to the language or culture or locale. Even when Latvia became a country of its own — "Your grandmother is finally from someplace," my aunt boasted — but no one invited any of us to apply for citizenship or come for a visit.

Riga represented the disappeared, the distant, and the undecipherable. When I was a tour guide at the United Nations, one of my colleagues was a perky young person from there. Žaneta had cropped platinum hair, a big smile, and a leather wallet embossed with the skyline of her hometown. I wanted it to resonate, but no.

Two generations back, I was from rubble and undoneness: Riga on my father's side and Bialystok, Poland, on my mother's — places that remained dead to us. Brooklyn and the Bronx had become makeshift homelands. The knish served as flag, emblem, flower, and bird. And now it, too, was endangered.

Outside Subway store number 37526, I slouched. Gramma was gone, Riga remained elusive, and my parents were in Queens, unobsessed with family history. Nonetheless, I needed answers. I had a few ideas about where to start my search for Mrs. Stahl's: the Internet, the Better Business Bureau, Community Board 13. But before any of that, I needed to combat the hollowness. Knishes were out of the question. I trolled the boule-

The former site of Mrs. Stahl's, as it appeared in late 2005.

vard in search of something edible, Jewish, and ceremonial. In the homes of Jewish mourners, it is customary to encounter foods that are round, to remind the bereaved — and all of us — of the circle of life, even if one would rather torque that circle of a food into an infinity sign.

Brighton Bazaar, a Russian grocery, displayed savory turnovers plump with cabbage, potatoes, and sweet cheese, each flavor identified primarily in Cyrillic. They were triangular, rectangular, and oblong.

All of these were cousins to the knish. None a knish.

Gone South

After the demise of Mrs. Stahl's, silence. No fruit basket or condolence card adorned the scene, no photograph or memento stuck itself into the shop's pull-down gate. No police officer cordoned off the area and no one recited kaddish.[4] But as with human beings, the loss rippled outward, troubled the tops of puddles, and put dings in the minds of women and men who did not always know what had hit them.

I called the community board. The community board directed me to Pat Singer, founder of the Brighton Beach Neighborhood Association, and also in mourning. Singer had long-standing ties to the area and knew the palates of the people around her were calibrated to flavors that predated glasnost. Newcomers to Brighton were Jews, too, but different.

"The Russians don't understand that this is our soul food," said Singer, about the knish. "It used to be shipped all over the country."[5] Nostalgia swaddled the gutters of Brooklyn. It trickled throughout the tristate area and plagued suburban side streets where the daughters and sons of Kings County had settled. Mrs. Stahl's knishes had entered the canon of the bygone. The absence of knishes echoed the absence of the Dodgers; it made for a black hole within a void, within the pit of a person's stomach. Even for those who saw it coming, the loss of Mrs. Stahl's was unthinkable. (So many unthinkables have graced Jewish history, you'd think one might learn to adjust.)

Pat Singer had to be diplomatic. It was her job to support business on the Avenue — all business — including the new Subway sandwich store. But Singer's heart was with the knish, and thus decimated.

From the 1920s to the 1950s and even after that, Brighton Beach and Coney Island were thick with knishes. Delis sold them. Corner shops set them on counters. Each knish concern cultivated its own clientele. Devotees of one knish place hardly acknowledged devotees of another. So deeply engraved were allegiances that it would be three decades before I understood Brooklyn had birthed and boasted knish makers who were not Mrs. Stahl.

It is worth noting that competing knish dynasties that took root along the Brooklyn shore used titles that ranged from the patronymic to the gender neutral. Mrs. Stahl's name was *heimish*, female, and just formal enough; through four decades of male ownership, the moniker remained the same.

"They had it combined with a pizza parlor," said Singer, about the shop.

Multicultural connections: Mrs. Stahl's in 2004.

"I didn't think it was the same consistency," said Singer, about the knish innards.

"When it became the Middle Eastern pizza thing, that was the beginning of the end," said Singer, about mortality.

I had to admit to the obvious signs of the shop's demise — and to my own denial.

Pat Singer spent her childhood summers in Brooklyn, beach-combing, bobbing in low tide, and downing "two-cents plain" (seltzer). She knew from the traditions of Brooklyn, which is to say, she had a handle on them, not just intellectually but viscer-ally. "To know from" is Yiddish-inflected New Yorkese that means to have a firsthand grasp on something that not everyone can know, because, simply stated, they weren't there. The term con-notes a familiarity in the bones and of the soil, even if one is sur-rounded only by pavement. It means to be steeped in, but not on purpose and not through study. It refers to experience acquired by osmosis, default, or both. It's not something that can be measured on a test; the wisdom, like the phrase itself, is tethered to time and place.

All this is to say: either you know Mrs. Stahl's or you don't. If you don't, don't worry. You can be brought up to speed. It won't be exactly the same, but you can get close. Or if you'd prefer, imagine a food you know intimately, up close, and over time.

Pat Singer knew from knishes the way she knew from egg creams, ring-a-levio, and potsy.[6] Her Brooklyn was the Brooklyn of her youth, which was nothing without Mrs. Stahl's. Though she knew from these knishes, Singer had neither dominion nor authority over them. She had no access to the recipe, nor to the business records. She was neither heir presumptive nor heir apparent, but she was there at the crossroads, in the epicenter of the void.

"This is our Ebbets Field," said Singer, who had lived through the decampment of the Dodgers and hoped to prevent another stain on the borough's psyche. She had even tried to broker an adoption with a local appetizing store run "by Russians," which meant the Russian Jewish population of Brighton, who could probably get by in Yiddish, but preferred their native tongue and who appreciated stuffed pastries, but harbored no affinity for the knish. The way Singer saw it, the stuffed pastry she grew up with could coexist with pierogi and blini and blintzes. She had even appealed to a local grocery store–café.

"M&I didn't want it."

She had appealed to Brooklyn's highest elected official.

"The borough president couldn't save it."[7]

Pat Singer did not give up easily.

"I've been trying to lobby for someone to bring it back," she said.

Mrs. Stahl's had stood on the corner of Brighton Beach and Coney Island avenues longer than Pat Singer had been alive. By dint of its existence it became family. Singer didn't have to explain. I knew. It was more than the food and the outdated décor. It was the waft of onions, cooked, and the Formica counter, orange, that lined the shop and led to the front windows, opaque from steam. It was a place to sit. Or not.

The People of the Mrs. Stahl's Knish had moved on. They had lawns, children, pets, aging parents, all of which required mowing or driving somewhere or other. The People of the Knish and their descendants had decamped to enclaves sans sidewalks; for ethnic cuisine, they had taken to dim sum, sushi, and tacos stuffed with fish.

Singer saw "a great deal of potential" in Mrs. Stahl's. The mere mention could make a person salivate. But when we spoke, the knish itself needed salvation. No denizen complained, and no one had come to inquire about a revival. In the Hebrew tradition, a tenet states that when all Jews are united in the same act of observance at the same time, this remarkable confluence will usher in the Messiah.[8]

Pat Singer did not suggest that all Jews join in a sacred ritual.

She didn't need many people, not even the traditional quorum of ten. She was in search of a singular soul who would shoulder the mantle of tradition, a knish savior. Pat Singer was talking to me on the phone, but her clarion call could have resonated from a deserted lifeguard stand on the wintry, wind-torn shores of Brighton Beach.

"Is there anybody out there who loves Brooklyn?"

Outlines of Kings County graced bibs, tote bags, and the façades of new boutiques. Families migrated from Manhattan, and real estate prices were on the rise. There were many people who loved Brooklyn, in many ways. But the borough's name, embroidered on a hooded sweatshirt, bore little resemblance to Pat Singer's *amour de* Kings County, which rooted itself in history and paid homage to a rough-and-tumble humble place where people spoke to their neighbors.

Singer gave me the name of the last-known owner of Mrs. Stahl's.

⊛ ⊛ ⊛ *Les Green was born in Brooklyn* and had since moved north of the city, to Rockland County. He knew from the knish and he knew from Mrs. Stahl's. "I was a patron there for years," he said in a phone conversation in 2005, after the shop had closed. "I thought it would be a good thing to be involved in."[9]

Green bought Mrs. Stahl's in 1985 from the Weingast brothers, Morris and Sam, who'd bought the store in the early 1960s from the original family. The Weingast brothers kept Mrs. Stahl's name in white sweeping script on the shop's marquee and mentioned themselves, in a smaller, modest typeface below it.

COCKTAIL KNISHES OUR SPECIALTY

Mrs. Stahl's Delicious Knishes

SAM MOR KNISH CORP.
WEINGAST BROS.

1001 Brighton Beach Av
Brooklyn, N. Y. 11235
NI 8-0210

Les Green never emblazoned his name anywhere, but the business bore the mark of his heart. In the 1980s, knishes remained a hands-on, handmade operation. "If you walked straight back on the right," said Green, "the women actually constructed each knish." When Green ran Mrs. Stahl's, the worker women no longer spoke Yiddish. But, whatever the language, they had their work cut out for them.

"Do you know what we did to a potato before we gave it to someone?" Green asked, then answered, "We cooked it, mashed it, mixed it."

And that was just the insides. "It's labor intensive," continued Green. "Dough has to be made and rolled, and rolled out."

By 2005, handmade was hardly the standard. Green had another knife to grind, too. "Most of the people, a good portion who are making knishes today" — I expected tales of bribery, collusion, and racketeering — "are using instant potatoes."

Green felt slighted. "They lump me in with the square fried crap," he said, of the flatter four-sided knish that got its start a few years before the advent of Mrs. Stahl's, a mile west, in Coney Island.

"Today you're better off to make horseshit and make a lot of money," ranted Green, who weaned himself from knishes when he left the business. "That's what people want: cheap. They don't care."

Plus, there was another factor at play: demographics.

"The Russian people didn't buy knishes," said Green. At first it didn't dawn on him. His shop was busy, but not with the growing population of Russian-speakers who inhabited Brighton Beach. The neighborhood buzzed with sounds of the Cyrillic alphabet, but those syllables rarely resonated inside his shop.

Veteran customers griped about the prices. In the course of twenty years, the costs of gasoline and rent and housing had all gone up. But old-time knish customers were mired in old-time prices. "People who love the knish, they want it, they want to eat it, but they don't want to pay for it," argued Green. "The knish should be going for three dollars, but wholesale, you have to sell it for a reduced price. In nineteen thirty-five, knishes went for a nickel; corned beef sandwiches, ten cents," remembered Green. "Now, corned beef is eight dollars and a knish is a dollar and a half."

There were other considerations: a difficult landlord, shady business partners, handshakes on deals that soured and stank. But a business like the knish, with a name like Mrs. Stahl's, surely it had the power to rebound.

If there had been only an influx of a new population but no price ceiling set by nostalgia, he might have made do. If there had been only a price ceiling set by nostalgia but not the flight of the regulars to the suburbs, he might have made do. But there was also the landlord and the expense and the time needed to make a hand-made product from scratch. And even without any of those things,

Green lacked the secret ingredient that had sustained Mrs. Stahl's from the start: family in the business.

"Face it," he said. "Not a lot of young Jewish people are looking to work behind the counter of a knish store."

He didn't want that for his own daughters. And they didn't want that for themselves. The regular customers had relocated to the suburbs. They didn't forget Mrs. Stahl's, but they certainly didn't visit as often as Green would have liked.

"People would come in once every two years for a dozen knishes," said Green. They would drive back to their suburban

The Weingast brothers (Morris is on the left, in white) ran Mrs. Stahl's from the early 1960s through the mid-1980s.

Printed in a Brooklyn paper during the Weingast era, this ad touts the shop's "Romantic Candlelight Atmosphere" and its specialty, "COCKTAIL KNISHES FOR YOUR 'SIMCHAS,'" or celebratory occasions.

homes, eat their knishes, and congratulate themselves for having gotten out of the old neighborhood when they did.

Meanwhile, at the intersection of avenues named for Coney Island and Brighton Beach, the knish, agent of nostalgia par excellence, withered. The people it had sustained forsook it in its time of need. And they complained.

"Now that we're not there, all of a sudden everyone is, 'What happened? Where are you?'" said Green. He remembered the accolades. "People said, 'the best this, that, the other.'"

He implicated the clientele. "Where were you when we were trying to make a living?"

He implicated himself. "Part of the problem is, it would have taken a tremendous amount of money and advertising.

Believe me, I was heartsick toward the end, trying to stay around and keep it going." Like his customers, Green had succumbed to nostalgia. "That's what sucked me in there for a lot longer. I would've never been doing it for as long as I was."

After the Brighton Beach store shut its doors, Green swore off knishes. "I can't find anything that's as good as I used to have," he said. "If you're used to driving a Rolls-Royce, it's kind of hard to get into a Ford."

⦾ ⦾ ⦾ *In 2005, he entrusted his legacy* to a pasta maker in Jersey.

"I basically bought the business after I learned how long the name and the reputation had been around," said Mike Conte, who ran Conte's Pasta, in Vineland, two hours south of Brighton Beach. "What I liked about it is that Les owned it for nineteen years," said Conte.[10]

"I don't know if he really understands what he has," said Les Green about Conte.

When Conte took on the knish, he brought in "the girls that worked in the back" of Green's operation to train his staff on the intricacies of knish assembly. Together, they practiced.

"Being that we're in the dough business, it wasn't very hard for us to pick up what they were doing," said Conte, who was committed to fresh ingredients and to profit. Conte made plans to integrate Mrs. Stahl's knish with his gnocchi, tortellini, and cavatelli. He made his kitchen kosher. Then and only then did the knishes return to the market. "Everyone was happy to hear that Mrs. Stahl's was still available," said Conte. "We were able to regain ninety percent of the customers."

Conte sold the knishes to distributors. Distributors delivered

the knishes to New Jersey, Long Island, and Manhattan. In delis and bagel stores, the knish continued to lie with the bagel and the lox, but the Brooklyn knish shop had become a thing of the past. Sure, you could get a knish at a dedicated shop within the confines of New York City — at Yonah Schimmel's on Manhattan's Lower East Side or at Knish Nosh on Queens Boulevard — just not near the ocean and not beneath an elevated subway line.

Mike Conte was born, in Abruzzi, Italy, "into food service." He came to the United States as a boy and grew up outside Boston. In 1978, his parents opened a pizza shop. It grew to a mega-pizzeria that seated five hundred, and after that, a pasta company that churned out ravioli by the thousands. Conte knew from big batches and he knew from big knishes. Buckwheat, as in kasha, is not widespread in Italian cooking, but similarities in the immigration patterns of Eastern European Jews and Italians meant that the two groups knew each other's foods. But what was the Italian equivalent of a knish? I was thinking of form. Conte went for function.

"Back in the Depression, in the war, this kind of food was the only thing available. . . . The Italians made polenta. All you need is corn and water; for the potato knish, all you need is potatoes and flour. I think every generation probably has some kind of food they came up with, with whatever was available."

Necessity may have birthed the knish, but Conte was the guardian of a particular lineage. He sent out small plastic signs to be displayed in shop windows and smaller placards for deli cases:

MRS. STAHL'S SOLD HERE

"When they see the little yellow tags," he said about end customers, "they know it's a good product."

The structure of his sentence reminded me of my relatives and their collective syntax. Perhaps Conte's questions came out as statements, too: *You like the knish(?). You want more(?).* Later it occurred to me, Jewish-infused New Yorkese and Italian-infused New Yorkese, they're not that different.

Gnocchi and "spaghetti with plain old sauce" were Conte's favorite foods, but he conceded that the knish, too, had its merits.

"I'll tell you," said Conte, "one of these babies will really fill you up."

The Self-Imposed Exile of the Coney Island Knish

Mrs. Stahl's was not the only Brooklyn knish to bow to the economic realities of the twenty-first century. In 2005, the "original Coney Island Knish," Gabila's, went east, to Long Island. On November 22, 2005, the *New York Post* proclaimed a turning point in New York, Jewish, and global culinary history with four syllables: "Knish Plant Bites Dust."[11]

Exile, that backbone of Jewish life, had riddled the spine of the knish and nicked holes in landscapes visible and internal.

Mrs. Stahl's: gone.

Gabila's: gone.

But "the square fried crap" (Les Green's term) would not be in traction for long. It had a forwarding address: Copiague, Long Island. Gabila's, the global leader in knish sales, was run by a grandson of the founder. Elliott Gabay (named for his grandfather, Elias) had been working in the business "forever and ever and ever."[12] He said finances motivated the move. Changing demographics had changed the business. Gabila's land had become more valuable than its plant. Luckily, the operation and its owners knew from relocating.

Gabay's paternal grandparents arrived in New York in 1919 from a small city called Niš (pronounced Nish), then Yugoslavia, now Serbia. His grandfather, Elias, was a custom shoemaker who sought work in the footwear factories of New York. When that didn't work out, Elias and his wife, Bella, went into restaurants. They opened up a basement eatery on Forsyth Street on the Lower East Side. Mrs. Gabay supervised the rolling pin and the stove. As the *New York Times* described, "She made dough so thin — without holes — that when you blew on it, it flew away." But the paper-thin dough had not always been destined for knishes. "A customer asked [Bella Gabay] if she could make blintzes with potatoes inside instead of cheese, and she began producing knishes. Then her husband took the goods out on a pushcart and sold them up and down Delancey Street."[13]

Delancey Street led to the Williamsburg Bridge, which straddled the East River and entered Brooklyn, foreign territory to Elias Gabay until he received an order from a restaurant on Roebling Street. In 1928, Elias took his business and his family east, to Brooklyn.

Once there, he set his sights on citizenship. His first attempt at becoming an official American was denied for "lack of knowledge."[14] On the second go-round, he played the royalty card. "I have five children," he told the judge, "and I'm a king already. I'll make a good citizen."[15] And thus, in 1926, Elia (né Elias) Gabay, ruler of his own burgeoning knish kingdom, renounced and abjured all allegiance and fidelity to every foreign prince, potentate, state, and sovereignty, and particularly to the "Kingdom of the Serbs, Croats & Slovenes."[16]

Dapper and debonair, Gabay could cut up a dance floor as quickly as he could concoct a knish. Business was good. In 1932, he brought on machinery to wash, peel, sort, steam, and mash potatoes. "We never got a patent," explained Gabay's business partner, "because if we got a patent we'd have to disclose."[17]

Better to keep the trade secrets under wraps. What the business partner *could* share was the number of employees (more than fifty in 1971), the automatic nature of "everything," and a commitment that rivaled that of postal workers: "When it rains, we go on working, and when it snows, we stay at the machines. If the employees can't get to work, we go out and get them. Nothing keeps knishes from the appointed place."[18]

Elliott Gabay, the grandson, learned the routine as a young man. He remembered the stories of back-to-back beachgoers who swarmed Coney Island.

> During the summertime in the early years, they used to have ten times the population. It was a place to go. On the boardwalk there were a lot of frankfurter stands. We were just a natural food item to go with the immigration that used to be down there. We used to truck the knishes down to Coney, Brighton, Manhattan Beach. Drivers would be out at six o'clock in the morning. Maybe two or three trucks. They'd sleep in the truck and let the cool air in. There'd be fresh knishes. At that time they didn't even have to put them into the oven. Refrigeration in 1920? What do you think there was? It was a different era. It was hard times.[19]

Eighty-five years later, times were less hard. Real estate was more valuable, and the way Gabay saw it, selling the factory was not just a good business decision, it was a mitzvah, a good deed. "I found a building that was one-third the cost of the property in Williamsburg," he said. "It's a Hasidic area and they need the housing. Being good-hearted people that we are here, we decided to sell the property to the Hasidic people with God sending blessings." That was 2005.

By 2012, it had become luxury condos, minus a *Shabbes* elevator.

Pilgrimage to Gabila's

I didn't know much about flat, square yellow knishes — I grew up in the circular tradition — but in the wake of Mrs. Stahl's demise, I set out to witness, and pay homage to, an alternate geometry of the knish.

Near the Long Island Railroad station in Copiague, Long Island, South American bakeries displayed arepas, empanadas, and *pan de bono*. But ten minutes in the opposite direction, past stacks of cars destined for demise, sat the world's largest knish production facility. (I was the only pedestrian in sight.) A cement walkway interrupted a lush lawn and led to a low brick building: the Home of the Original Coney Island Square Knish. Inside, men in scrubs and hairnets pulsed through a doorway beneath a 1980s-era license plate:

MR KNISH

NEW YORK

Every surface of the reception area was prone to memorabilia: photos of Gabila's workers; photos of Gabila's trucks; photos of the factory in Brooklyn in the early days; articles framed, laminated, and lacquered. I had entered a scrapbook and found myself happily trapped in several decades at once: a photo from the Sixteenth Annual Banquet of the Interborough Delicatessen Dealers Association in 1955, an image of the elder Gabays adorned with Hawaiian-style leis, and a plaque from a Florida synagogue, since decommissioned:

IN LOVING MEMORY OF

ELI GABAY

BELOVED HUSBAND FATHER

GRANDFATHER AND GREAT GRANDFATHER

MARCH 3, 1971. ADAR 6, 5731

Elliott Gabay, the third-generation owner, ushered me to his office. I asked after his competition.

"We've got none." He shrugged. "Not by the volume."

"You know those signs at McDonald's that say 'five billion sold'?" Gabay's business partner chimed in from the next desk, beneath an ancient-looking "Ask Gabila's for Knishes" sign. "We sold over a billion knishes in the last hundred years."

Or, rather, "Almost one hundred years," as noted on the boxes of frozen knishes sold in supermarkets.

"You know why I did that?" said Gabay. "I made boxes up fifteen, twenty years ago. They said 'Nineteen twenty-one to two thousand and one.' It was eighty years. And son of a bitch, they expired. I had ordered hundreds of thousands of boxes like this. So for the next one I said, 'Let's make it, "almost one hundred years."'"

Gabay gave me one of his business cards and riffed about the image of the man in the saddle on his grandfather's card. "Maybe he thinks he was on a horse, going somewhere, my grandfather," said Gabay, who got started in the business just before the death of his namesake.

In 2012, Gabila's was galloping forward. Its knish line had expanded to include bonbon-sized "Knishettes," sixteen to a box,

Elia Gabay likened his knish kingdom to that of King William III of England.

His grandson was more literal.

and round puffy, standard-sized knishes in kasha, spinach, and broccoli. They looked vaguely like Mrs. Stahl's to me, but Gabay had another name for them. "The fragile is the opposite of the square," he stated, as if handing down a commandment. "The square is what brought us where we are."

Cases of the original Coney Island knish sat on pallets in walk-in freezers. But the road ahead was not paved solely with yellow squares. "You can't sit on your laurels," said Gabay. "You gotta make sure you progress. We do pancakes and blintzes, all good kosher food."

For holidays, he made matzoh balls, kosher, but not for Passover. That would require a separate facility, untouched by leaven.

"For one week, does it pay?"

(In Canada, the megalithic bakery operation Montreal Kosher makes a kosher-for-Passover knish in a kosher-for-Passover factory. It's pretty much all potato.)

Gabila's found its own way to cater to a Shabbat-observant crowd. King David knishes pass the highest tests of *kashrut*, or kosherness, and bear two *hecshers,* or kosher certifications: the Orthodox KOF-K mark, and a designation as *Pas Yisroel.*[20] (The term, literally "bread of a Jew," means a Sabbath-observant person has participated in the knish-making process.)

Elliott Gabay is third generation, and his son Andrew, vice president and CEO of Gabila's, is fourth. Andrew Gabay is an attorney; ditto his wife, who works as the company's chief legal counsel. Andrew occupied the big office in the back, but had to leave on a delivery.

I was starting to understand the allure — and the reach — of the square knish. It would never plug the round hole left by Mrs. Stahl's, but knish lineage is knish lineage and Gabila's was going strong.

"Life moves on and so do we," said Elliott Gabay. "Now we're in all the supermarkets, thank God — Costco, BJ's, Sam's Club, Shop-Rite. We keep on trucking."

Toward an Expanded Knish Consciousness

Mrs. Stahl's and Gabila's weren't the only knish giants to leave Brooklyn in the twenty-first century, just the most recent exiles in a long history. Marcel Proust had his madeleine, Jewish New Yorkers had their knishes. They were bigger, heavier, less refined, and made sans mold or frilled pan. The more I mentioned knishes to Jews of a certain age, the more stories I discovered lodged just beneath the skin. Connections kept cropping up. You could call them coincidences, but that seems silly, since the connections came from my parents, their friends, and friends of their friends, most of whom are Jews who came of age in the New York of the knish-laden fifties and sixties.

A Star of David has six points, but the degrees of separation between a New York Jew and a knish shop hovered around three. One connection begat another, which begat another, and yet another. Mention of Mrs. Stahl's begat mention of Brighton Beach, which begat mention of Andrea, my mother's friend who grew up there, which begat mention of her brother who knew someone in the business. Knish, the food, and "knish," the word, were linchpins and signifiers. Hint at the knish and you could unleash a litany of links to a common history. We traced our roots to Eastern Europe, to the Pale of Settlement, a geographic blob that defied geopolitical boundaries and defined Jewish life in the shtetls of the nineteenth and early twentieth centuries. Some parts of the Old Country proved more dense with knish inclinations. Some New York neighborhoods had been more knish-laden than others, and some individuals more knish-inclined. But a person needn't have come from knish stock to beget knish connections.

Case in point: My mother grew up on Morris Avenue in the Bronx, not known as a knish district. Her mother's round-trips to the bakery yielded cookies in the shape of puffed bowties, yellow rolls stuffed with onion, and salt sticks, distant cousins to the croissant, made with a breadier dough, wrenched straight and scattered with kosher salt and caraway seeds. As far as I could gather, my mother gained her knish connection through marriage. But even before that, by dint of her lineage and the circles in

35

which she traveled, she was destined to become a carrier of knish information.

Shatzkin's Knishes

The backstory: My mother's sister, may she rest in peace, married into a family with ties to a central address in the Borscht Belt. That was a strip of upstate New York greenery that stuffed itself with a small horde of hotels that served a predominantly Jewish clientele. The place was thick with beet soup, comedy routines, poolside splendor, and chandeliers, not necessarily in that order. The Concord Hotel — its name forever fused to the eponymous flavor of Manischewitz wine — also meant jobs. My cousins worked as waitresses at the coffee shop; I served a stint as junior hostess in the Imperial Room (Rodney Dangerfield and Joan Rivers in the same week) and my mother consecrated several summers to work in the vault. Moneyed ladies came to check their pearls and fur coats; my mother made friends with Priscilla, who had the same job.

Fast-forward forty years. Priscilla had a daughter who had a friend who had a dad who, in his youth, had worked in Coney Island, in knishes.

As soon as I started to inquire after Shatzkin's, the stories heated up. Joseph Heller, author of *Catch-22*, grew up on those knishes and lauded the place in his autobiography, *Now and Then: From Coney Island to Here:*

> It was futile to search anywhere in the universe for a tastier potato knish than Shatzkin's when they were still made by hand by old

In 1953 this Coney Island knishery lured noshers of all ages.

women who were relatives or friends of the family. (Although I still run into mulish people, hogs, who didn't mind the thicker, yellow Gabila's, and to people brought up in adjacent Brighton Beach who still salivate at the mention of Mrs. Stahl's, the queen of potato knishes there.)[21]

Inspired by Heller's attempt at diplomacy, I set out to make contact with descendants of a competing knish lineage.

"There isn't a culture in the world that didn't take a dough and fill it with something," said Mort Shatzkin, whose family ended up in the business out of need.[22]

"When it got started was really during the Depression," said Shatzkin. "My grandmother was a really good cook." His grandfather, a skilled tinsmith, sustained an injury that prevented him from working, so it was his wife, Mort's grandmother, who took to the kitchen. "We fried knishes. We had two flavors in the beginning," said Shatzkin. "Potato was fully round. Kasha was half round, so you knew what you were serving."

After a while, they opened a branch on 15th Street and Surf Avenue, also in Coney Island. Mort became partners with his brother Bill, who had a chemical engineering degree. "There was a lot of anti-Semitism at the time," remembered Shatzkin. His brother had trouble finding work in his field, so "he went into knishes." Mort studied law and passed the bar. Bill continued in knishes.

Mort moved to California's San Fernando Valley, where he took on cases in tort legislation and medical malpractice and worked in the district attorney's office. His career blossomed, but his proximity to the knish dwindled to nil.

Where could a person get a knish in Los Angeles?

"You can't," said Shatzkin "unless you make them."

He didn't.

But in 2006, he had no problem remembering the products he had proffered a half century earlier. "We introduced the baked knish — blueberry, cherry, pineapple. Then we did cocktail knishes. Frankfurter knishes. Cocktail franks."

The Shatzkin's legacy, like Mrs. Stahl's, provoked whiffs of nostalgia across the country. "People still remember them," said Shatzkin. "Even in California.

"From the time I moved out here, I had people come up to me and say, 'Open up a store.'"

He didn't.

In the 1990s, some transplanted New York accountants *did*—a branch of Mrs. Stahl's Knishes, in Los Angeles.[23] In 2012, I left messages, asking them to call back.

They didn't.

"By the time I was thirteen, I was handling a frankfurter grill on my own," said Shatzkin. Food service was family tradition, passed down, like the words of the Torah and the heft of the scroll, from generation to generation. And blessed by ancestors. "Grandma was a really smart woman, powerful. When she was ninety, she could sit outside, and at the end of the day," said Shatzkin, "she could tell me what my gross was."

Back then, the crowds were infinite. "For many years after the Second World War there was still no air-conditioning," said Shatzkin. "The only place you could come to breathe was by the ocean. You had a million people at the beach. You had no room to put your blanket down."

I knew the scene from the black-and-white photograph by Weegee: people shoulder-to-shoulder, thigh-to-thigh, arms raised, waving at the camera.[24]

Hirsch's Knishes

Next knish connection: My mother's friend Andrea had a brother who, through his sailing club, knew an heir to another bygone knish kingdom of the Brooklyn boardwalk. Marvin Hirsch, as it turned out, was also a knish maker turned attorney. I called him with some questions, but he beat me to it:

"How old are you?

"Where did you grow up?

"How did you get involved in this?"[25]

The law offices of Flamhaft Levy Kamins & Hirsch occupy the second floor of a two-story office building in the Long Island town of Mineola. I could not separate the place from a 1980s jingle for a car dealership: "Honda of Mineola. We'll give you the shirts off our backs."

So embedded was the jingle in my psyche that I half expected a handful of bare-chested hunks to greet me in a fleet of late-model Acuras.

Mano Hirsch at his eponymous Brighton Beach knish shop in the 1980s.

No such welcome, but the jingle persisted: *Honda of Mineola . . . we'll give you the knish off our backs.*

En route to the law offices of Flamhaft Levy Kamins & Hirsch, I walked past Mineola's "New York Deli" to check on the knish situation.

Nope.

Hirsch had his own trove. Not knishes, but clippings: yellowed newsprint and purpled mimeographs, stored in a mahogany-colored accordion file. Back in the day, politicians would go out of their way to be photographed at Hirsch's knish establishment.[26] Marvin's father, Mano (short for Emmanuel), was profiled in numerous papers of the day and hailed as a philanthropist of the highest order. Summers, he worked days that stretched endless; winters, he sat on committees at Israel Bonds and UJA-Federation.[27]

It had been decades since Marvin Hirsch had concerned himself with the knish, but he maintained tradition. Once a year he took his son and grandson to Brighton, and every few months he got together with the guys from Brighton, about a dozen, many of whom had worked, at one time or another, in his father's shop. One more vestige of the boardwalk stuck with him.

"In my family," said Hirsch, "whenever we would write a letter to each other, we would sign it 'love and knish.'"

Ruby the Knish Man

"Love and Knishes" was also the name of a folk trio I'd discovered in my research. The group, based in Rochester, New York, developed a repertoire of traditional and new Jewish songs, including a paean to a certain beloved knish vendor.

Bonnie Abrams, songwriter and lead singer of the group, penned lyrics to honor the man who made the knishes that came from a truck she encountered as a kid. Abrams grew up in the Bronx, but girlhood summers in the Catskills in the mid-1960s made her a devotee of Ruby the Knish Man, so much so that later on, she considered a similar livelihood.

"In the 1980s, when bagel stores were opening up everywhere, my husband and I thought we wanted to start a chain of knish stores, because so many people in the world don't know from knishes," said Abrams, who was able to pinpoint the soft underbelly of her beloved food.[28] "We were worried that with healthy food sensibilities, maybe it wouldn't be politically correct."

Abrams, who became the director of the Center for Holocaust Awareness and Information in Rochester, never forgot about Ruby, who drove around in a black car with "something like an oven in the back." In the town of Woodbourne, New York, at about three p.m. Ruby would pull up to Wiener's Bungalow Colony. "Usually the fathers weren't even there and the mothers were busy making dinner," said Abrams, whose memory of that event can be relived in film. *A Walk on the Moon,* set in the Catskills in the summer of 1969, includes a public address announcement broadcast throughout the vacation community: "The knish man is on the premises."[29]

But these weren't just run-of-the-mill potato pies. "Most knishes that people are familiar with are yellow pillows or they have a flaky pastry," said Abrams, whose memories were unaltered by time. "These were fried somehow. The outside doughy thing seemed like a donut. The inside was this very tender mashed potato. It wasn't really spiced — maybe a little salt and pepper or onion powder."

The color, "plain, just brown," was also reminiscent of a donut, the kind one finds at a fall festival and downs along with a cup of apple cider. A Ruby's knish was round. "About five inches in diameter," according to Abrams, who found a knish comparable to that of her youth in another part of the Catskills, at Izzy's Knishes in Loch Sheldrake, New York. "They have all the kinds of knishes — the pillow ones [Ruby's style], the pastry ones, and the round ones. And this is run by ultra-Orthodox women," reported Abrams. Izzy, who runs the kosher knish stand, claimed that his recipe came from some relative of Ruby's. Abrams could taste a resemblance. "Maybe because they're fried, the potato part is more moist. They really are different than knishes you find anywhere else."

"The Ruby lore is very strong," said Abrams, who memorialized it in song.

Ruby Oshinsky, the knish man, had a wife and three children — a daughter and two sons. One son, Jerry Oshinsky, was not convinced about Izzy and the Ruby's recipe. "That's just one of the imposters," he said. "I don't dispute the situation, but it had nothing to do with my dad."[30]

Jerry said the family knish formula originated, like his grandfather Hershel Oshinsky, in Kiev and gained a foothold on Amboy

Ruby's Knishes

By Bonnie Abrams

I want to sing of Ruby's knishes
It's been one of my fondest wishes
To taste the potato and the kasha
I ate when I was a *klayner nosher* [small eater/little kid]
Now if you don't know what a knish is
It's a Jewish dish that is delicious
It's like a thick potato pancake
Wrapped in dough that's fried or baked

CHORUS

Now you can get a knish at any supermarket
That has a deli or a kosher food department
But those yellow pillows and mashed potato rounds
Are nothing like the sight, the smell, the sound
Oh—ho—when Ruby brought the pushcart around

Ruby bring the pushcart around
Ruby hollered, "Hot potato, kasha!"
Di kinder [the children] gave a big *geshrey* [scream], ay!
Mama, mama—give me a quarter dollar
A Ruby's knish I wanna buy
The dough was brown just like a fried cake

And the first bite that you'd take

Was tender *kartoffel un a bisl—fefer, zaltz un schmaltz un tsibl*

[potato and a little pepper, salt, fat, and onion]

CHORUS

It's been thirty years now since I tasted

Oy, all the calories I wasted

On cheap imitations that were no good

Still I tried every knish I could

Hoping for a moment to recapture

My childhood gastronomic rapture

I went to the great Rabbi of Woodbourne

Ruby's whereabouts to learn

And he said . . .

CHORUS

He sent me to Loch Sheldrake to the *mikvah* [ritual bath]

I said, "Rabbi, this is not the answer!"

He said, "There you will find just what you long for

Hunger for Ruby's knish no more!"

Down to Loch Sheldrake on a Sunday

Chasidim were crowded in the doorway

Of Izzie's Knishes, now I knew why

It's good to listen to the Rabbi

They said . . .

CHORUS

Bonnie Abrams, "Ruby's Knishes," from *Welcome to My Mid-Life Crisis*, 2007, MP3 audio file, http://www.allenhopkins.org/loveandknishes.html (accessed July 18, 2008).

Street in Brownsville, Brooklyn. There was no longer a trace of the building, but Ruby, who died in 1987 at age seventy, left a legacy that wafted through strands of time and tubes of the Internet. It lent itself to a dedicated website, a simple affair set up by Bruce Brodinsky, who needed to teach himself HTML for his job.[31] Ruby's former customers clicked in droves. Grown-ups relived the aromas of their youth. More than a hundred people posted their recollections:

> Ruby would be there every day at lunchtime shouting, "COME BUY MY KNISHES. I HAVE TO SEND MY WIFE TO THE COUNTRY."

> I can still remember Ruby cutting the knish in the middle, mustard placed in the middle and of course, salt sprinkled on top from that beat-up old can.

> Every Sunday after attending Church at Our Lady of Loreto, I would RUN to the corner of Pacific St. and Eastern Parkway to buy Ruby's Knishes. They were only 20 cents at the time. That was in 1966.

> He always gave me credit when I was broke but told me not to tell anybody. And his fav[orite] joke: Do you like flowers? Put your two lips around this.

> In the mid-1980s my mom opened a small knish-eatery in the food court of the (now-defunct) Busy Bee Mall in Massapequa on Long Island. . . . She got them from various knish bakers around New York, including driving every week to Brooklyn to get "authentic pushcart knishes" from Ruby at a place called "Mom's." . . . People

came from miles to eat them and some literally *cried* at the counter and stated "that it was like re-living their childhood in Brooklyn."[32]

Ruby Oshinsky sold knishes in the Carnarsie section of Brooklyn in the 1950s and '60s. His customers were rarely over the age of fifteen; those who could not afford the nickel per knish received a sprinkle of salt, gratis. "Everyone knows Ruby the Knish Man with a salt shaker," said his son. "The only thing that held him back from real greatness was the poverty that his family had."

The salt Ruby kept on his cart brought out the taste of his potato delicacies and let kids without coins join in the ritual. In Jewish religious tradition, salt marks a different mitzvah. In the Holy

Temple of Jerusalem, sacrifices required salt; by extrapolation, so does a person's dining room table. Salt reminds us of the Temple, of sacrifices to the Almighty, and serves as a modern incarnation of an altar. Most important, it links us to what came before.[33]

Before he made knishes, Ruby worked in a slaughterhouse, as a breaker of cows' necks. Before that, he fought in World War II.[34] Ruby served in General Patton's Third Army and interrogated German prisoners. But that's not all. "He was in the infantry," said his son. "Then he went into the MP [military police]. At that point, most of the MPs were from the South and they didn't care for the Jews too much, but my father was such an exceptional person that they accepted him beyond his Judaism.

"Everyone has a picture of this poor, old, dirty man selling knishes," said his son. "The person he was, was a very intelligent man who was ahead of his time. He was a very good baker. At one point in time, he made a pastry knish, a cherry cheese, and a dessert knish with jellies or jams, some with fruit filling and some with applesauce."

Ruby's son Jerry had not abdicated his upbringing. He prided himself on being the maker of the southernmost knish in the United States, in Key Largo, Florida, where in 1994, he did some baking of his own. Knishes, of course. It continued for three or four years, until illness forced him to stop. "I had taken the formula," he said. "I was baking the knishes: forty-one different varieties. It was a trip and a half, the most fun I ever had." The menu, as he described it, included:

The McKnish: A baked potato knish, with an egg on it and mozzarella on top. The egg would get mixed up with the potato and it would become like a breakfast knish.

The Key Lime Knish: A potato knish, but it had a key lime topping, in a custard-type form. No whipped cream.

Charlie Knish: Tuna casserole supreme in a knish.

The Ruby: A Reuben knish with corned beef and sauerkraut. The dressing was *milchedich* [dairy]. (It's not the *frum* that were going to eat it.)[35]

Frum, which comes from the German *frumm,* meaning devout or pious, refers to someone who will not ingest milk with meat. Jerry Oshinsky was becoming receptive to religion. Whether a higher degree of observance could help knish sales was another question altogether.

In the environs of Miami, former New Yorkers of Jewish extraction have long flocked to early-bird specials. And in nearby Broward, Dade, and Palm Beach counties, knish connoisseurs have been known to dominate the polls. But a few hours south, all that changed. "The Keys was not exceptionally Jewish," said Oshinsky. "For people to figure out what a knish was, it took a lot of selling."

Lucky for him, entrepreneurship ran in the family. "My father was the first one to put a speaker on the top of a truck," said Oshinsky. "And he also created a way to keep knishes warm during transport."

I told him what Bonnie Abrams said. He filled me in on the nitty-gritty.

"My father's car was a 1952 black Plymouth," remembered Oshinsky. "He took out the trunk and he modified the proofing box to become an oven. It had trays and compartment drawers he made. What he would do is put charcoal briquettes in the bottom to heat it up."

In 2008, when I spoke to Jerry Oshinsky, there was still hope for a knish revival in Key Largo. "Right now some of my friends down here, they're urging me to start making them again," said Oshinsky, who passed away in 2013. "It's my generation. There was nothing better. Eating one of them with an Orange Crush, that was one of my favorite memories of the summer in the Catskills."

Yonah Schimmel's

A HUNDRED YEARS ON THE LOWER EAST SIDE

The knish may have blanketed Brooklyn and summered in the Catskills, but its center of gravity hovered over the foot of Manhattan. At the turn of the twentieth century, streets like Delancey, Rivington, and Stanton were dense with people and thick with knishes. Jewish immigrants from Eastern Europe — Austria-Hungary, Russia, and Poland — accounted for nearly a quarter of Manhattan's population. They were largely laborers and largely unskilled, crammed, at work and at home, into small, lightless spaces.

A single block on the Lower East Side weighed in as the most crowded place on earth. The environs birthed knish carts and knish shops; peddlers and purveyors inserted themselves into

*Sunday morning on the corner of Orchard and Rivington streets
was prime time for shopping in the early 1900s.*

street and gut. Even with minimal elbow room, the populace
strove, again and again, to lift knishes mouthward.

The knish tradition wove itself into the urban landscape. When
the masses morphed and the population thinned, knish constitu-
encies spread themselves far and wide, and the potato pie fabric
of the neighborhood frayed. One place remained. In 2010, Yonah
Schimmel's Knish Bakery marked one hundred years on Houston Street. In the century since the knishery came into being, its

competition had crossed the river, churned to a halt, or slipped into oblivion. The closest rival knish concern was across the East River, nine miles northeast. Knish Nosh, established in 1952, held court on Queens Boulevard in Rego Park (and ran concessions inside Central Park). Closer to Schimmel's, there were other places for knishes — down Houston Street at Katz's and up Second Avenue at B&H Dairy restaurant — but no businesses dedicated to the exclusive care and feeding of the knish-minded individual.

Schimmel's steeped itself in nostalgia and nodded to the future with flavors that would have sounded foreign to its forebears: *Jalapeño-cheddar? Chocolate?* It kept its dumbwaiter and lured tourists and old-timers with thick knishes and long narrow tables, where the silverware waited in upright metal cylinders from the dishwashing machine. The knishes were large and not quite Mrs. Stahl's. I found consolation in the dumbwaiter and the wall decorations (another walk-in scrapbook), and gravitated there for Thanksgiving, Christmas, and Erev Yom Kippur. Schimmel's stayed open late. It catered to hipster moviegoers and to suburbanites who came to commune with the past.

But with road construction on Houston Street in 2012 came a threat to Schimmel's receipts. That may seem counterintuitive for an enterprise so ensconced in the city and less than a block from mass transit, but remember: memory. Half of Schimmel's customers came from beyond the city limits. They pulled up, ran in, placed their orders, grabbed their bags, and ran back to the car. Sometimes, to quicken the sprint, they phoned in advance or kept someone in the car to avoid a ticket. The shop's co-owner Ellen

Anistratov (her business partner is her father) knew her clientele parked illegally. She knew their motivation was benign. They needed to access their fix as quickly as possible. It had been that way for years.[36]

Tradition.

To be fair, ex–Lower East Siders of the Jewish persuasion and the people who love them were not the only ones drawn to Schimmel's. Visitors from Japan, Australia, and Germany (always Germany) flocked to the place; teenagers came for the cheap eats; and passersby stopped in to make peace with their curiosity.

Tradition.

The city was with the knish. It heard the cry of its owners and vindicated it. Schimmel's — consider its age — stood for small business, local history, and the essence of New York City, a place worth preserving.

The street construction was set to last two years.

At the rate things were going, said Anistratov, the neighborhood could be sitting *shiva* for Schimmel's by then. City Council member Margaret Chin didn't like the sound of that. Her office petitioned city agencies whose leaders, if they were worth their mettle, had meddled, one time or another, in knishes.[37]

Yonah Schimmel's *kvetched,* and officials took note. Around the corner from the shop, on Forsyth Street, were created two parking spots, destined especially for knish picker-uppers. The parking spots, it should be noted, had meters.

Roots tourism to the Lower East Side was nothing new. Even before the area became a swank hangout for vegan chocolate chip cookies and their disciples, it drew onlookers: chroniclers and writers, artists and people predisposed to grasp at the past, myself included.

The first time I went to the Lower East Side solo was spring break, sophomore year. My peers flew off to keg stands in bikiniland; I took the F train to Delancey and Essex and wandered in search of the familiar, whatever that meant. The eastern wall of the Bialystoker Home for the Aged greeted me with a mural: immigrants with beards and suitcases, a woman with Shabbat candles, a picket line with Yiddish signs and images of ordinary people clustered above this phrase:

OUR STRENGTH IS OUR HERITAGE

OUR HERITAGE IS OUR LIFE.

In 1990, the mural marked my arrival. By 2012, it had molted. The immigrants and their suitcases bore the scuffs of time. The sky next to them got rubbed out. Above the woman with the Shabbat candles, another woman's face had turned to brick.

"'Jewish Heritage Mural' is what it's called," said Susan Caruso Green, who, in the 1970s, directed the project and recruited young people from the neighborhood to make it happen.[38]

To restore it would cost fifty thousand dollars. Untouched, the mural would fade beyond recognition.

"It's hard to see it deteriorating," said Caruso Green. "But it's like everything — time takes its toll."

Luckily, other impressions of Lower East Side knish history

have been better sheltered from the elements. Artist Hedy Pagremanski immortalized Schimmel's storefront in an oil painting that found a home uptown, at the Museum of the City of New York. Pagremanski did not come of age on the Lower East Side, nor did she pass through the neighborhood in its heyday, but she had been enthralled by it since girlhood, thanks to all the stories. Born in Vienna in 1920 — "Hitler came when I was eight" — Pagremanski arrived in the United States a few years later, via Panama.[39] She lived on Herzl Street in East New York, Brooklyn, married, had two children, and moved to Long Beach, Long Island, but thought of the Lower East Side as "the beginning of America." In the 1970s, she went there daily, with an easel and a palette to paint portraits of neighborhood places, including a knishery — Yonah Schimmel's.

"I loved that building," said Pagremanski. "It was one long, skinny building."

When the Museum of the City of New York accessioned her painting, she sent three pages of notes, handwritten in flowing script.

"Incidentally, there is no 'c' in Schimmel in the big yellow sign," she wrote to the curator. "Mrs. Berger [Lillian Berger, an owner of Yonah Schimmel's] told me that the sign painter ran out of room."

That was just the start of what the artist gleaned from her conversations.

The original Yonah Schimmel was a part-time Hebrew teacher — a *"melamed"* [a religious instructor for children]. He began the business with a pushcart, then rented a small store in partnership with his cousin Joseph Berger.

Two years later Joseph Berger took it over completely and ran it up to the present generation. His wife Rose (originally Schimmel) worked with him and they were instrumental in making the store famous. He passed away in the 1930s, leaving the restaurant to his son Arthur and his wife Lillian.

When I began this painting, Arthur Berger had passed away and his wife, Lillian, and the two sons, Joseph and Harold, were running the business. The area had deteriorated, but the restaurant had not. Famous people in the industrial, political and show-business worlds still ate there and on the Sunday there were waiting lines. But that's not what I was interested in. There was a sense of history in that building and I needed to show that. At first I did the painting without people . . . but it looked so lonely. Then I put in Lillian Berger (the tall blond woman in front of the door) and then some neighborhood people, but something was still not right . . . and then I met Fannie Svendlick and everything fell into place. In the painting, Mrs. Svedlick can be identified as the elderly woman in a patterned dress.[40]

Pagremanski shared Mrs. Svendlick's reminiscences:

I came to America as Fannie Kaufman, age 10, in 1902. I came via Ellis Island. In those days men and women were put into separate sections and I can still remember how my mother and I wept because we were afraid of never seeing my father and brother again.[41]

Pagremanski met Mrs. Svendlick on Long Island, but that was a mere quirk of geography. Mrs. Svendlick was of the Lower East Side, a New Yorker by way of Eastern Europe. In her I saw my grandmothers. She was older than they were but not by much. Pagremanski also met Mrs. Svendlick's grandson and wrote down his story: "Seventy years after my grandmother left the Lower East Side I came to Soho to live. . . . I wandered through the streets, remembering vaguely stories told to me by all of my grandparents. I spoke to new waves of immigrants and watched the profiles change. I guess when I left, the circle had come full term around."[42]

But even before a Lower East Side knish shop was immortalized in oils, the neighborhood's stuffed pies were no strangers to art. As part of the Works Progress Administration (WPA) Federal Writers' Project, knishes were seen as sustenance and muse. In the 1940s, folklorist, historian, and humorist Nathan Ausubel cast his gaze on the area and wrote a series of essays — never published but long enshrined in the microfilm cabinets of New York City's Municipal Archives. Just north of New York's City Hall, in the ornate building on the north side of Chambers Street, visitors, even if they have been there before, must have their photos taken and affixed, as stickers, on their person, as if not to lose themselves amid the miles of microfilm. Visitors fill out forms, tug at metal drawers, and pluck faded cardboard boxes from shallow drawers.

Visitors thread and rethread the film and thread it yet again — it has a habit of slipping — until it sticks in the plastic spool and whirs firmly under the glass platen until the past laps at the present and reveals itself on a square screen:

Yoineh Shimmel is dead. But he has left behind him an everlasting monument — of knishes. Knishes are more than an indigenous food of the Jewish East Side. They are even more than an expression of local culinary patriotism. Knishes in fact are a passion, an ambrosial ecstasy. . . . Yoineh Shimmel was a rabbi, so legend claims for him posthumously. . . .

It was really his good wife who blazoned for him the knish way: she made excellent knishes. Expansive and hospitable she used to invite her neighbors to eat them. The news of her knishes swept the neighborhood like wildfire. Now there are two million Jews in New York City — and if every Jew ate at least one knish a day — at five cents a knish — just figure it out for yourselves!

So Rabbi Yoineh Shimmel, praising God for his everlasting mercy, opened a little knish shop on Allen Street. The neighborhood began to ring with a new exhortation:

C'mon folks: Something new — something delicious —
We call 'em — knishes!

Soon he did a land-office business. The grateful East Side descended upon him like an avalanche. What could a pious man do: So in 1910 he moved to larger quarters on East Houston Street between 1st and 2nd Avenues. And as Holy Writ would say: "the Lord was with Rabbi Yoineh Shimmel and he prospered."

. . . Yoineh Schimmel's wife really was not the inventor of the knish. Like all elements of folklore it sprang spontaneously from the Jewish people. . . . In reality, Yoineh Shimmel was only the Americaniser of the knish. He performed a great public service by applying modern industrial mass-production methods to the ancient knish, thus making it available to the poor in pocket and rich in appetite for a few paltry pennies. So much deliciousness for so little! . . .

Oh! The place has become quite a landmark, just as recherché as the Stork Club or 21. No need of advertising any more. All who hunger for knishes find their way to the East Houston Street address. Yiddish poets with little money and enormous appetites haunt the restaurant for hours at a time, chewing the rag about the arts and munching knishes.

In conclusion: first came the knish to the East Side — and culture followed presto prestissimo.[43]

In the 1970s, Schimmel's catered to long-time customers and newcomers to the neighborhood. A sign in the window proclaimed, "TRY IT, YOU'LL LIKE IT."

Once upon a time, one block west of Yonah Schimmel's, Second Avenue sat blanketed with Yiddish theaters and dairy restaurants, places that packed themselves with actors and audience members. In a song, "The Whole World Is a Theater," actress Molly Picon ticked off types of people who attended the show: the latecomer, the overeater, and the boy who asked his mother, rhetorically, about the lady onstage: "You think she's delicious? She isn't as good as Yoineh Shmitnik's knishes."[44]

Rivalry on Rivington Street

The fracas did not originate with Schimmel's and it didn't contain itself to the stage. In January 1916, a few blocks east of Second Avenue, the knish elicited drama *en plein air* and pastry made headlines in the *New York Times*:

RIVINGTON ST. SEES WAR
Rival Restaurant Men Cut Prices on the Succulent Knish[45]

Across Rivington Street, Max Green and Morris London fought knish to knish. One sold his goods at five cents, the other went down to three. One lured customers with cabaret, the other summoned an oompah band. One put up signs, the other followed suit. Eventually, détente seemed to fill the air between them.

Eleven months later, the *New York Sun* revived the story: "'Knishe' Founder Cheers East Siders: Declines to Boost Price of the Edible to Please H. C. O'Living." London, the newcomer, had succumbed under pressure. Green, the soi-disant inventor of the knish, put posterity over profit: "He didn't care to have future generations accuse him of taking an unfair advantage of their forefathers."[46]

In 1919, *The Messenger*, a trade journal "published weekly by bakers for bakers," ran a primer on knishes and the continuing hostilities. "The East Side," it declared, "has gone clean crazy about these knisches." The dispute remained heated.[47]

To help keep his knishes hot, Morris London of the United Knish Bakery stockpiled ideas for a steam chest and sought a patent. Green, whose knishes had warmed Rivington Street for thirteen years, retaliated with a gigantic hand-painted placard rendered, in Yiddish, by a prominent sign maker of the day called Rosenthal:

THE TEN KNISCH COMMANDMENTS

1 All good pure food.

2 Everything strictly fresh.

3 All bread, etc., baked on premises.

4 At any time hot knisches.

5 Strictly union waiters and bakers.

6 All articles used are strictly union-made goods.

7 I sympathize with organized labor.

8 My place is big, clean, and elegant.

9 Good music every evening.

10 Coupons with every knisch.[48]

It is not clear how — or if — those hostilities ended. But decades later, when neither Green nor London remained on Rivington, Schimmel's stood firm. So what if the rabbi who lent his name to the shop had abandoned knishes to return to Torah? The shop was involved in a different tradition: the Electoral College.

"No New York politician in the last fifty years has been elected to public office without having at least one photograph taken showing him on the Lower East Side with a knish in his face," wrote Milton Glaser and Jerome Snyder in *The Underground Gourmet* in 1966. Izzy Finkelstein, a career waiter at Schimmel's, corroborated their observation. In fact, he remembered a day when Franklin Delano Roosevelt was campaigning downtown; Eleanor entered the shop on a de rigueur visit and left with a bagful of potato pies.[49]

For the knish, it was a golden age, but no one dreamt this — and the hardship that preceded it — could become the stuff of longing. No one dreamt hindsight could make squalor shine or that the knish might lose its prominence. No one imagined that the humble knish might one day loosen its grasp on the populace and be threatened by the very people it helped to elect. But years hence, in 1996, under the Giuliani administration, cooked potatoes landed on a list of "potentially hazardous foods." New York City's Department of Health argued that the guts of a knish could support the "rapid and progressive growth of infectious or toxigenic microorganisms, or growth of C. botulinum."[50] Potato pies were restricted to carts with warming ovens, more cumbersome and more costly to operate than those without.[51] The knish population — we're talking about squares, here — diminished but survived. Eventually, the regulations were relaxed and knishes returned to simple lithe carts that pock Manhattan from the South Street Seaport to the upper end of Midtown.

But once upon a time, the knish blanketed the East Side. Max Green of Rivington Street pronounced himself king of knishes. Morris London tried, with vehemence, to unseat him. On Forsyth Street, Elias Gabay claimed dominion over his own knish kingdom. And four blocks east of Yonah Schimmel's, on Houston Street, sat another, nearly forgotten stronghold.

The Queen of Knishes

Gussie Sussman arrived in New York from Borislav, Romania (present-day Ukraine), at the turn of the century. In 1904 she married Abraham Schwebel and worked in a factory, nothing special.[52] Then a *landsman* approached her with a business idea. Not only was he a fellow Borislaver, but also he was her husband's sister's brother-in-law. Yiddish, which uses the word *makheteneste* to describe the familial relation of one mother-in-law to the other, does not have a description for the rapport between these particular branches of a family tree. But Mrs. Schwebel did. "A piece of relative," she called him.[53] This "piece of relative" (the term wasn't a slur) suggested they go into business together: knishes. He put up the dough; she baked it.

The way she saw it, their establishment was the first to produce knishes in the Land of Opportunity. "You couldn't buy a knish for love or money in those days," she said of Houston Street in the early 1900s. (Perhaps she had never ventured the four blocks west toward Schimmel's, or if she did, averted her eyes.) Mrs. Schwebel was nonetheless a keen observer of her surroundings. She noticed that the street teemed with pickpockets and she knew who walked through the doors of her shop: politicos, entertainers, and ne'er-do-wells of the highest order. Jewish organized crime operator Abe Reles, a.k.a. Kid Twist, was a repeat customer until he pulled a gun on Mrs. Schwebel. The tools of her trade could double as weapons, but first she opened a round of verbal artillery. "I told him with a knife in my hand . . . he shouldn't come here anymore." And that wasn't all. "I told him, 'If you don't get out, Kid, I'll cut off your head like from a chicken.'"[54] That tough-on-crime attitude could have been instilled in her by another illustrious customer, New York City Police Chief Teddy Roosevelt, who, at the end of the nineteenth century, was said to punctuate his late-night rounds with a knish or two. The future president of the United States roamed darkened downtown streets with a distinguished guide, journalist Jacob Riis. Perhaps, in their wanderings through the world of the "The Other Half," they split a kasha.

For decades Mrs. Schwebel relayed accolades she received — from the police chief, Enrico Caruso, and Leon Trotsky — to the press. On Saturdays, like the neighborhood, she rested. But the following day, business boomed. "On a Sunday is lined up Rolls-Royces from one corner to another corner," gushed Mrs. Schwebel to the *New York Post* in 1941. "From all over, from Jersey, from the Bronx, from Pennsylvania, just to eat by me a knish. It smells like gold." The crowds inflated Mrs. Schwebel's sense of pride — and her feet, which swelled beyond the berths of her shoes. No problem: she flitted amid ovens in slippers, as if a knish incarnate:

Mrs. Schwebel in the kitchen of
her Houston Street restaurant, 1942.
"Sweetheart, you must eat them,"
she told a reporter, about her knishes.
"It's something out of this world . . ."
(rest of sentence is: "as my youngest
would say.")

stout, robust, and stuffed with warmth. Her build may have been stocky, but her touch was light. That's what the papers said.[55]

In 1942, Houston Street was widened, Mrs. Schwebel's table count doubled to ten, and plants were added for ambiance.[56] Her kids, four of them, were older and needed less attention, so she and her husband tag-teamed the night shift. After midnight, she'd roll a new batch of knishes. At two a.m. she went to bed. Two hours later, her husband started baking. Men en route to work at the city's markets succumbed to the aroma. A knish — with a cup of coffee — went for six cents. (Izzy Finkelstein, of Schimmel's, remembered when one went for three.)[57] Clementine Paddleford, the pioneering, non-Jewish food columnist for the *New York Herald Tribune*, grasped the proper protocol: "Knishes should be eaten while blistering hot. Tantalizing things, too hot to eat and too good to wait for. Carry them home, but reheat for serving."[58]

Not everyone was delighted. An Oregon paper condemned the knish along with Paddleford and her "food poems," but ultimately made peace with the stuffed pastry (even if it did pale in comparison with native foodstuffs of the Northwest):

> Well, of course, food is food, and then again it can be something much more than just food, for without the personality of that fine artist, "Ma" Schwebel, a "knishe" might just be something to produce bad dreams. On second thought, we will adhere to the fresh Oregon peaches with cream and the bacon and eggs. They fit into the Oregon landscape of ours just as the "knishes" fit that of New York's East Side.[59]

For Mrs. Schwebel, the knish signified a locale and a livelihood. It was an instrument of acculturation par excellence, useful for luring reporters. "When I came here at seventeen, I didn't know a knishe from a pig's knuckle," she told *the Herald Tribune*.[60] But as an adult she was confident enough to share her recipe:

> First there's the potatoes. You peel them, but good. Then you boil them and afterwards, mash. When they're cool mix in some onions that have been fried in butter. Season to taste. Make a dough, roll the mixture up in it and bake slowly for an hour and fifteen minutes. That's all, God bless me, and it's all I want that people should like them."[61]

Thirty-five knishes fit on a baking tray, huddled shoulder-to-shoulder, with only bits of pan peeking through. Knishes were common food for common people, but Gussie Schwebel had an idea on how to catapult them to a new echelon.

From: Mrs. Gussie Schwebel
191 East Houston St.,
New York City
Jan. 6, 1942

My Dear Mrs. Roosevelt:

I take the liberty of sending you a newspaper clipping dealing with my humble self.

The purpose of this letter is two-fold. First: It is my most sincere hope that I may be permitted to send you a sample of my dish, the knish, which, believe me, my dear Mrs. Roosevelt, is really worth tasting. Also, I wonder if I may not be able to be of service to my beloved land, by way of introducing the knish, which is very wholesome and not costly to produce, into the diet of our armed forces. I shall be most happy to devote all of my time and my energy to this end.

Again, I pray that you may accept a boxful of knishes from me and will let me know when and where I can send them, I am

Your most respectful servant
Mrs. Gussie Schwebel[62]

The first lady was familiar with the customs of the Lower East Side and not just from her knish shopping trip to Schimmel's; as a young woman, Eleanor Roosevelt had volunteered at the University Settlement as a dance instructor.[63]

January 12, 1942

Dear Mrs. Schwebel:

Mrs. Roosevelt has received your letter of January 6 and wants you to know how much she appreciates your kind offer to send her a sample of your knishes.

Mrs. Roosevelt expects to be in New York around January 16 and 17, and if you care to send some knishes to 49 East 65 Street, where she will be staying, she will be very glad to have them.

Very sincerely yours,
Secretary to Mrs. Roosevelt[64]

Two days later, Mrs. Schwebel sent an overnight telegram:

MRS MALVINA C THOMPSON=

THANK YOU SO MUCH FOR INFORMING ME ABOUT MRS ROOSEVELTS WILLINGNESS TO TASTE MY KNISHES. THEY ARE BEST OVENHOT AND FOR THAT REASON I BEG YOU TO LET ME KNOW THE EXACT HOUR FRIDAY OR SATURDAY WHEN I SHOULD DELIVER THEM TO HER HOME. GRATEFULLY WIRE ANSWER BY WESTERN UNION COLLECT[65]

A week after that, a letter arrived on Houston Street, by mail:

Dear Mrs. Schwebel:

Mrs. Roosevelt has your telegram and asks me to say that she will be glad to receive the knishes at her house, 49 East 65th Street, at 5:00 p.m. on Tuesday, January 27th.

Very sincerely yours,
Secretary to Mrs. Roosevelt[66]

In anticipation of the delivery, the *Sun* ran an early edition headline, "First Lady to Get a Taste of Knish," and relayed the play-by-play for that afternoon: "At 4:30, Mrs. Schwebel will snatch three dozen of the delicacies from her old-fashioned oven. . . . Golden brown, the knishes will be loaded into a car and she and Jack [her son] will be off." The eldest of her four children told a reporter, "Ma's only 55 years old but she's been cooking knishes more than forty years and she knows her stuff."[67]

The following day Mrs. Schwebel made the news again, in Yiddish. Her photo ran on the front page of the *Forverts*, beneath the headline "Mrs. Roosevelt Would Like to Taste Jewish Knishes, but . . ." The paper reported:

> *Nu, nu!* So Mrs. Schwebel got very busy — as fired up as a little match. [A *shvebl* is a kitchen match in Yiddish.]"[68]
>
> In the meantime, the knish story was receiving a lot of publicity.
>
> Reporters swarmed the presidential residence. Things began heating up.
>
> By the time Mrs. Schwebel arrived at Mrs. Roosevelt's home last night with three trays of hot knishes in tow she faced disappointment.
>
> One report states that the first lady's secretary would not accept the knishes on the grounds that too much of a big deal was made of it. The home on 65th Street was beleaguered by a crowd of curiosity seekers who were eager to accompany the parade of knishes.[69]

Who could blame them? Finally, one of their own had provided entrée (almost) to an upper rung, and not just of society, but of government. How else but with the knish could the masses gain such proximity to such a person?

The thwarted mission did not deter Mrs. Schwebel; it just greased her resolve and spurred her PR apparatus. She did not stop baking knishes, nor did she stop using them to build bridges and open doors. Several years after the failed bid for the first lady's table, Mrs. Schwebel renewed her efforts at knish diplomacy. In 1945, the *Washington Post* reported on her intention to celebrate the end of World War II with mass production, but these weren't ordinary knishes, these pastries were catalysts for détente. They were to be baked in jars and downed with vodka, in the spirit of international camaraderie.

Closer to home, too, Mrs. Schwebel's special dish had the power to replace political rifts with a rare form of bipartisanship. Or, as she put it, "Republican and Democratic knishes — the delicious dishes." [70]

In Search of the First Knish

● ● ●

From the Holy Land to the Old Country

In New York, the knish shaped a generation, then another and another. But what shaped the knish? The hunk of stuffed dough, like those who consumed it, was of European extraction. It arrived in New York as an immigrant and remained tethered to its humble beginnings. The knish, after all, had traveled in steerage.

I searched for a trace at Ellis Island. Records documented the arrival of several knishes — but not the one I had in mind: Jan Knish, a Russian laborer, arrived from Blschjar [*sic*], Russia, on August 17, 1907, and headed to Jessup, Pennsylvania. Magnus Knish, a Swede from Tinnammon [*sic*], Sweden, landed on October 1, 1913, and headed to — where else? — Brooklyn.[1]

I had no indication that either of these men was Jewish or had as much as a passing affiliation with the potato pie. But the migration of Knishes underscored my theory that the knish and knish derivatives existed on every shore. Empanadas, samosas, gyoza, and calzones were part of the global family of dough wrapped around a filling: knishing cousins. If the knish came from Eastern European Jewish stock, perhaps its peregrinations could help me reconstruct the places and inclinations that shaped my people.

Ancient Israelite coins bore images of sustenance: sheaths of wheat, grains of barley, and pomegranates; but at the Israel Museum in Jerusalem, the Antiquities Wing held no evidence of a petrified potato pie. Knish-like foods, though, reared their heads in unexpected places. In rural Senegal, the *fatayer*, a sealed, thin-skinned bun, won the love of women and children who made it for monthly gatherings (imagine a Tupperware party with vigorous dancing). If a knish-like pie could surface in a predominantly Muslim country in West Africa, surely the knish had left a trace of some sort in the lands of my ancestors. I schemed about future knish explorations.

"How about an *article* on the knish?" suggested a friend.

"Why not a book on schmaltz herring or lox?" urged my dad.

Even those who (ostensibly) cared for the knish waxed cautious when I mentioned an around-the-world hunt.

What are you going to find? they chided.

For that, you have to go so far?

What's wrong with Crown Heights? Borough Park? Monsey?[2]

Naysayers only fueled the flame on the proverbial Sterno. (A propos, heating knishes in a chafing dish, over Sterno? Don't do it. Well, only in a pinch—if and only if the knishes are already warmed to the core. But it's never ideal.)

I was convinced that clues lay somewhere in region of the so-called Old Country. My Internet queries revealed a resurgence of the pastry—in Moldova. In 2008, the former Soviet Republic boasted a form of knish that went under the name *placinta* or *pateu*.[3] In Chișinău, the Moldovan capital, even McDonald's served up a knish-like food (think sealed rectangular apple pies with bubbled skins, served in red cardboard packets puckered shut). I decided the reflowering of the baked good echoed the rebirth of a Jewish community.

In 1903, Chișinău, then Kishinev, witnessed one of the bloodiest pogroms to tear through Eastern Europe. ("Pogrom," I have learned, is not necessarily part of common parlance. The first time I discovered someone for whom the term was new, we were equally taken aback: she by the long trail of anti-Semitism that preceded the Holocaust, and I by the fact that she hadn't heard of it.) The rampage in Kishinev left more than one hundred Jews dead and five times that number wounded. The *New York Times* chronicled the event.[4] As did a man sent by the Jewish Historical Commission in Odessa to interview survivors. Decades later that man, Chaim Nachman Bialik, would become known as Israel's national poet.

> Get up and go to the city of slaughter,
> See with your own eyes.
> Feel with your hands in the courtyards,
> On trees, stones, walls,
> The dried blood and brains of the dead.[5]

By 2009, Chişinău had become home to a Jewish community center, a Jewish day care facility, and bonfires in honor of Lag B'Omer, Jewish holiday.[6] I never made it there, but virtual knish crumbs led to Escazú, Costa Rica (potato and feta, baked at a place, since gone out of business, called Little Israel);[7] to Tokyo (sort of: a puffball pastry jammed with saccharine potato salad);[8] and to a canine (a blue-eyed, deaf Australian shepherd, up for adoption in Florida). In Washington, D.C., the Library of Congress had a hankering for knishes. Its Music Division had accessioned a double ocarina — or fipple flute — in the shape of a flattened round potato pie.

Montreal, Melbourne, and London boasted standard-issue knishes, as did most places with a handful of Ashkenazi Jews. Medical literature highlighted the dish as a serendipitous salve for acoustic trauma.[9]

My quest was not an international knish census (though I have been tempted). Simply put, I was on a hunt for ancestors.

If the pastry had indeed sprung "fully formed from the head of the Jewish people," as suggested by folklorist Nathan Ausubel, chances were that happened within the Pale of Settlement.[10] The Pale once encompassed modern-day Poland, Latvia, and Lithuania, which translates to the lands of my grandparents. Much of modern-day Ukraine and Belarus also fell within the area. In 1791, Catherine the Great carved out the Pale as a way to corral and control the growing Jewish population. The masses were expelled from large cities, urged toward small towns, and subjected to taxes disproportionate to their poverty. Regulations excluded Jews from business, higher education, and ownership of land.[11]

As a term, "Pale of Settlement" has come to connote a place of shared origins and near endearment, but nothing about that corridor was quaint or *heimish*. In the nineteenth century, 90 percent of world Jewry lived in close proximity to one another, under strict laws and limitations.[12] It's not hard to see how that helped set the stage for what came next.

(I don't mean to get all heavy on you, but let's face it: the knish, it's a little heavy.)

I first landed in the area formerly known as the Pale on a whim. After a year of study abroad in Paris and a few weeks as a volunteer on a château reconstruction project, my new Polish friends invited me for a visit. (Or, rather, I hung around the bus station in Lyon until they figured out I wanted a glimpse of their country.) I traveled thirty hours by bus with a handwritten lexicon:

Please — Proszę. And instructions on using a making a call: *First you need: żeton A* (a token for a pay phone).

In Warsaw's main train station, I stood before the departures board and picked out the names of my grandmothers' towns. I vowed to see them, but instead laid eyes on mountain spas, beer halls, and Auschwitz. I learned the word *gołampki*, which meant both "little pigeon" *and* "stuffed cabbage," my grandmother's specialty. I didn't find what I was looking for on that trip. It would be years before I realized it was — among other things — the knish. Four times in two decades, Poland lured me back. I saw friends, sleuthed for family history and looked for signs of Jewish life. Marcel Proust's homeland beckoned, not only thanks to the madeleine; a scholarly hypothesis suggested that French Jews could have invented the knish before being forced east by the Inquisition.[13] In the Middle East, the possibility of a proto-knish enticed me. I remembered seeing a mustard plant in a Bible-era landscape in Israel, which led to conjecture about a before–Common Era (BCE) knish. Perhaps that was a reach. But, anyway, I was going to visit relatives.

Land of Falafel and Bourekas

TEL AVIV, NOVEMBER 2009

"*Ma zeh*, knish?"

I'd heard the Hebrew for "What's a knish?" often enough to develop a knee-jerk response.

"Ashkenazi bourekas."

Occasionally I continued, "Dough, with a filling, sealed and baked."

Every so often that description elicited a flicker of recognition. "Ahhh . . . blintzes?"

Let's look at this objectively. A blintz begins life crepe-like as a near-transparent skin of dough. It ends up rolled into the shape of a sleeping bag, tail ends tucked neatly into its torso, and, more often than not, doused in sour cream. Blintzes tend toward the slippery and thus invite both fork and knife. If you really tried, you could walk around with a blintz, but that would not be in the spirit of the food. A knish you can eat at a counter, on a sidewalk, en route to just about anywhere, which is very much in the spirit of the food, but perhaps less in accordance with Jewish law. Street food is frowned upon and is considered an indicator of unreliability. He who is seen eating certain wheat-based snacks while walking may be deemed deficient in self-respect and thus unfit to serve as a witness in court.[14] (Clearly the High Court of Jerusalem had never been to New York's Chinatown.)

At Tel Aviv's Carmel Market, a vendor surrounded by a congress of buns, beignets, and baguette-like objects beckoned to me. The circles, triangles, and stretched squares of stuffed dough were called *sambusek* and *bourek*. They were delicious, she said. How many did I want?

Bourekas, a flakier Sephardic version of the knish, blanketed the landscape, as did falafel. What the knish once was to the Lower East Side, falafel was to modern-day Israel: street food, cheap food, food of peddlers, and backbone of on-the-go snacking. The cry of the falafel man followed me on main drags and through alleys. The chickpea was ubiquitous; the knish nowhere to be found.

My mother's mother, Nana, went, in 1977, on pilgrimage, as it was called, to Israel. She had arrived in New York in 1914, and left the Bronx mostly to see siblings in New Jersey. To get citizenship papers, Nana needed a birth certificate. Communist Poland sent a letter dappled in official seals and stamps and signatures and the message *"Nie figure."* Nope. Nothing. No trace.

Thanks to an assemblyman, Nana acquired papers, a passport, and then a seat on a group tour to Tel Aviv, Jerusalem, and the Dead Sea.

Fifteen years after that, I went to Israel to volunteer and to visit the sites that mattered most to her: the Wailing Wall and Simcha, her cousin.

Simcha, of airmail letters in Yiddish and that single visit, lived in Kiryat Bialystok (literally, the City of Bialystok) in Yehud, a Tel Aviv suburb next to the airport.

Outside Haifa, at Kibbutz Ramat Yochanan, I peeled eggplants for baba ghanoush. Smushed eggplants seasoned with tahini go by the name *hatzilim.* I confused it with *haloutzim,* the word for pioneers. The eggplants — steamed, mashed, macerated — got desalted in a Jacuzzi-sized vat before they met the strong hands of the head cook. Yehuda was stout and tan. His name filled the kitchen.

Yehuda, taste this.

Yehuda, what do I stir this with?

Yehuda, is this done?

Yehuda seasoned the eggplants with powder from a plastic jar the size of his forearm. *Ashan,* it said. Smoke.

Thump. Thump. Thump.

Years later, back in Israel on a quick trip, I went looking for knishes but found only bourekas. At the Tel Aviv equivalent of 7-Eleven, they populated layers of baking trays and filled shelves of tall rolling carts. Tribes of flaky pastries arranged themselves by flavor: spinach, corn, olive, Bulgarian cheese, yellow cheese, and pizza, in the shape of a pinwheel.

I sought expert advice.

"Knishes are quite rare here," Janna Gur, author of *The Book of New Israeli Food: A Culinary Journey*, told me via e-mail. "Your best bet would be Bnei Brak and the Mea She'arim Quarter in Jerusalem, time capsules of the Eastern European shtetl."[15]

I made calls to the bakeries of Bnei Brak and had even packed a requisite below-the-knee skirt. But on my free day, a Friday, I hemmed, hawed, and balked. Instead of heading to an orthodox community in search of knishes, I met Janna Gur in Jaffa, at Leon Bakery, her favorite place for bourekas. They came in a familiar array of flavors and appeared, from a distance — you'll forgive me — like knishes. The owners, third generation, shuttled platter after bourekas platter to our table (white plastic, with a red-and-white-checked cloth). Bourekas had a thinner skin than knishes, a similar array of flavors, and the same "Eat, eat, eat" ethos. Bourekas had roots in Bulgaria and, according to Janna, a place in rituals linked to mourning. "They were served at *shiva*," she said. The men of Leon Bakery gathered napkin dispensers, folded tablecloths, and piled chairs upon chairs. The sun began its descent. The day dimmed, the week tucked itself in. The third generation of boureka men herded their goods into plastic containers, paper bags, and the hands of grateful customers relieved to have something to serve for Shabbat. Down the block, the sun slipped into the Mediterranean. The waves glistened, the horizon went pink.

I tried to rethink the eclipse of the knish. Perhaps bourekas were not as militant as I had imagined. They, too, were immigrant fare, and, like the knish, simple street food. And just like knishes, bourekas had provided a livelihood and a foothold for new arrivals.

In the Holy Land, most of my conversations about the knish provoked incredulousness, curiosity, or plain confusion. But one group knew what I was talking about: the older generation, especially those from Romania, Poland, and the Pale. At a park on

Tel Aviv's swank Sheinkin Street, a chorus of chess players and bench sitters in their seventies and eighties shared their takes on the knish situation.

"I love it and I haven't eaten it for years."

"Why don't they make it anymore?"

"Once upon a time people had behinds that were . . ." (extending his hands about a meter apart).

"You have to know it from your family, from home."

"Knish is not really Israeli, but it's tasty."

"It didn't catch on in Israel because it is a lot of work."

"All this food is for older people."[16]

Less than two miles from the cabal of knish cognoscenti, in the neighboring municipality of Ramat Gan, sat a professional knish maker emerita. Bella Sherman was born in 1922 in Kovel, Poland (historically part of the Volhynia region, called Volin in Yiddish), and as young person, acted in Yiddish plays. In Israel she earned a living as a cook, but long before that, she was an understudy in the kitchen of her mother. Bella spent the war in Russia and the forests of Lithuania and arrived in Tel Aviv in 1948. She went to work at Café Batya, which predated the state of Israel. The food was familiar; it reminded Bella of what her uncle cooked at the Hotel Versailles, his own place, back in Kovel.

Bella encountered huge metal pots brimming with weapons used by the Jewish underground military organization, the Haganah.

For seven and a half years, Bella worked in the cauldron-hot kitchen. For seven and half years, she commuted by public trans-

In 1941, Café Batya opened on Tel Aviv's Dizengoff Street. In 2013, it moved to make room for a boutique hotel.

portation. For seven and half years, she formed knishes and kreplach and cholent and traded her sick days for pay. She put a son through medical school. He had since moved and was a doctor in Los Angeles.

"The dough has to be elastic," continued Bella. "If the flour is too dry, you add some water to it."[17] Shabbat, we sat around. Her niece Leah, whom I met in Poland and who tipped me off to her familial knish connection, kept interjecting, to make sure I understood. I did. Shabbat, no public transportation. Leah had picked me up at the home of my relatives who happened to live right near her boyfriend. (It's hard to tell if anything is really a coincidence or if everything is.) Shabbat, people dropped in. Bella's former daughter-in-law came by for a visit, too.

"You knead the dough," said Bella, "make it as thin as a tablecloth — that's what we call it, 'a tablecloth of dough' — then you put the meat not at the center [of the dough], but all around." A discussion ensued about innards. "There's the meat filling and there's varenike," declared Bella. Varenike were made with the same dough but stuffed with fruit or with cheese, which meant knishes filled with fruit could also be called varenike. I found this alarming but tried not to let on. "Use a glass to press around it," continued Bella. "The size depends on what you fill it with."

Café Batya, A Whiff of History

TEL AVIV, DECEMBER 2010

Before Shabbat, old army buddies gathered on the patio for their weekly lunch. Diagonally across from a Pizza Hut, at the intersection of Dizengoff and Arlosoroff, Café Batya bustled. Inside, waiters called out orders, the takeout line snaked past diners at tables, and yellowed clippings adorned the walls. The display smacked of Mrs. Stahl's, it should rest in peace. At Café Batya the photos showcased customers synonymous with the city: politicians, soldiers, writers, and actors. Bella had not worked in the kitchen for decades, but gefilte fish, which had been her specialty, was still on the menu and on the tables of faithful customers. I saw no trace of the knish, but the guy behind the counter assured me that knishes did exist on the premises, under the name *leviva memulet*, stuffed latke. (Were knishes really stuffed latkes? If that was the case, perhaps I shouldn't have gotten into such a huff when the Huffington Post paired my article about the knish with an image of a potato pancake.) The so-called knishes, oblong, with breaded skins, hardly resembled latkes. They looked like miniature footballs of the Nerf variety. One arrived at my table, warm, with a side of silverware.

Out of the fryer, onto the plate. At Café Batya, a knish has meat at its core.

We contemplated each other for a minor eternity.

Eventually, I delved in.

Beneath the fried exterior, a clump of mashed potatoes huddled around a dollop of meat. Homeland, *schmomeland*. This was foreign territory. The knish in my presence had little to do with Bella Sherman's tablecloth of dough. It looked like a dish sponge.

Two days later, I sat in the living room of Batya Yom Tov, the restaurant's namesake. Ensconced in her leather couch, the nonagenarian asked her aide to shuttle fruit and cakes from the kitchen. The knish, said Batya — with clementines, pears, and biscuits as her witnesses — was inextricably linked to *Yiddishkeit* and akin to a ritual object. "Catholics go to church and wear a cross, they cross themselves when they pass even a picture of Jesus or Mary," said Batya. "But Jews, Jews find the sacred in other places."[18]

Batya rarely made the three-block walk to her restaurant. Instead it came to her. Her aide, Michelle, traversed the few blocks to Café Batya several times a day, and returned with containers full of kasha and schnitzel and kugels. "There aren't that many locations where you can say, 'I ate here with my grandmother,'" said Batya, age ninety-three.

Batya Yom Tov was born in 1918 in the town of Kolaczyce, Poland, on the Russian border, in modern times, halfway between Kraków and Lviv. At age eighty, she went back there on a *tiyul shoreshim*, or roots trip. She located the house and asked, in Polish, if she might have a look.

She went in and thought, 'Too bad.' The dirt floor made her sad. It made her miss those times. It made a part of her unravel a little. "I could have stayed with my memories," Batya lamented. "But life isn't like that." Her hometown had become devoid of knishes. In Tel Aviv, too, Batya had noticed the deficiency. Her theory: In Israel Mizrahim, Jews with roots in the Middle East, outnumbered Ashkenazim. No wonder than that the pastries followed suit.

Shmil Holland, a Jerusalem-based chef, restaurant owner, and authority on Eastern European food, didn't see the cuisines as in competition. It was more of a collaboration, and one unique to his country. "It's the only place in the world that's a mixture of East European and Middle Eastern food," said the Jerusalem native and son of Polish Jews.[19] "In my house you could find herring with kreplach with tahini with eggplant and Israeli chopped salad. It lives nicely together." His cookbook *Schmaltz* paid homage to the cooking of his Ashkenazi grandmother and included a recipe for petite knishes, stuffed with cheese, in the form of half circles. ("Schmaltz," which, like "knish," is an everyday term in

New York, was, for Israeli bookstore clerks, an enigma.)[20] I entered three stores in search of the book and was greeted, three times, with quizzical looks.

Adventures in Antiquity

With slim findings under my belt, I set out to explore the knish in antiquity. Susan Weingarten, a scholar of ancient Israeli foods, drew my attention to a discussion in the Babylonian Talmud (circa fourth and fifth centuries CE) of *kisanin*, a type of roasted wheat that could be used as a stuffing inside bread.[21] That sounded promising, like a centuries-old kind of kasha. And given the Hebrew word for pocket is *kis*, *kisanin* seemed like a logical name for a key ingredient in an ancient pastry pocket. I tried to imagine what form a knish-like food might have taken in the third century CE; taste would be another matter altogether. And I wasn't the first to contemplate a pastry from Late Antiquity. Through the ages rabbis debated *kisanin* — and the bread they came with — in order to figure out what they were and what they weren't and which blessings to recite over them. Some said *kisanin* could benefit the heart and stop negative thoughts. (Any leftovers, by chance?)[22]

Around 1000 CE, another group of rabbis shared a recipe for the bread served — or stuffed — with *kisanin*:

> You bring fruit and white bread and put in it oil and honey and nuts and sesame and knead them in their covering and bake them in the oven and make of them several shapes such as birds and trees.[23]

It sounded like something out of Martha Stewart.

But those stuffed breads didn't have to be that ornate. They could also radiate beauty, or rather, flavor, from the inside. A rabbi from twelfth century Tunisia wrote about a simple pastry filled with sugar, almonds, and walnuts as a delicacy served on special occasions.[24]

Rabbis who came after that said that the special bread related to *kisanin* was made with oil, honey, or wine and was served with dessert. (A possible precursor to the cherry cheese knish?) My Talmudic food contacts couldn't establish a direct link between the *kisanim* of Talmudic times and knishes that came later. I latched on to a line from the e-mail, "the similarity in form and name makes one wonder a little . . ."[25]

Even if it didn't have a clearly defined antecedent, at least the knish was not entirely alone in the canon of pocket foods. At least it had ancestors.

I got a falafel and went, as is my custom, to visit Simcha.

Simcha who, every time, asks me to extend, on his behalf, warm
  regards to each member, individually, of the extended family
Simcha who, every time, makes me promise I will distribute these
  regards, individually
Simcha who, during intermission at Footloose on Broadway, told me,
  in Hebrew, his story
Simcha who, during the war, served in the Red Army
Simcha who remembered my nana's address from addressing letters for
  his grandmother
Simcha who, on seeing the Twin Towers, gazed up in awe

Simcha who considered my grandmother as if a mother. As if his
   mother

Simcha who visited her grave in New Jersey

Simcha who went also to her parents' graves in Brooklyn

Simcha who, in his neighborhood, took me for bike rides

Simcha whose birthday, on the Gregorian calendar, is the day before
   mine

Simcha who, after the war, returned to Bialystok to find no one

Simcha who arrived in Palestine after the war and became a medic in
   the army

Simcha who married Cohava, another medic, from Tunisia

Simcha whose name in Hebrew means joy or celebration

Simcha who submitted the names of fifty murdered family members to
   Yad Vashem

Simcha who bought a parcel of land near the airfield, before there was
   plumbing

Simcha who still mentions the uncle, Joe Mines, who helped him buy
   the land

Simcha who saved all the letters from my nana

Simcha who reads the Yiddish Forverts with a magnifying glass

Simcha who says, about his health: it shouldn't get worse

Simcha who wants to hear from us rak shurot tovot, only good
   things

Simcha who, to talk on the phone, turns down the radio

Simcha who calls me Larushka

Simcha whose doorway is flanked by a tree of kumquats

That visit, as always, Simcha asked after my work. I did my best to explain.

"*Ma zeh*, knishes?" asked Simcha.

His son was waiting to take me to the airport.

"*Lo hashuv*," I said. *No big deal.*

In Search of Knishes Past

"*Le* knish? *Qu'est-ce que c'est?*"

Again, that question. What was the knish?

I had come prepared with a location-specific answer.

C'est un chausson aux pommes, mais avec pommes de terre. It's an apple turnover, but with potatoes.

Chausson aux pommes means apple slipper, but it's really a fancified turnover, flaky, puffed up with apples, and dappled in cinnamon, butter, and sweetness. I thought I was being clever. In French, the response might seem more nuanced. Delivered correctly, it could convey a sense of a proletarian takeover of a glamorous pastry. If that didn't work, I was prepared to invoke Marcel Proust, whose obsession with the past was well known, legendary, and made mine seem like a blip. I could simply say I was in search not of lost time, but of lost knishes.

In Paris, I went straight to the Boutique Jaune to assess the knish population. Sacha Finkelsztajn, the owner, had been cordial on the phone. He confirmed he sold knishes and said he would be happy to meet. I should just give a call when I arrived in town. The Boutique Jaune, or Yellow Boutique, sat on a historically Jewish street in a historically Jewish neighborhood, not entirely unlike New York's Lower East Side. The Marais (it means swamp) had also turned trendy, studded with gay bars, nightclubs, and falafel shops. On Sundays, when the streets closed to cars, pedestrians swarmed the place. Certain tourists gabbed in accents often associated with Brooklyn or the Bronx.

The surfaces of the Boutique Jaune were covered in pastries. Photographs of Finkelsztajn forebears adorned the wall; but, alas, they were the only family members on the premises.

When might he return? I asked.

Uncertain.

Could I leave a message?

Oui. And a shrug.

I cursed the Eternal Knish. *You lure me to the place where the first knish purportedly took hold and voilà: the void.*

I went to meet Jean Zilberman, at the Ashkenazi food restaurant he owned nearby, Pitchi Poï. He said the name connoted a kind of neutral never-never land, but, a Jewish woman who lived through the war in France, said "Pitchi Poï" was not all positive. It had come to mean a scary place, exactly where Jews *didn't* want to be. It was, in any case, according to Zilberman, unattainable. Ditto the subject of my quest.

"Knish?" he took off his glasses and squinted his blue-brown eyes. "That's Russian. My parents were Polish, but I'll talk to you anyhow."[26]

Zilberman, born in France, had been "back" to Poland a few years prior. He recounted the arithmetic of death that had divided his family and decimated his parents' towns. The style of recitation resonated, familiar but with a different spin.

"All of us, we were in France during the war," said Zilberman. "What remained in Poland, we don't speak about anymore."

What he did speak of, in Yiddish, was food.

"*Gehachte leber*," said Zilberman. I thought he was referring to a broken heart. It took three repetitions for me to understand he was talking about chopped liver. "*Gehachte leber*," he said, "as in *gehachte tsuris*, chopped-up worries."

He knew from those. Zilberman first learned, at age forty, that he was Jewish. He learned, at the death of his father, about the *kaddish* and recited it.

Zilberman, trained as a chemical engineer, could not, at age sixty, find the food of his youth. "When you have forgotten everything," he said, "the last thing you remember is the schmaltz herring and the *gehachte leber*." Chopped liver was de rigueur; not so the object of my quest.

"In France, no, we don't care about the knish," said Zilberman, sans emotion. What mattered was "schmaltz herring with schnapps, soup with knaidlach [matzoh balls]. Or vodka."

Zilberman's restaurant served twenty flavors of the potato-derived spirit, which in its unadulterated form is colorless and without taste. But Zilberman was in it for flavor. His list included anise, banana, peppercorn, and vanilla and honey. It reminded me of the twenty-four varieties of stuffed pastries listed in Regina Frishwasser's *Jewish-American Cookbook*, from 1946.[27] The knish list featured flavors like banana, pepper, green pea, and molasses.

People who had never inherited cookbooks relied on Zilberman for ancestral recipes. His restaurant welcomed a diverse clientele, and on big holidays he hosted communal meals for locals. But one population was conspicuously absent from his restaurant: Jewish intellectuals.

It was, explained Zilberman, akin to the difference between red wine and vodka.

In another part of Paris, intellectual curiosity and the knish *did* intersect. Bibliothèque Medem, home to Europe's largest Yiddish-language library, and, I hoped, some references to the knish. Before I entered, I stopped in at a bakery. The woman behind the counter greeted me in a frilled smock.

"For the lady?"

She put one *chausson aux pommes* in a square of bakery paper and spun the ends like the handles of a jump rope. It looked like a froofy distended bonbon. The moment I left the shop, I downed it. For something called an apple slipper, it felt more like a clog. In a good way. The sliced apples inside — tart and firm — reminded me of family trips to upstate orchards for "picking season," and of my year as a student in Paris, when a few pastries counted as a full meal. (In the absence of knishes, I assigned memories to the baked goods at hand.) The *chausson aux pommes* — flaky, manicured, and glistening with an egg wash — felt like the antithesis of a knish. It was showy, more expensive than a croissant or a *pain au chocolat* — and, I had to admit, delicious.

At the Bibliothèque Medem I met Yitskhok Niborski, a native Yiddish speaker, who, by dint of his upbringing, understood my quest. Niborski was familiar with the roadblocks one could encounter when trying to discuss stuffed dough in France. Case in point: the snafu that ensued when he introduced adult students to a Yiddish proverb about food and Torah.

Az Vayakhel iz a knish,
iz Pikudei a vareniki.[28]

As he had done with the secular French Jews in his Yiddish class, Niborski began the explanation from scratch:

The Torah comprises five books of Moses.

Each book is divided into sections.

Each week on the Sabbath, one section or Torah portion — a *parsha* — is read in synagogue.

The last two portions of the Book of Exodus are *Vayakhel* and *Pikudei*, which are usually read on the same week.[29] *Vayakhel* means "and he assembled," referring to Moses, who got his people together to build the holy Tabernacle; *Pikudei* means "amounts of," as in the quantities of gold, silver, and copper needed to adorn the sanctuary, the spools of thread needed to stitch priestly vestments, and the sheer energy needed get the place up and running.

Aknish comes from Aramaic. Aramaic is the language of the Talmud and one, according to scholars, that Jesus spoke in his lifetime. Jewish marriage contracts are written in Aramaic. Ditto the mourner's *kaddish* and the Dead Sea Scrolls. In Aramaic, "a knish," or rather *aknish*, meant a coming together, a joining of people, a community. *Knishta* meant synagogue.

Whoa. Perhaps my quest was not as far-fetched as I had originally envisioned. My family's secular pilgrimages made us de facto members of a de facto knish community, but I had never thought that the knish, at its core, might have anything to do with getting people into the same room.

> If *Vayakhel* is a knish,
> then *Pikudei* is a varenike.

If you believe *Vayakhel* is about a knish (which is to say, if you don't know your Torah, or your Aramaic), then you must think *Pikudei* deals with those small dumplings called varenike. Or, in modern terms: If you believe the Torah portion *Vayakhel* is about a knish, I have a bridge to sell you.

Niborski explained each of the two Torah portions. He explained the Aramaic and the Yiddish and the syntax. The students nodded politely, but they didn't get it. Niborski explained again, methodically, from the beginning. No dice. Eventually he figured it out: the students didn't know from knishes.

But for me, Niborski had more to dish. He pulled out a mini-encyclopedia of Yiddish foods from 1958. The listing for "knish" fell beneath the heading for "pierogi":

KNISH in Polish is *knysz*, Ukrininan, *knys*, *gefilte klyotske* [stuffed block], and in Russian [*knish*], a cake baked in butter or fat. Goes back to German dialect *knitsch*. Something which is pressed together, *knitschen,* to press together.

The description included an excerpt from a memoir by a man born on the border of Ukraine and Poland, circa 1842. "The cemetery man had an additional source of income. He used to sell *knishek-lekh* [little knishes] in town."[30]

Hunh. At the same time that knishes came to prominence on the Lower East Side and Coney Island, they were a source of entrepreneurship in the town of Terespol, one hundred miles south of Bialystok. (I didn't realize it then, but, in the 1920s, before the shop at Brighton, Mrs. Stahl had already begun her knish business, in a rooming house in Spring Valley, New York.)[31]

In Paris, I went to the Mémorial de la Shoah.[32] I went to the Mémorial des Martyrs de la Déportation, underground, behind Notre-Dame. I went to the Centre de Documentation Juive Contemporaine and stood before a bulletin board of notes written by people who were looking for other people in search of the same lost relatives. No sign of a knish. And no sign of Finkelsztajn.

La Boutique Jaune greeted me with matzoh. It was half a year before and half a year after Passover. "From Father to Son," proclaimed the black letters on the sun-colored shop, "since 1946."

Inside, the knishes sat among pierogi, which were called *pierojki* and came in strange flavors like eggplant, salmon, and leek. Dora and Itzik Finkelsztajn, Sacha's grandparents, arrived in Paris from Poland in the early 1930s. Itzik Finkelsztajn was known for apple strudel and *vatrushka*, a sweet-cheese-filled mega-knish. In the early seventies, his son Henri took over. And after that, Henri's son Sacha, who hoped to pass the tradition to a fourth generation.[33] The place was the Mrs. Stahl's, the Yonah Schimmel's, and the Gabila's of Paris, all rolled into one, minus the grit, and heavy on the egg yolks.

A stout, potbellied isosceles knish stared at me from atop a bakery case. It sat there, primped, plump, and undeniable. The dough glowed as yellow as the storefront. It looked like the plucky love child of Brioche and Hamantaschen. On the inside though, it was pureed potato, with bits of onion to provide a whiff of the familiar. I lifted it to my lips. If this was the French knish, so be it.

Au Revoir, Pitchi Poï

PARIS, DECEMBER 2010

I went back, but not for Finkelsztajn. Zilberman's restaurant was closing. *Fin.* End of an era. Good-byes can be so disappointing. One comes for catharsis and leaves empty-handed. (At the farewell to Ratner's on Delancey in 2004, the restaurant had been stripped of its booths and cookie counter; hors d'oeuvres huddled in chafing dishes.) Pitchi Poï was ushered out with bouquets of smoked fish, an ocean of vodka, and dancing of every denomination. People stood in coats for hours, trying to take their leave — and avoiding it.

The next day, I stopped in on the knishes. They were as I remembered, yellow triangles, as if parts of stars, pulled from clothing — detached, elongated, and stuffed with things we would never discuss.

To Poland, with Ambivalence

WARSAW, AUGUST 2009

In Helsinki, the woman at the duty-free shop demanded my boarding pass, and an answer. "Is Warsaw your final destination?"

Interesting word choice. Can I go home?

The year before, in Warsaw, I had seen the banners for the Singer Cultural Festival. Singer, as in Isaac Bashevis (I knew him to be a resident of Seagate, Brooklyn, next to Coney Island, and later, the Upper West Side).

I had seen banners, but no living, breathing Jews.

In Helsinki, the duty-free shop cashier — blond, compact, and expressionless — gripped my receipt and boarding pass.

Is Warsaw your final destination?

The café in the Helsinki airport sat there, expansive, fancy, and welcoming. Low-backed benches and round tables beckoned. I made my way toward the baked goods. I urged a set of tongs into a Plexiglas box and retrieved a flattened brown rowboat of crust stuffed with mush the color of bone.

I didn't know it at the time, but the *karjalanpiirakka* is the preferred pastry of the Karelia region of Finland. Something about it felt familiar. Something about it offered comfort.

The puckered edge of dough recalled a picture frame. I contemplated an about-face to New York, then imagined ancestors staring up a me, each vying for a spot on the trip. A momentous occasion deserved a memento. Suddenly I wished for custom-printed yarmulkes I could distribute as proof of my visit.

MISSION TO KNYSZYN

AUGUST 28, 2009

◦ ◦ ◦ *Warsaw was streaked in a* yellow-pink haze, as if lit by a distant bulb. The public bus ran smooth and swift, straight shot into the center of town. The city looked, I had to admit, pretty. I would have a go at it. I would try to shed at least one layer of resentment. I would try to make friends, with the city and perhaps a person or two. Aleje Jerozolimskie greeted me with a five-story palm tree.

"It looks like a joke," said a map I'd picked up the year before, "but in fact . . . 'Greetings from Jerusalem Avenue' is meant to remind passersby of the void left by the absence of the Jewish community from Warsaw."[34]

Cheery.

"Erected as a temporary installation on a traffic island in 2003, it became a landmark and stayed for good."[35] I envisioned a supersized memorial to the knish (preferably kasha) to be erected on the opposite corner. "Greetings from the Old Country."

The next morning found me on Ulica Dobra, Good Street, opposite the University of Warsaw Library. The building was Statue of Liberty green, with inscriptions on its façade that paid homage to music, math, and electromagnetism. Between swaths of Sanskrit and Arabic, a phrase in Hebrew greeted me. But the very thing that welcomed me made me feel estranged.

Oh, you cunning calligraphy. You lure me with your ancient letters and then, shalom, *the void.* My street Hebrew was no match for sacred texts: I could make out letters and words, but not meaning. If only I had studied harder in Hebrew school, and spent less time trying to decide which of the Turner twins (fraternal) was cuter. If I had grown up observant or gone to *shul* with some hint of regularity, then maybe I would have understood the biblical message set before me. Maybe I could finally fit in (with whom exactly remained to be seen). Nonetheless, I was determined to flaunt my heritage in a rebuilt, glittering Warsaw.

Above the Vistula River, clouds floated aimless, a bridge rose in strings. One block away, I stood on the lookout for an ally and a guide. Across the street, a young man pointed at the Hebrew lettering on the library façade. *A Jew,* I thought, certain that the Almighty or Nana — or both, in cahoots — were looking down at me. The young man gesticulated to his friends.

I stepped off the curb.

And back on.

Off.

On.

I blamed my surroundings. It was Poland's fault that I couldn't speak its language or read the holy text that beckoned me on so-called Good Street. Poland's fault that I couldn't speak a fluent *mamaloshen.* Poland's fault that I had no relatives on its soil, no real ancestral home, and that my SIM card from the previous year had expired. I resented the fact that I had traveled so far to pick at shards of what once was.

Off.

On.

Each foot carved a question mark in the air. I snaked from sidewalk to gutter. The three young people distanced themselves from the Hebrew.

I bounded across Good Street.

"*Dzień dobry.* Umm. Hello? Hi. Umm. Do you speak English?"

They did.

"Do you, umm, understand what that says?" I waved an arm at the Hebrew panel.

The guy who had been pointing at the letters had seen them at the Chabad House downtown. He wore a shoulder bag emblazoned with red letters that slunk and dripped like wet paint, or blood: "Welcome to Destruction."

He wanted to know why certain Hebrew letters were wider than others. It was an artful form of right justification, I explained, relieved to be able to answer the question.

I wanted to know if he was Jewish.

He wanted to know if I was.

Did he speak Hebrew?

Did I keep kosher?

Did he know about the Singer Festival?

Did I?

We exchanged names (his was Maciek) and arranged to meet later in the week.

● ● ● *Again, matzoh. The plaza outside* the Ester Rachel Kamińska and Ida Kamińska State Jewish Theater was covered in the
stuff. Passersby pressed boxes of matzoh to their bosom. Kids
clung to it. People waited on line to aquire it. It was half a year before and half a year after Passover. Rosh Hashanah was around the
corner and with it the promise of plump, round challah, designed
to remind us of the circle of life.

I muttered something about knishes. Someone thrust a box of
matzoh in my direction. I tried to get tickets for a sold-out show.
Denied. I explained how I had e-mailed and called and phoned and
sent messages from New York.

I flashed my press pass.

I smiled.

I squirmed and hesitated.

"But," I paused. "I'm Jewish."

The blond guy at the box office squelched a smile (or was it
a smirk?). *"Sold out" meant "sold out."* Other parts of the festival
were free and open to the public. A park across the street boasted
a freestanding cutout of Isaac Bashevis Singer. (His countenance
reminded me of a similarly cardboard Princess Leia I had encountered at a bar mitzvah on Long Island.) Próżna Street, whose
buildings had survived the Ghetto, were gussied up for the festival. Scrims covered windows with quaint portraits of people who
would never return. The festival's main drag was decked out in
ersatz nostalgia and faux-old pop-up shops. At the café on the corner, hand-dipped chocolates were topped with the Hebrew letters
that spelled *chai,* which is to say, life.

Friday evening: A plastic table under a white cloth extended over the better part of Próżna Street, with forty folding plastic chairs tucked into each side. Finally I would find my people.

Men milled around in Day-Glo vests, emblazoned with a word I looked up later, "Security."

Festive.

Seats were reserved, but not for me. I hovered among the gathering crowd, increasingly indignant. Nana kept kosher, kept separate dishes for Passover milk and Passover meat. (I didn't know it then, but so did Mrs. Stahl.) Nana's candy store stayed open on Shabbat. (So did Mrs. Stahl's.)[36] On Rosh Hashanah and Yom Kippur, Nana and my grandfather closed the shop; Friday night, she lit candles. I stood ready to rattle off this lineage to anyone who might want to know. No one did. I stood shoulder-to-shoulder with onlookers, annoyed that I had to jockey for a seat at a ceremony that was my birthright.

Golden challah rolls lolled on the Sabbath table on Próżna Street. In the tradition of the older ladies of Ratner's Lower East Side Dairy Restaurant, the woman next to me squirreled rolls into her bag. She gathered napkins and shuttled desserts to her handbag. She drooled the Hebrew-ish words of a song. I commandeered a hunk of cake, passed it to Maciek (standing behind me), and asked him to find out how the humming lady knew the words to the song. (Was she Jewish?) She zipped her handbag, and almost smiled. The lyrics, said Maciek, she had learned from a record.

The next day I found a bakery that smelled like the Bronx:

Kingsbridge, where Nana went for errands. I knew the beauty parlor, supermarket, and sacrosanct bakeshop that emitted canary-colored rolls, thick with onions. In Warsaw, the same aroma radiated from small ovals. Each round of baked dough was crowned with strips of onion, translucent, burnt at the tips. I pointed.

"*Procszę,*" I said, as in please. Please, may I have one?

I pointed again and smiled again. I pointed and smiled, smiled and pointed. I uttered the word "four" in Polish, *cztery*, because it was the number I remembered and it seemed like a reasonable quantity. The crowd stepped back, and I pointed at the onion-stomached pastries from closer range.

"*Cebularze?*" asked the bakery woman. "Little oniony things?"

Yes. Please. *Those.*

A memory from the Bronx: In the kitchen of the apartment on Morris Avenue, Nana at the table next to the window. In the alley, the laundry line clanked in a breeze. Nana sat there, all eyelids. Her knife did double time.

"Why are your eyes closed?"

"I'm just looking down."

"Are you crying?"

"Oh, am I? Must be the onions."

Before Poland, I went back to her building on Morris Avenue. The buzzers listed Ramirez, Santiago, and Colón. Someone came out; I walked in. The stairwell had shrunk and darkened. I knew Nana's was the apartment in the corner, facing the street, but couldn't remember which floor. I searched for proof of a mezuzah. The smell of arroz con frijoles overtook me and the hallway.

Warsaw made me mute and clueless, but, I had to admit, the place smacked of home. Under the spell of the *cebularze*, I let my knish quest languish and spent days at the cafés along Good Street. I lurked around the university library and learned the meaning of its Hebrew inscription, from Ezekiel: "And He said unto me: 'Son of man, cause thy belly to eat, and fill thy bowels with this roll that I give thee.' Then did I eat it; and it was in my mouth as honey for sweetness."

In Poland, I pronounced the knish ethereal, ephemeral, and gone. I would have to content myself with the aftertaste. Then, through a friend of a friend of my cousin, I met a man who mentioned Agnieszka Kręglicka. She owned a slew of restaurants in the city, was a leader in Poland's Slow Food movement, and had just been to New York, where she encountered, yep, knishes. We met at Chianti, one of her restaurants, on a Saturday, before it opened. Agnieszka took notes and made calls and wrote down all we could unearth of the knish in Poland. She knew people who might know of the knish: her former neighbors (Jewish), a friend who had moved to Israel, and the restaurant critic for Warsaw's biggest daily paper. Agnieszka introduced me to him later that evening. When I mentioned the knish, he nodded in recognition.

"It's for the ancestors," he bellowed. "And it's served on November first."

I knew about November first, All Saints' Day, or Day of the Dead, when Mexican bakers turn out colorful breads to placate the departed. As a kid, I had even attended a mass for the occasion. After a Halloween slumber party, I spent the following day in church with my friend, and with strict instructions from my grandmother: *Don't kneel*. During the Eucharist, I clung to the pew in front of me. I teetered in deference and disbelief. My feet wedged themselves against the fold-out step, a carpeted ledge the likes of which I'd never met in synagogue. (It was called a kneeler, my friend told me.)

In Poland, All Saints' Day is holy and dedicated to remembrance. People crisscross the country by car, driving hours to get to the graves of their ancestors (not entirely unlike the Jewish ritual of visiting the dead in advance of the High Holidays). At a bar in Warsaw, the food critic sketched a knish, a round thing, he said, that had to be filled with meat. He bought rounds of the cherry liqueur called *wisniak*. I remembered it from my first time in Poland. Before we left the house for a day trip, to Auschwitz, the mother of my friend gave me a nip.

Family Reunion, Once Removed

BIALYSTOK, AUGUST 2008

Given a day to visit the graves of my people, I would traverse New York City suburbs, stop in the less-than-sexy parts of Queens and Brooklyn, and sprint to Florida.

I had no relatives buried in Bialystok, but I did have a past, worthy of a visit. Before I arrived, the guy next to me on the train wanted to know if I had relatives in the city.

My family, I told him, was (pause for emphasis) *Jewish*.

But at that moment, I *did*, in fact, have family in Bialystok. Five of my relatives peopled the place. We were first and second cousins, several times removed. (Some of us had not seen one another in twenty years.) Proximity kept us apart — they lived in Jersey,

A Friday afternoon in Bialystok, 1932. Women bring their Sabbath meal, pots of a stew called cholent, to a local bakery.

we were in New York — but Bialystok brought us together. At the Hotel Branicki, the descendants of Celia and Max Levy gathered at the breakfast buffet. Tomasz Wiśniewski — the same guide Mimi Sheraton had for her exploration of the bialy, I bragged, to anyone who would listen — sank into a tufted couch in the lobby and explained our itinerary. He had found nothing with regard to our family history — not in the cemetery, not in the burial records, and not in the many databases he had compiled of the area's Jewish dead. But there was still plenty to see. The six of us, plus Tomasz, would spend two days in his Kia Carens, zooming around the region surrounding Bialystok. It was called Podlasie. We were to call him Tomek.

The descendants of Celia and Max Levy piled in and out of the car on cue. We asked questions and laughed at Tomek's jokes. We combed the countryside, ate at an old-fashioned organic restaurant with dimmed lights, and acted like everything was fine. At the synagogue cum museum at Tykocin, we stared at prayers painted on the walls. (We didn't know it then, but a menorah on display came from the same place as our people.) In Bialystok, we passed through the gates of the Jewish cemetery into a sea of gravestones, leaning, as if in prayer or exhausted from it. We came across a black obelisk chiseled, in Yiddish, with names of nearly one hundred people killed in the 1906 pogrom. (Our family left in 1914 and 1920. "Bialystok," they'd mutter occasionally, but the monument and the horror they never mentioned.)

We downed tea with mint and lemon, dumplings with meat and cabbage, and posed for photographs with wide eyes and smiles.

We wedged ourselves into the Kia and pried ourselves from it with fitness and finesse. After one lunch, a group of tourists, Polish, ambled toward Europe's oldest Muslim cemetery (we'd been, earlier). Our trip was half over. We had found scant trace of our relatives, they should rest in peace. The tourists — kerchiefed, umbrella-laden, and expressionless — slunk across the road. We sat buckled into the Kia. I rode shotgun and found myself, for the first time in forty-eight hours, a full three feet from any living relative — which might explain the sudden yearning for a busload of cousins.

And a shofar. To disperse the crowd.

One sturdy blast — *Tekiah gedola!* — would assert our presence, reinsert a Jewish element into the landscape, and clear a path for the car.[37] At that moment, though, I had only mounting frustration and my voice, which blurted kazoo-like: "Jews, coming through!"

❖ ❖ ❖ *Three times I asked Tomek* to introduce us to live Jews. Three times he said there were only six in the city, none of whom were born there.

The descendants of Celia and Max Levy were five women and one man, from New York, New Jersey, and California, born, all of us, in the tristate area. Celia and Max Levy were buried in Brooklyn, at Washington Cemetery, beneath six-foot grave markers with blatant block letters: LEVY. Cousin Ed said, according to his father, brother of my grandmother, the last name, in Poland, had been Czapnik. I considered myself a decent keeper of family records and a decent keeper of the peace. I wasn't convinced about Czapnik, but had no evidence to the contrary. Plus, we Levys had to stick together.

At dusk on our third and final night in Bialystok, my mother's cousin, named for Max Levy, remembered about the birth certificate. Maxine (she goes by Max) had traveled from San Diego to New York, through Prague and Warsaw, with a large brown duffel bag, a.k.a. the Beast. The Beast contained, among many other things, a Ziploc bag with a sheet of beige parchment, imprinted with official stamps, official seals, and official signatures.

At dusk on our last night in Bialystok, the sky went pink —
translucent and then opaque, the color of a "While You Were Out"
pad. No one had telephoned. No one called to see us. No one had
left a message. I called Simcha from the hotel lobby, to verify de-
tails, but they were all moot: his high school, home, and street had
been erased, repaved, and renamed. Even the memorial to the
Great Synagogue was a reconstructed skeleton of the dome that
once pierced the city's skyline.

The wall behind the hotel glowed red. Our train was set to
depart at ten the following morning. Tomek unfolded the beige
parchment harvested from the Fort Lauderdale condominium of
Aunt Jean, may she rest in peace.

Aunt Jean who knit cardigans, scarves, and matching hats

Aunt Jean who balanced her neighbors' checkbooks

Aunt Jean who listened, on phonograph, to Mel Brooks in The 2000
Year Old Man

Aunt Jean who, whenever she could, said Yizkor[38]

Aunt Jean who snuck cigarettes in the bathroom with the silver-dancer
wallpaper

Aunt Jean who got knishes at the Festival Flea Market in Pompano
Beach

Aunt Jean who, the youngest of seven, remembered the bread lines in
Poland

Aunt Jean who, as a girl, didn't remember her father or eldest sister
who left Bialystok in 1914

*Aunt Jean who, with her mother and siblings, arrived in New York six
  years later*

*Aunt Jean who thought Nana, in blue taffeta, was "the most beautiful
  woman" she'd seen*

*Aunt Jean who, on Rosh Hashanah and Passover, sent money to Simcha
  in Israel*

Aunt Jean, who at ninety-two, went again to visit him

*Aunt Jean who, a life member of Hadassah, wrote notes on its
  stationery*

Aunt Jean who would make thirty hard-boiled eggs for a seder

*Aunt Jean who said, in lieu of her birthplace, that she was "brought up
  in Brooklyn"*

Aunt Jean who liked the onion loaf at Red Lobster

Aunt Jean who made a mean matzoh brei

*Aunt Jean who kept a list on her fridge: In case of emergency: daughter,
  son, grandsons*

Aunt Jean who beat us all at Scrabble

"It says here," said Tomek, "Knyszyn."

The sun slipped into oblivion. Thirty-seven kilometers northwest of Bialystok, Knyszyn was waiting. I knew, from Tomek's
book, that it had one of the few surviving Jewish cemeteries in Poland and a woman who remembered the Jews.

"We'll wake up at dawn and drive there," I suggested, giddy as a
kid for Disneyland.

A Jewish family from Knyszyn at a celebration, circa 1920–1930.

Mission to Knyszyn

POLAND, AUGUST 2009

A year later, in Warsaw (via Helsinki) I scanned the city for a copy shop. I had to print out images of knishes: square ones, round ones, fried and baked, split and whole, exposed and encased in aluminum foil. Photos could help dismantle the language barrier and at least give people an idea of what I had in mind when I said, "knish." Karol — Jewish, from Warsaw, wearing a Yankees cap — became my friend at the Singer Festival. He wasn't sure he knew knishes, had never heard of Knysyzn, but came along, to translate.

Tomek picked us up in Bialystok. Wooden churches, bales of hay, and endless sky marked the way to Knyszyn. I braced myself for the local Hadassah chapter and the decades-old cholent they had kept warm for just this occasion. *So you're the great-niece of Szejna Czapnik? She was a small child, but feisty.* The name, in Yiddish, meant "pretty."

Tomek ushered us to Town Hall, to the office of a man who resembled Gene Wilder as Willy Wonka. Krzysztof Bagiński didn't greet me with a somersault, but he did bend over backwards. The head of public relations for Knyszyn glanced at my knish headshots with a smile and a question mark. I kept hoping he would unlock the key to my past. His town had about two thousand inhabitants; before World War II, twice that number, nearly half of whom were Jews.

The town historian arrived by bicycle, in a sport coat. The men purred and sputtered. They asked for Aunt Jean's birth certifi-

cate and murmured, "Czapnik." I plucked words from the Polish: *Płacząca* (weeping, as in willow). *Pamiętać* (remember). *Żydowski* (Jewish). The men stood and sat, raised their voices and lowered them, opened books and urged them shut. I stared at the lace curtains and decided they conjured Nana's kitchen, and its split pea soups, kugels with cornflake roofs, and matzoh balls fluffy from seltzer. My nana, Eva Farbstein née Levy, she should rest in peace, never served knishes and never mentioned Knyszyn.

Pan Henryk the historian (we addressed him with the everyday honorific) took us to the cemetery. On the outskirts, we unfolded a quick picnic: local beer plus baked rolls with vegetable guts.

Pan Henryk tucked the cuffs of his slacks into his socks, turned up his collar, and led us through a forest studded with tombstones. We saw markers from the 1700s and Hebrew inscriptions worn to near oblivion. Tomek, who is not Jewish, had transcribed and transliterated names from seven hundred *matzevot*, or grave markers, in the forest.

My family did not figure in, but the knish did. According to local legend, professional mourners hired to cry at funerals distributed filled pastries to the bereaved, to acknowledge grief and assuage it. Another legend linked the name of the town with the name of the pastry. Until then, I thought I was only connected to the knish via proclivities that came from my *father*'s side of the family.

In town, plums clung to every tree. Hand-painted letters on a trash can called out, KNYSZYN, lest we forget. Pan Henryk

Knishes from Knyszyn? Not quite, but good in a pinch.

On a mission: (from left) Knyszyn town historian Henryk Stasiewicz, Karol Kempnerski of Warsaw, and the author, 2009.

wanted me to pump water from the well in the center of town. After a few rounds of resistance, it came quick. We drank. Even without the Hadassah ladies, the day became a homecoming. I kept pumping—for water, then information—in what I would later recognize as that excited, impatient, verge-of-irritated tone that took over when I asked my grandma questions on tape. There

The Legend of the Knyszyn Knish

The day was sunny; the summer sun showed noon. In a darkened room, women busied themselves with preparations for a meal for peasants who worked in the fields. From beneath thatched roofs an aroma familiar and alluring teased nostrils. The women chatted happily; their hands and arms moved with grace and speed. They chopped, they kneaded dough into cakes and fried it. They rarely had to look down at their hands, so familiar were they with the work.

Not far from the huts, at the very edge of the forest, major routes led to Warsaw, to Vilnius, and to Ukraine. The routes led to the north of Podlasie Province and well beyond. But not many visitors came to this little village with the marvelous smells.

Then, amid the silence of the forest and the fields, the villagers began to hear the sound of hoofs, advancing gradually and steadily, not fading into the distance, but coming toward them. Men on horseback were coming closer and closer to their village.

Were these their own people or were they enemies? Should the townspeople welcome them or flee? A skilled eye left no doubt. These were indeed their own people.

The procession approached.

The women emerged with several children in tow. They greeted the guests according to tradition. The peasants stayed behind, according to their instinct for self-preservation.

"We are exhausted," proclaimed the men on horseback. "Pray, good lady, give us food and drink and we will pay you back."

"We are pleased you're here," replied one woman. "Welcome, great and honorable guests. Our home is your home."

The women bustled around briskly. They set the table with milk and mead. For dinner, they served dumplings on horseradish leaves, with home-baked cakes for dessert. The travelers ate. They admired the food and offered compliments. As a measure of gratitude, the horsemen left a golden coin. The horsemen thanked their hosts and, before riding away, addressed one woman: "Pray, good lady. What is the delicacy with which you welcomed us?"

"It is knish, my lord," replied the woman, clutching the golden coin to her breast. "Knish." She thanked the visitors and bowed deeply until they vanished from sight.

Another day, the men on horseback passed the place where they had eaten knishes. They remembered the taste of the savory dumplings with onion and game meat served on horseradish leaves. They'd liked the dumplings very much and wished to stop again.

"Pray, good lady, what do you call those dumplings?" asked the most important horseman, who was the king.

"It is knish, my lord," said the woman as she bowed. "Knish."

"Pray, good lady, what do you call this hamlet?"

"We are forest people and this is a forest hamlet," said the woman. "That is what we call ourselves."

"That is not a name," declared the king. "From today onward this forested hamlet will be called Knyszyn."

And so it remained.

From that day forward, people asked, "Where does one eat knishes?"

"In Knyszyn!"

Later that year, the king built his manor house in that hamlet and it became his favorite place to stay. The surroundings were beautiful and bucolic with a large forest and a river. The game was abundant and the waters clear. The king came often to relax and to hunt. Knyszyn came to be an important seat in the region of Podlasie. It was a town rich in wealth and capital, but with no resource as great as its handsome knish.

Tomasz Krawczuk, "Knysze Jak Knyszyn" (October 6, 1995), in *Knysze Jak Knyszyn: Legendy I gawędy* (Knyszyn: Biblioteka Gońca Knyszyńskiego, 2006), 11–13. Translated by Mateusz Zurawik.

In 1897, musicians from Knyszyn played a pre-Purim concert as a fund-raiser.

was never enough detail in her responses, and what detail there was, was piecemeal, confusing, and contradictory. (I didn't know it then, but I would detect a similar lilt — eagerness, frustration, dismay — in the voice of the great-granddaughter of Mrs. Stahl, in interviews recorded with her grandmother and great-aunt, about the family and the knish business.)³⁹ But that day in Knyszyn, I prattled and prodded, as if my questions could revive stories that had, long ago, dwindled in size.

Of Family Trees and Paperwork

POLAND, 2010

The hard, bright, uninterrupted light of a November morning made Warsaw shimmer. I hadn't planned to return, but when a Warsaw nonprofit invited me on an official trip, I couldn't resist.

The Forum for Dialogue among Nations (as in Jews and Poles) had arranged a week of meetings with ambassadors and distinguished speakers. We participated in the organization's work with youth, visited Auschwitz, and partook in a Shabbat dinner in Kraków.

After that we made a beeline for Knyszyn, with a stop in Bialystok to search the State Archives for my people. If Aunt Jean was from Knyszyn, perhaps others were, too.

I wrote the words "Levy" and "Czapnik" in shaky Cyrillic and unfolded the paper for a clerk.

"What is your confession?" she asked.

When I first visited Poland, in 1991, my friend's aunt said I really should go hear the pope in Czestochowa. Nearly two decades later, the woman at the archives in Bialystok asked for my confession ...

Right there, in her open office.

Then she left.

Ablutions, I concluded.

She returned. "Confession. It means religion."

I filled in official state forms with the Polish words for birth, marriage, and death. Those forms brought binders, which brought more binders, which brought books of birth records handwritten in Old Russian and dribs of Hebrew and revealed a name I had never encountered: *Riwa Mordkowna* (Riva, daughter of Mordechai), alongside one I had just warmed to, *Czapnik,* hatmaker. My mother's mother was born not in Bialystok but in Knyszyn.

The next day, I scurried back to the archives for documents, official stamps, official signatures, and an official receipt. The bookstore on Bialystok's main square had added ceiling lamps, a coat

*The author, right, and
her nana, Eva Farbstein, née
Riva Czapnik, late 1970s.*

*Jewish cemetery
restoration project,
Knyszyn, 2009.*

rack, and a café. Soon it would host a Scrabble tournament (hello, Aunt Jean). Outside, on the square, a man sold cards for Christmas. His table was blanketed with images of angels and evergreens.

I asked Karol, who had come from Warsaw, to ask the guy what he had for Chanukah.

Upstairs, at a *bar mlechny*, which translates as "milk bar" but meant "food like Nana's," I took a cup of compote and a small mountain of kasha — no knishes. And no time for Knyszyn. The sky grayed early. People were waiting for us in Warsaw. Plus, what did I need to prove? I was a direct descendant of Knyszyn, which explained my penchant for wide sky, heavy carbohydrates, and haggling with the past.

The Prehistory of the Knish

I knew the knish was my elder, but just how old was it?

To find the answer, I would have to delve deeper into its dense heart. I consulted dictionaries, conferred with food scholars, and called on historians of Jewish life. Pinpointing the exact origins of the knish, warned Hasia Diner, would be near impossible.[40]

HERE LIE THE BOWL, BOARD, AND ROLLING PIN,

WHICH, ALONG WITH THE HANDS OF ITS MAKER(S),

BIRTHED THE FIRST KNISH.

I gave up hoping to find such a plaque at the site of the pastry's debut; better to gauge the relevance of the humble pie based on its sphere of influence over time. The knish's tenacity was a mark of its importance to one generation, a next, and then another. In the face of adversity, the knish just kept going. It was, after all, a gift — tweaked, reconfigured, and passed down from one generation to the next (without reclaimed wrapping paper, as was the tradition of a beloved relative. For years I ripped open presents with abandon and poked fun, and then, in matters of wrapping paper, *became* her).

In matters of food, evolution was a good thing, said Diner, a sign of strength and malleability. Longevity signified relevance, vibrancy, and integration into the larger society. Case in point: a T-shirt from a Jewish deli in Brookline, Massachusetts: kelly green, screened with a shamrock, white lettering, and a cross-cultural directive:

KNISH ME, I'M IRISH

I'm often mistaken for Irish (freckles) but never figured the land of potatoes could have anything to do with the Land of My People. According to the *New Oxford American Dictionary,* the word "pale," as in Pale of Settlement, came from the slats of the fence used to define physical or political areas, like the one that surrounded the part of Ireland under English rule before it was conquered by Queen Elizabeth I. These linguistic investigations were a warm-up for the word crunching necessary to get at the ancestry of the knish. The earliest reference I'd found hovered around the Lower East Side, circa 1900. But carbon-dating a kasha knish from Yonah Schimmel's would be futile. To get at the early days of the knish, I would have to rely on literature. I sifted through knish definitions. Yiddishist Leo Rosten called it a "little dumpling filled with groats, grated potatoes, onions, chopped liver, or cheese, from Ukrainian," and cited other meanings, new to me. A term of abuse: "He has the brains of a knish." And a kind of prize: "When you say you hit someone 'with a knish,' you mean reward." *Huh?* Plus, a below-the-belt reference still in circulation, especially among men of a certain age: "vulgarism: vagina."[41]

Etymologically Speaking

Oxford English Dictionary first published "knish" in 1976, defined it as "a dumpling of flaky dough filled with chopped liver, potato, or cheese, and baked or fried," and attributed its etymology to Yiddish, from Russian, *knish, knysh* a kind of cake.

Webster's traces the first known use of "knish" to 1916 — likely from the *Times'* report of the price wars that ravaged Rivington Street — and calls it "a small round or square of dough stuffed with a filling (as potato) and baked or fried," with etymological roots in Yiddish, from Polish *knysz*.

For good measure, I also checked the French. There is no mention of "knish," "knisch," or "knitsch" in the *Larousse Gastronomique* or the online *Dictionnaire de l'Académie Française*. Even *Encyclopedia Judaica* gave it short shrift. Or, rather, no shrift at all. The YIVO *Encyclopedia of Jews in Eastern Europe* mentions the knish under "Food and Drink," as one part of the potato-saturated diet that Jews ate before World War I in the area that corresponds to modern-day Lithuania.

In 2011, the knish, in its Jewish rendition, was in the midst of a subtle renaissance in Poland. A book on Jewish cooking mentioned the revival of coming-of-age celebrations, and with them, the requisite hors d'oeuvres, including our favorite humble pastry.[42]

That same year, five hundred miles east, two kinds of homemade knish (spelled *knysh*) of Ukrainian extraction were included in an exhibition of ritual breads in Kiev. The first version was a bulbous loaf that looked like a beanbag chair folded in on itself.

This Ukrainian knysh or "bread with soul," was baked in the village of Honcharivka, one hundred miles south of Zhitomir.

This form of Ukrainian knysh comes from the eastern part of Ukraine, from a village of Zozuli, near Zolochiv.

The other version of *knysh*, from a different region, seemed to be a stout, glistening column of challah, popped from a pan with a delineated *pipik*, or belly button. Lubow Wolynetz, an expert on Ukrainian food, informed me that every kind of *knysh* honored those who had come before. "You cut off a little piece of dough for the ancestors," she said. That was the part that got stuffed back into the top of the loaf to form the belly button part of the bread.

"A few times a year, ancestors descend and see how you are living," said Lubow, who indicated a certain kind of behavior was required in their presence. "When you do all this, you have to have positive thoughts. You can't gossip."[43]

The Ukrainian *knysh* not only came with a protocol of behavior, it had a habit of inserting itself into the vernacular. Think of the word "pie" in American expressions like "easy as pie," "pie in the sky," and "piece of the pie." I liked the idea of *knysh* in common parlance, but the Ukrainian knyshisms, even when rendered into English, remained foreign, funky, and plain old impenetrable. I enlisted Lubow's help.

> *Berries from the same field; knish from the same dough.*
> LUBOW: The equivalent of "cut from the same cloth" or "peas in a pod."[44]

> *There's a full stove of loaves of bread and knish is in the middle.*
> LUBOW: "Full stove of loaves" was probably a commentary on a meeting of sorts, or a gathering where the chief honcho would be referred to as the *knysh*, the most important person in attendance, or someone who thinks of himself that way.

> *When grandmother finishes cooking knish, grandfather won't have a soul.*
> LUBOW: It takes a long time to prepare a *knysh*, and the food is prepared only on special occasions, so the joke is: by the time the *knysh* is done, grandfather might have expired after waiting so long.

Grandfathers who survived the anticipation would be greeted with a treat made from hard-to-find ingredients like wheat flour and hemp oil, which only increased the allure. Each region had its own twist on the *knysh*. In the Carpathian Mountains, a recipe made during Lent called for a mashed-potato dough filled with *bryndzia* — a sheep's milk cheese, mixed with thyme, parsley, and garlic — and basted with butter or pork fat.[45] (Clearly not a Jewish dish.) The same region gave rise to *knyszyk* (KNISH-ek).[46] These diminutive pastries — yeast rolls stuffed with cheese and dill and onion or cabbage — were eaten on Pentecost. The Christian holiday fifty days after Easter corresponds to the Jewish holiday of Shavuot, which celebrates the giving of the Ten Commandments on Mount Sinai, and is gastronomically observed with blintzes, whose shape recalls the scrolls of the Torah. Carpathians also issued a special-edition knish — replete with fruits, cheese, or poppy seeds — to appease the dead. On All Saints' Day (again, that holiday), the people of Bukovina had their own knish traditions. In a region that corresponds to modern-day Romania and Ukraine, locals brought regular-sized pastries, *knysz*, to the cemetery, to give to beggars assembled there, in the realm of the ancestors.

I didn't make the connection right away — it took months — but eventually remembered that I, too, had used the knish to honor and conjure the departed — my grandmother — with a Mrs. Stahl's, on a jetty overlooking the ocean.

Kasha, wasn't just the stuff of the knish I used to summon my grandmother, the grain had a significant history in Eastern Europe, including this recipe from a 1910 Polish cookery book:

Cook half a liter of buckwheat groats and bake them in a tube shape, adding two tablespoons of goose fat and the same amount of cracklings [or in Yiddish, *gribenes*] with finely minced onion. If you don't have goose fat, you can use the same amount of melted pork fat. Before that, prepare strudel dough, stretch it on top of a tablecloth, drizzle with melted butter, and spread the buckwheat groats on top of it. Lightly fold the dough, lay it down in a buttered pan sprinkled with bread crumbs, and bake it in the oven. Serve the knish with bouillon, mushroom, anchovy, or caper sauce.[47]

Those knishes weren't exactly Mrs. Stahl's (ahem, pork . . .), but I remembered the words of professor Diner: If a food morphs over time and adapts to its surroundings, that's a good sign.

Rewind to 1845 in the region of Volhynia, which corresponds to the northwestern corner of modern-day Ukraine, on the edge of Poland and Belarus. In the middle of the nineteenth century, during the periods of Advent and Lent, monks rode from one manor house to the next, trick-or-treat style, asking for offerings. Yes, knishes. The monks, if they liked the snacks, gathered leftovers in their bags — not unlike the women at Ratner's on Delancey Street, but unlike the ladies on Delancey Street, the monks uttered Latin verses attesting to the strength of their faith.[48]

Pagans and Pastries

The knish wasn't always Christian. The Ukrainian *knysh* was mentioned in quite a few Christmas songs, said Lubow, but those ditties were less about baby Jesus and more inspired by the season, winter songs, with roots in pagan times.[49] In Poland, too, before Christianity took hold, December 24 was celebrated as Day of the Dead and the eve of winter solstice, prime time for ancestor worship.[50] On that night, pagans believed that the spirits of dead relatives arrived at their homes for supper. Some Polish families still set an empty plate on the Christmas table to welcome the ancestors and the stranger — *Let those who are hungry come and eat.* It made me think of the seder-table tradition of pouring a glass of wine for the prophet Elijah. (Year after year, it saddens me to see the contents of his cup splashed, after the fact, into the sink.)

In Ukraine, too, the knish commemorated loss of loved ones. In 1798, Ukrainian poet Ivan Kotliarevsky recalled the pastry as a key part of the memorial meal held a year after the passing of a loved one, in this case, his father.

> At once, they all went out
> To shop for brandy. They filled crates
> With bread and buns [*knyshi*], and sauerkraut
> Besides, they bought some dinner plates.
> They boiled shelled wheat with poppy seed,
> Prepared a drink with mead;
> Each one invited to that feast
> His hospitable host
> They brought from street, the poor foremost,
> As well, invited were the cantor and the priest.[51]

Before that, in 1768, a German dictionary used the word *knitschen* to define *knautschen*, which means to crumple or stuff, or in less

polite contexts, to grope. *Knautschen* was also found in an Alsa-
tian expression relating to dough, *im teige knautschen,* "to pinch or
cinch in dough."[52]

But our story of knish history unrolls further back in time and
farther to the east. From the year 1614, in the Polish language, from
the shelves of the Statue of Liberty-hued university library of
Warsaw, came tales of melting pots, multicultural tendencies, and
tolerance, including a poem, "Krakowiec Guild," about a mish-
mash of a village on the outskirts of present-day Lviv, Ukraine.

Like New York, Krakowiec was known for its inhabitants' extraordinary diversity, unusual alliances, and headstrong ways.
Founded by shoemakers, tailors, and furriers, the local crafts
union was composed of heretics who lived side by side and generally ignored the town church. Each inhabitant observed a mélange
of rituals made up of personal whims and inclinations.

> They get so confused, they know not their own minds,
> One celebrates with a Jew, and at night with a Lutheran dines.
> The next day, it's knishes with the Orthodox priest-man,
> And so each one knows not where he stands.[53]

Since its beginnings, the knish has been a crosser of borders and
a citizen of the world. It has been a prod for conversations, barbs,
and jokes and an invitation to lean over the fence. The knish, at
its origin, just might have been the articulation of what Gussie
Schwebel proposed during World War II: a catalyst for a coming
together.

If "Krakowiec Guild" counts as the first mention of the knish, the year 2014 marks the pastry's quadricentennial. But not so quick—hints at knish underpinnings appeared even earlier. Before 1500, Poland boasted more than a half-dozen place-names reminiscent of knish or *knysz*. The first, Knyszka, in western Greater Poland, was recorded in 1347, Knyszyno, near Poznań, in 1387. And my ancestral town of Knyszyn landed on the map in 1569.

Biblical Underpinnings Revisited

Still, I held out hope that "knish," the word, had been built on Judeo-linguistic underpinnings. Remember the talk of a Talmudic pocket-food predecessor to the knish?

Debunked. By the researchers themselves, thanks to new findings, relayed to me in an e-mail.[54] "Unfortunately, *kisnin* is not knish," wrote Tova Dickstein. "The Septuaginta (the Greek translation of the Old Testament) translated *nikudim* from the Bible as *kisnin* and so did the Aramaic translation, both from the first century."[55]

Nikudim can be described as hardtack, an indestructible biscuit suitable for sailors. If *nikudim* was akin to *kisnin*, then *kisnin* could not connote anything as heavenly as a knish, unless the knish in question had been heated and reheated to utter rigidity. (I've seen it happen, and it's not pretty.) With any connection between "knish" and ancient Jewish texts dissipated, I turned to Aramaic. Surely the earliest knish encapsulated—in food or word—some shard of Jewishness.

In Aramaic, as in Hebrew, words are built on a system of three root letters. Prefixes get added, suffixes get tacked on, past and future tenses alter the sound, but the three-letter core holds strong. Yona Sabar, author of *A Jewish Neo-Aramaic Dictionary* and the leading scholar on the language, said that the Aramaic root, K-N-SH, was related to the Hebrew root, K-N-S, meaning to assemble, or to come in, as in:

Knesset, Israeli Parliament or Assembly

bet knesset, synagogue

knesiya, church

In Aramaic, *knishta* did indeed mean synagogue. The term was also used in a pejorative sense, by gentiles, said Sabar, to connote a noisy place.[56]

But did "knish," the word, come from this K-N-SH family of words and thus from the ancient language of Jewish marriage contracts?

"I cannot say for sure if knish is Aramaic," Sabar told me. "Theoretically it could be a short form of *knishta*, but if there is a better Slavic explanation, it would be preferable."

In Aramaic, *knishta* is also the word for another agent of gathering, the broom: bristles on a stick urge forgotten bits of things into a central location for pickup, kind of like what I have done with found crumbs of seemingly unrelated information.

Knish history has yet to be codified, and barring the discovery of a fossilized pie of potato or kasha, we will likely remain ignorant of the exact circumstances that gave rise to the first pastry. But at the intersection of lore, legend, etymology, and literature lie the guts of the knish: a thickly textured story culled from a chorus of voices across continents; a recipe delivered via translation, tradition, and hard work. At its core, in addition to potatoes or groats, the knish consists of bringing voice and heft and attention to experiences that could have easily been swept under a rug.

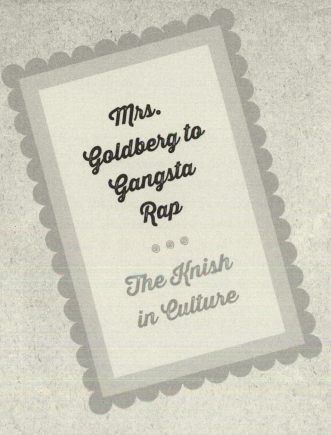

Mrs. Goldberg to Gangsta Rap

The Knish in Culture

Borscht Belt nightclubs, Yiddish theaters, and prime-time television are no strangers to the knish. The hunk of stuffed dough has graced stages and screens with its multi-faceted roles: comic foil, naughty lady, and trusted sidekick. It has touched the guts of audience members with humor and, yes, dyspepsia. From mobster comedy films to the *New York Times* crossword puzzle, the knish goes from lowbrow to high.[1] It has seized the zeitgeist of more than one era and more than one place. It has become synonymous with New York, Jewishness, and the intersection thereof, but as a cultural icon, it has also spiraled outward to Pittsburgh, London, and Winnipeg.

Yoo-Hoo, Mrs. Knish Maker

In one 1950s sitcom, the squat pastry was an outgrowth of ethnic identity that doubled as a gauge of personality. *The Goldbergs* invited viewers into the home of housewife, cook, and Jewish immigrant mother (or *balebosteh*) extraordinaire, Molly Goldberg. Gertrude Berg, who wrote the show and acted in it, portrayed Molly as a selfless matriarch whose Yiddish-inflected speech was laced with malapropisms and not-so-hidden truths.

In a preface to recipes for knishes (cheese and potato) in *The Molly Goldberg Jewish Cookbook,* the lady of the house lauded the pastry as a divining rod for kindness and a salve for less-than-perfect familial relations.

Who is Sylvia? She's Tante Elka's middle boy Georgie's wife. When she and Georgie got married it looked like she was going to be a regular daughter-in-law. But she turned out fine. How? *Knishes.* That was the turning point. Elka thought Sylvia was stuck-up and she was very worried that it would be contagious to Georgie, but one afternoon Elka fell into Sylvia's apartment and found her making *knishes*, so everything was all right from that moment on. Like Elka says: "You couldn't be stuck-up and make knishes too." And that's the truth. Show me someone who can make knishes and

I'll show you a person. No matter what they call them or how they serve them, a *knish* is a *knish* and that's all.[2]

A day spent measuring, mixing, rolling, stuffing, and coaxing dough into knishes could be interpreted as only one thing: an act of devotion to family and heritage.

Puppetry of the Pastry

The knish would continue to serve itself up in prime-time sitcoms of the 1970s and '80s. But long before then, its Jewish-sounding name resounded on the set of a children's television show and in homes throughout Pittsburgh.

In 1952, the host of a popular kids' program invited a former World War II navy pilot turned television personality for a tryout. Hank Stohl (no relation to Mrs. Stahl of Brooklyn) arrived at the interview sans puppets (his flock was back in Ohio). Forced to improvise, Stohl cobbled together a character from a decapitated floor mop and a darning egg.

"The puppet was named Clarence," he remembered, "but Mitzi [the show's host] said, 'He looks like a knish.'"[3]

Perhaps the character's unkempt tresses made Mitzi think of a bunch of rebellious shoestring fries that would be better off inside a skin of dough. Or maybe she found herself captivated by Clarence's homemade quality, his down-home vibe, or his Semitic profile. Whatever it was, in that puppet she saw a knish. And so that's what he was called.

Mitzi McCall (née Steiner), from a Jewish family in Pittsburgh, was not "brought up particularly religious," but "latke" and "brisket" were second nature, as foods and phrases. Ditto "knish."[4]

"It's a funny word," said McCall from Studio City, California, where she moved soon after she christened 'Knish.' "It just came out. It's just one of those crazy things."

At the time Stohl thought, "Anything you want, lady."[5]

It stuck. Stohl and Knish starred on *Mitzi's Kiddie Castle* and went on to host their own daily program. Knish took on an adviser, Rodney Nugent Buster Hackenflash III, a hand puppet inspired by W. C. Fields. They introduced cartoons and welcomed live guests the likes of Sammy Davis Jr. and Jack Lemmon. After that, Stohl created a show around cartoons of a spinach-eating sailor. For

Knish, the puppet, garnered a huge following in his day and proved easier to preserve than the average potato pie.

more than a decade, until the early 1960s, the kids of Pittsburgh clamored for "Popeye 'N Knish."[6]

Conceived "as a mischievous boy with hair in his face, always challenging his mentor,"[7] Knish took pleasure in "attending Yo-Yo tournaments and Frisbee seminars."[8] At first he bore no obvious connection to the food that lent him its name, but eventually he, too, became a knee-jerk prompt for nostalgia. Mention "knish" to someone who grew up in Pittsburgh of the 1950s or 1960s and stories suddenly pour forth. Knish is no longer on the air, but he has not strayed far; his physical incarnation lives on at the Heinz History Center in his hometown, flanked by the commandments he passed down to his fans.

KNISH GOOD KID CLUB RULES

1 I will always obey Mother and Dad.

2 I will be extra-careful crossing streets.

3 I will be kind to animals.

4 I will be careful of other people's property.

5 I will clean my plate at mealtime.

6 I will be truthful.

7 I will go to bed on time.

8 I will always be a good sport when playing with my friends.[9]

For the knish, it wasn't all fun and games. On television, the potato pie graduated to adolescence and grappled with teenage problems. On the 1970s sitcom *Welcome Back, Kotter*, the knish entered the inner sanctum of the Sweathogs, a multiethnic group of high school misfits. In season two, Juan Epstein, the Puerto Rican Jew, confessed his nicotine addiction. Mr. Kotter seized the moment as teachable and fessed up about a weakness from his youth.

> I was hooked on potato knishes.
>
> It all started out innocent, ya know.
>
> I was in Coney Island, a young guy walking around Coney Island.
>
> This guy came up to me, he said, "Hey, kid, come here, you want a free knish?"
>
> I said, "Sure, why not?" It was free, so I took it.
>
> Next day, same guy: "Hey, kid, come here. Want another free knish?"
>
> I said, "Great."
>
> It was free and easy. I was rolling in clover — a free knish every day.
>
> When was it going to stop?[10]

When the knish vendor started charging for his wares, the young Kotter consecrated his entire allowance to the cause. Eventually he had to go cold turkey, literally. (Five days, nothing but cold cuts.)

Cut to lunchtime: the Sweathogs are getting ready to feast on their own deli meats. Each one introduces the contents of his sandwich.

HORSHACK: Liverwurst and chocolate sauce on date-nut bread
BARBARINO: Peanut butter and squid on pumpernickel
WASHINGTON: Pig knuckles on Jewish rye with Virgin Island dressing

Mr. Kotter squirms, but not because of what he's just heard. All the knish talk has triggered a relapse. The teacher knows he must, once again, swear off the stuff of his addiction. He challenges Epstein to follow suit.

> Kotter dislodges a knish from his desk drawer.
>
> Epstein pulls a cigarette from his hair.
>
> Kotter fetches a "Bicentennial knish" from behind the flagpole.
>
> Epstein frees cigarettes from behind a picture frame.
>
> Kotter excavates a knish from a bookshelf and pulls another from the trapdoor in the classroom radiator.
>
> Epstein pulls down a window shade; a squadron of cigarettes parachutes into a trash can.
>
> And cut.

Mere mention of the knish elicited laughter and required no definition. The food was a feature in the urban landscape, as common as a package of smokes or the highway sign in the show's opening credits: "Welcome to Brooklyn: Fourth Largest City in America."

The knish could also skew heavy and cater to an older crowd. On *The Golden Girls*, it complemented mortality, regret, and forgiveness.

In season four, Sophia Petrillo (Estelle Getty) learns of the death of her closest friend and returns to Brooklyn for Esther's funeral. Years prior, Estelle's husband, Max, admitted to gambling away profits from the business — pizza and knishes — he ran with Sophia's husband, Sal. During the condolence call, a tray of knishes (the round kind) reignites Sophia's grudge. Max is forced to explain that, in fact, he took the flak to cover for Sal, who lost that cash at the horse races. Friendship is revived and sparks fly.

Max woos Sophia, moves to Florida, and marries her. Together they revive the old ethno-eatery. But less than a day after it opens, the Judeo-Italian snack shack goes up in flames.[11]

Heat can bring humor and pathos, but not every televised knish reference linked itself to outbursts of laughter or threads of melancholia. Sometimes a knish is, well, just a knish, or the simple sum of its ingredients. Just ask the Muppets. In 1996, an adult-centered spin-off of *The Muppet Show* presented a punk rock parody that has lived on via YouTube. On *Muppets Tonight,* Gonzo introduced "Sid Knishes and His Mosh Pit-tatoes" to the roar of a crowd. Done up in blue Mohawk and gold chain, the spud belted out lyrics that set his audience in motion. In this case, it's best not to underestimate the effects of potato-on-potato friction. When Sid Knishes propelled himself into the mosh pit, he encountered a sea of fans who were, umm, rather mashed.[12]

"It was a goofy pun on Sid Vicious and Johnny Rotten and mashed potatoes," said the script's creator, Kirk Thatcher.[13] "Sometimes that's all we needed."

From Inside Joke to Badge of Honor

The knish has remained an agent of Jewish humor and in-the-know jokes on prime-time television. "That's somebody's knish!" hooted an older man, after encountering a digital image of female private parts (long story) on a Canadian comedy series set in Winnipeg. The passing exclamation became the title of the episode, which aired in 2010. The show, *Less Than Kind*, took its title from

Love at first bite.
Norman Wisdom and
Britt Eckland in The Night
They Raided Minsky's.

Shakespeare (*Hamlet*, act 1, scene 2: "A little more than kin, and less than kind").[14]

The knish's big-screen debut came in 1968, in a musical comedy filmed on the Lower East Side and set a half century earlier in the same neighborhood. *The Night They Raided Minsky's* was a fictionalized version of the invention of the striptease; its promotional poster touted: "In 1925, there was this real religious girl, and by accident — she invented the striptease. This real religious girl."[15]

The devout damsel was not an Orthodox *maidele* defying the tenets of her faith, but rather a singer-dancer from Amish country. In the film, Rachel Schpitendavel (Britt Ekland) arrives in New York City from a Pennsylvania farm with her self-choreographed "Bible Dances." She meets up with Chick Williams (Norman Wisdom), who parlays her innocence into "theatrical experience." In a scene following the couple as they walk through the Lower East Side, he sidles up to a pushcart and purchases a knish. And voilà, it's that easy to indoctrinate his companion in the ways of the neighborhood.

Woody Allen, too, has used the knish as a gauge of urban savvy and as a conduit for neurosis. In Allen's 2009 comedy *Whatever Works*, a physics professor turned children's chess instructor takes on a new-to-New York ingénue as a tenant. Boris Yellnikoff (Larry David) shows Melodie St. Ann Celestine (Evan Rachel Wood) the sites: Grant's Tomb, Washington Square Park — and Yonah Schimmel's knishery.

> MELODY: What is this?
> BORIS: A knish.
> MELODY: What's it made of?
> BORIS: I've been eating these things for sixty years. They're delicious! I don't know what's in them and I don't *want* to know what's in them. Don't even talk about it![16]

Heather Quinlan *did* want to talk about knishes. And about New York accents. Her 2013 documentary *If These Knishes Could Talk* recognized the street cred of the knish and used the food as a metaphor for New Yorkers and their accents. Notable interviewees — and accents — include author Pete Hamill and Harvard law professor Alan Dershowitz, who, incidentally, catalyzed a bit of knish history during the early chapters of his career. Mavens Kosher Court, a deli that graced Cambridge, Massachusetts, in 1988, was founded by sixteen partners, six of whom, including Dershowitz, were attorneys. The short-lived deli exhibited evidence of knishes (potato, meat, kasha, and spinach) in a section of the menu consecrated to "Supporting Memoranda — Side Dishes."[17]

Quinlan, the filmmaker, tasted her first knish at age five, in Staten Island, at the zoo. "I loved it," she said about the Jewish food given to her "by an Irish dad in a heavily Italian borough." That kind of cultural mélange was nothing new. "In New York all the ethnic boundaries are blurred," said Quinlan, who, case in point, made the *Knishes* movie as a tribute to her grandfathers, "even though they're Irish and the knish is not an Irish food." She predicted that New York City's accents, like its street food, will be forever tethered to new immigrants and ascribed her own fondness for the knish to a bygone time. Said Quinlan, "I think I've been reincarnated as a Jewish vaudevillian."[18]

Knish Alley, Reconsidered

Yiddish theater, too, has been reincarnated and with it, whiffs of the knish. In 2009, the Broward Stage Door Theater in Coral Springs, Florida, premiered *Knish Alley!* The musical, directed by Tony Finstrom, hinged on a journey of theatrically minded Jewish immigrants headed for stardom on the stages of New York's Second Avenue. They traveled steerage, and at night, took to the ship's deck to rehearse plays that would, or so they hoped, secure their fortunes.

Knish Alley, named for the many dairy restaurants that once catered to actors and audience members, is nearly devoid of knishes, which explains how I came to pay homage to the all-but-eclipsed history of the strip. In a knish costume. In 2010, as part of a downtown arts festival I led a somber processional. Nearly a dozen yellow-clad individuals filed past sites that once defined Second Avenue. We paid homage to a Yiddish theater-turned-movie house (the cornerstone is engraved with the Hebrew date) and the Yiddish Walk of Fame where actors' names are embedded in the sidewalk, à la Hollywood, minus the handprints. Some passersby stopped and watched, some got it; others thought I was dressed like a slice of cheese.

A few weeks after that, Second Avenue came alive a mile north, on East 25th Street, when the National Yiddish Theater/Folksbeine put on *Fyvush Finkel Live!*, a variety show featuring the octogenarian star of Yiddish theater. Alongside classics, the vaudeville acts included a new skit with a familiar flavor, "Reuben the Knish Man." Reading the part of the narrator, in Yiddish, was Fyvush

Knish Alley Revival: a performance project to honor the hidden history of a street that once buzzed with Yiddish.

Finkel, who, as it so happened, in 1936 or so, had read an on-air advertisement for knishes on WEVD: *"Yoineh Schimmel's Knish . . . is my favorite dish."*[19]

The knish man skit, written by his son Ian Finkel and mimed by actor Merwin Goldsmith, depicted a man who had worked fifteen-hour days for fifty years. "No one on the face of the earth had his genius for putting a filling in dough. After people would come to his shop and eat one of his creations they left with their feet six inches from the ground. They could taste the artistry, the soul in his food."[20]

Reuben shares his wares with actors, gratis, but wants to be more enmeshed with the theater. In a dream sequence, he takes to the stage and gains the favor and the applause of the public, but without his wife and knish fixings, becomes despondent. The knish maker wakes up with a newfound appreciation for his lot.

According to Ian Finkel, the character is a composite of three carbohydrate pushers from his past: Ruby the Knish Man of Brooklyn; a man who would bring bread to the Jewish theaters on Second Avenue; and Finkel's own favorite boyhood knish maker, who had a shop on Utica Avenue in central Brooklyn. Finkel did not remember the man's name, but his baked goods had left a mark. "He had fabulous potato and kasha. He had a specialty, a cabbage knish. It was something from another planet. Period. Anyone and everyone who ate it freaked," remembered Finkel.

"That guy was the Heifetz of knishes."[21]

History, Firsthand

If knishes be the food of memory, play on. Nosh on. Bake on. Or all of the above. That's what writer David Wise did. Starting in 2002, he brought his great-grandmother's recipe to life with *Momma's Knishes*, a solo show performed in home kitchens in New York, New Jersey, and Pennsylvania. The roving participatory dinner theater — $600 for a ninety-minute performance ($800 on weekends) — welcomed up to a dozen audience members cum baking assistants to each seating.[22]

Wise got the idea on a cruise in honor of his grandmother's eightieth birthday. "I was interested in exploring my own family and how this immigrant culture resulted in me."[23] He arrived at gigs with premixed dough, premixed filling, and his own baking sheets (best to eliminate as many variables as possible). Before guests arrived, Wise familiarized himself with his host's kitchen and doled out basic instructions. Then he donned an apron and a wig and became Sarah Grabel, a character inspired by his great-grandmother, the knish maker. Wise fine-tuned his Yiddish accent by listening to radio episodes of *The Goldbergs*. He experimented with a new breed of performance — cross-dressing with gravitas — and tried out the show on family and friends. Wise created strands of monologues that he could modify on the basis of goings-on in the room during a show. One of Mrs. Grabel's topics of discussion was an essay assignment received in night school: What would you put in a time capsule?

Knishes, of course. But even an experienced cook had to contend with obstacles.

David Wise whips up some dough before showtime in a Connecticut kitchen.

"Things in a time capsule are supposed to last for five thousand years, and in my kitchen, knishes don't last for more than five minutes."[24]

At each performance, Wise generated two trays of knishes, but not solo. Audience members plunged their hands into dough and premashed potatoes, part of their role as thirteen-year-olds of 1938, learning the art of knish making from the mother of a classmate.

Snafus found their way into the action. "Dough changes so much," said Wise, "and cooking it in a different kitchen every single time is a challenge." Once he set a potholder on fire. "Luckily, the kitchen was in another room."[25]

Wise, who last performed *Momma's Knishes* in 2005, had not partaken in many of the pastries since then. "It's interesting to think that multiple times a week I was doing a 'Time to make the donuts' kind of thing," he said, seven years after throwing in the dish towel.

As for the possibility of a knish comeback, he'd told himself that he would consider reviving the show when he reached the age at which he had portrayed his great-grandmother, his mid-thirties.

"That's where I am now," he said. "I'm thinking about it."

Either way, David Wise has already secured a spot in the pantheon of knish-inspired entertainers. The lineage goes back to musician and parodist Mickey Katz, known for his irreverent Yiddish-and-English parodies of songs of the 1950s. Katz (the father of Joel Grey) packed his ditties with references to Yiddish and Jewish culture, expressed in sayings that defied obvious translation. He melded Jewish identity with American identity and did not hesitate to poke fun at his own traditions. Inspired while "trudging along with lox and bagel through darkest Delancey," Katz converted the 1958 hit "The Witch Doctor" into "The Knish Doctor" and gave those with Lower East Side roots a chance to consider the exoticism of their own ways.

> Way down in Africa
> *a dortn* [over there] in the jungle,
> you'll find a Knish Doctor
> who looks just like your uncle
> the natives know him by the name of Jungle Yankl.[26]

Katz converted the nonsense lyric of the refrain into a rallying cry for Jewish food.

> Oo ee ooo aah aah, ting tang Walla Walla, bing bang[27]

became

Ooh ha ya hoo ha *farvolte er veranikes* [he wants *varenikis*, stuffed
dumplings] too[28]

The Yiddish doctor treated *kvetchers* (whiners) and *krankes* (the
sick) with remedies like schmaltz (chicken fat) and *bankes* (cups
for medical cupping) and a smack in the head. Maladies of the ab-
dominal region required special attention.

For those with *pipik* [belly button] trouble
He prescribes *af* [with] knishes

For audience members, "The Knish Doctor" also offered a salve: it
invited them to be on the inside of bilingual, cross-cultural gags.
But not everyone wanted to join in the humor. On the heels of
World War II, Jewish audiences preferred to keep a low profile.[29]

Katz's next paean to the knish converted a song of romantic
longing into a ballad studded with reflections on loneliness. "The
Little White Knish That Cried," a parody of Johnny Ray's 1950s hit
"The Little White Cloud That Cried," told of a lone potato pie left to
wither in a deli case. Katz's narrator purchases the glum dumpling
for "a nickel a *shtikl*" (five cents the piece).

You should have seen that sad little *punim* (face)
The little white knish that cried.[30]

Lewd, Lascivious, and Liberated

Beyond the elegiac, "knish" has also encapsulated — and still
does — racier meanings. Its iteration as Yiddish slang for female
genitalia was documented in *Call It Sleep*, Henry Roth's 1936 novel

of Lower East Side squalor. In a chapter called "The Cellar," in dialogue that captures the immigrant-infused speech patterns of the day, a neighborhood girl invites the story's young protagonist to play "bad."

> "Yuh know w'ea babies comm from?"
> "N-no."
> "From de knish."
> " — *Knish?*"
> "Between de legs. Who puts id in is de poppa. De poppa's god de petzel."[31]

Those connotations stuck and inserted themselves into off-color invitations and hints at less-than-scrupulous behavior. Consider Yaacov Shapiro's "Ich Hob Leib a Knish" (I Love a Knish). Ahem.

O, come over here
Give Uncle Meyer a knish
When I detect your scent
I burn hotter than a fire[32]

Shapiro's lyrics, delivered only in Yiddish, converted the word "knish" into an inside joke within an inside joke: the term referred to private parts, in private parlance. Shapiro was not the only one to use it as such.

Nightclub performer Pearl Williams made no effort to couch the knish in pleasantries. She said it loud, proud, and repeatedly. Her 1961 album *A Trip around the World Is Not a Cruise,* oozed innuendos.

I asked a guy, which is saltier, herring or knish.

He said, "I've never eaten herring."[33]

A secretary turned pianist turned nightclub star, Williams filled her act with unvarnished, unapologetic references to a new form of feminine wiles.

> I found a new way to do it.
>
> For money.
>
> Don't laugh. For years . . . I was doing it for love. Then one day I took a ride through the Holland Tunnel and I saw a *big* sign: "Pay as you enter." What an idea hit my brain. Now I have a tattoo above the knish: "Pay as you enter." Underneath, I have a tattoo: "Thank you, call again. Member of the Diners Club."[34]

As a *nom de* private parts, "knish" allowed Jewish women comedians of the nineteen fifties and sixties to be outspoken, ribald, and unashamed about sexuality. Four decades after Pearl Williams performed her loose-lipped late-night act in the nightclubs of southern Florida, a troupe of performers in the UK reclaimed the knish as a term of pride.

In London, a quartet of creative women were looking for a catchy title for their collaboration. The year was 2007. One member of the group had been working on several projects in Yiddish.

"I found the knish was the Yiddish term for a woman's vagina," recalled humorist Judy Batalion, who, with her collaborators, christened themselves the Knish Collective.[35] They produced and directed *I Am Ruthie Segal, Hear Me Roar*, a "musical comedy, feminist, Jewish coming-of-age film" about a young woman relegated to a minor role in her own coming-of-age ceremony. In the ten-minute film, Ruthie rebelled and soliloquized in song — and led the congregation in a dance-off.

Today I am a woman
What does it really mean?
I'm wearing a bra for the first time
I'm three weeks off thirteen
Should I get my period or cook a meal?
If that's all there is to womanhood,
Then tell me, what's the big deal?[36]

In an interview with the Knish Collective, "Sounds Jewish" podcast host Jason Solomons inquired about the group's name and on learning of its anatomical undertones, opined, "Most Jewish boys don't know where that is. Somewhere near Minsk?"[37]

The Knish Collective's logo offered a handy diagram: the "i" in "knish" was styled to look like labia and a clitoris.

It's not just in England. Jewish American comedian Sarah Silverman proposed a hot-off-the-presses moniker for female members of the Jewish tribe in her Twitter feed:

New word: Judithy: (joo-dith-ee) A strong handsome woman who smells vaguely of knish.[38]

Like social media, real life is rife with inference and innuendo. I've heard stories of a grandfather with a faulty hearing aid who, wanting to convey the female equivalent of *putz*, shouted the English translation of "knish" across a crowded deli.[39]

And, even closer to home, when a fellow diner at a late-night dumpling joint on Essex Street found out about my research, he offered a question — "What *kind* of knish are you writing about?" — a smirk, and an offer of a ride home. The hole-in-the-wall place where this exchange took place could have been a knish shop of yore: it housed a narrow counter and two sit-down tables where strangers in forced proximity shared meals and conversation.

You Don't Have to Be Jewish . . .

Traditions morph, migrate, and rub up against one another. It's no surprise that the knish has found its way into hip-hop, street slang, and lyrics that would clank incomprehensible to knish aficionados of yesteryear. One hip-hop artist known for heavy-duty masks and a super-villain persona gave the potato pie a shout out on a 2004 album *Mm . . . Food*. Daniel Dumile, stage name MF DOOM — note the anagram — used the pastry pie's moniker to rhyme with "bitches." The song, "Rapp Snitch Knishes," skips niceties and nostalgia; it describes street crimes and the futility of rapping about acts that could land a person behind bars.

Long Island–born hip-hop artist SD3 (an abbreviation for Sammy Davis the Third) bills himself as "America's favorite Black-Jewish rapper" and uses the knish to bridge cultural and culinary gaps. Weaned on bar mitzvahs, SD3 was nonetheless not born into the faith so he runs his material by friends who are "really Jewish."

Synagogue-centric subjects form the backbone of his repertoire. In one music video, SD3 (né Derek Brantley) and his posse crash a bar mitzvah party to regale the young man of the hour with a live performance, including these lyrics:

> One Potato, Two Potato, Three Knish
> A table full of Bubbe's goodies is what I wish[40]

"My whole concept was to integrate hip-hop with the Jewish culture," said Brantley, "The best place to start was to celebrate Jewish cuisine. Knish is a staple."[41]

The food was never a mainstay in Barbra Streisand's repertoire, but she incorporated it in her sold-out "back to Brooklyn" concerts at the Barclays Center in 2012. The lyrics of "As If We Never Said Goodbye" from the musical *Sunset Boulevard*, took on the flavor of Brighton Beach Avenue.

> Yes, a world to rediscover
> But I'm not in any hurry

became

> Yes, a world with hot knishes
> Is incredibly delicious

The crowd erupted, proving that the mere mention of soul food can spark a memory, generate a connection, or bring on the warm fuzzies. But that's nothing new.

Consider these lines written by Sholem Aleichem at the tail end of the nineteenth century: "We'll have knishes or kreplach or *knaidlach* or maybe even blintzes," said Tevye the Dairyman, to a stranger cum long-lost relative who appeared in his town of Kasrilivke out of the blue. "You can decide, but be quick about it."[42]

In literature as in life, the knish went from the Old Country to the New World. The pastry survived a transatlantic journey and thrived in its new environment, where it was chronicled by another generation of Sholem Aleichem's characters. Tevye's son-in-law Motl has an in-law, Yoneh, a baker, who was warned against opening a bakery — too expensive, too complicated, and too embroiled in union rules. Motl reports:

> He receives advice that instead of baking bread and challah he should make knishes, homemade knishes, dairy knishes with cheese, or parve knishes with cabbage. What can I say? Our in-law isn't doing badly at all, not at all! His knishes have a reputation all over the East Side. If you go down to Essex Street, you'll see a sign in the window written in large Yiddish letters — HOMEMADE KNISHES SOLD HERE — and you'll know that's our in-law, my brother Elyahu's father-in-law, Yoneh the baker. And if you see on the same street, right across the way, another Yiddish sign with the same large letters — HOMEMADE KNISHES SOLD HERE — you'll know it isn't our in-law Yoneh the baker. He now has a competitor, so don't go there.[43]

As the knish came to prominence in the United States, it held its own in Eastern Europe and was used to entertain the younger set. A collection of Yiddish verse for children published in 1921 Kovno (Kaunas, in modern-day Lithuania) takes its title from the poem

"Der Groyser Knish" (The Big Knish) and tells of a grandmother who lives in a forest with her grandson and a big dog. The grandmother bakes a litany of knishes, but tiny ones, which invariably leave the boy wanting more.

> As the grandchild goes to the table, he cries:
> I want, I want a big knish
> It's always one, one by one,
> Always little ones!!![44]

When the boy comes eye-to-eye with a gargantuan knish, he enlists his canine sidekick to hoist the megalith to the table; but when he, the boy, takes a bite, there is yet another surprise: the sprawling skin of dough gives way to seven golden-beaked birds, who circle around the room squawking gibberish.

> *Tartar, tartar, tartar, tar.*
> All you wanted was a big knish?
> *Karkar, karkar, karkar, kar.*
> Here you go — here's your big knish![45]

Be careful what you wish for, especially in the realm of knishes. Issac Bashevis Singer also referenced the knish as the stuff of longing. His novel *Meshugah* (Crazy) depicts a community of Holocaust survivors living on New York City's Upper West Side. At lunch at Rappaport's on Second Avenue, a former Warsaw patron of the arts orders cold carp in jellied broth, but his thoughts turn to other delicacies.

"I am not allowed to eat much" he said. "My heart does not pump as well as it should. But when I'm served those Jewish dishes, I forget everything. In that sense I resemble our forefather Isaac. When Jacob served Isaac blintzes and knishes and kasha varnishkes, Isaac pretended to be blind and gave Jacob the blessing that was Esau's."[46]

In Singer's oeuvre, the knish also bears witness to personal crises of biblical proportions. In *Lost in America*, the last part of *Love and Exile: An Autobiographical Trilogy*, Singer recounts his first days in New York. On a trip from Seagate, Brooklyn, to Manhattan with his brother, they stopped in at Café Royal, another Second Avenue hangout of Yiddish literati. Immobilized by homesickness, Singer stared at his food.

> The waiter came up and asked, "Why aren't you eating your blintzes? Don't they look good?"
>
> "Thank you. Maybe later" [said Singer].
>
> "When blintzes get cold they turn into knishes," the waiter joked.
>
> Those at the nearby tables who had heard laughed and repeated the joke to others. They wagged their fingers at me.[47]

In literature, the knish has not always been allied with emotion or humor; it can simply be skin and innards, or that thing on the counter. *Teitelbaum's Window,* a novel set in Brighton Beach in the 1930s and early 1940s, touches on the knish as an inevitable accomplice to teenagers' hijinks and an unremarkable element in the local landscape.

The boys ordered one knishe [*sic*] with four forks, half a half-sour tomato, one Mason Mint wrapped and in a double bag, and toothpicks from a fresh box.

On separate checks.[48]

The 1970 novel by Wallace Markfield mentions the neighborhood's resident knish purveyor, the Knishe Queen, a shop and a person, known for her tenacity, gutsiness, and presidentially oriented PR stunts. The Knishe Queen closes early for Passover, promotes new flavors — "apple-cherry, sour lemon, nutty onion" — and sends communiqués to world leaders. The White House writes back on official stationery:

> We herewith acknowledge receipt of your parcel and its contents. Regrettably, neither the President nor members of his personal or official family can in any way whatsoever lend his/their endorsement to a specific product/item/foodstuff.[49]

Undeterred, the fictitious Knishe Queen not only writes to Mahatma Gandhi but also pens a follow-up missive imploring the pacifist to consider his health — and her establishment.

> We want to once again wish you good luck in your freeing of India. Our biggest hope of the Brighton Beach Jewish community is that you don't overdo it with your fasting because your country is not going to appreciate if you come out of prison a nervous wreck. May we therefore suggest that you think of yourself and do what is good for you by breaking your fast on one of our blackberry or gooseberry currant knishes which are so lightly fried in the finest

quality peanut oil that the word *fried* doesn't even apply. As made in our modern kitchens, these knishes are strictly *parveh*, meat doesn't go anywhere near them.[50]

In her desire to make her local delicacies global, the Knishe Queen harnesses the essence of her product: an ethnic dish that caters to the populace and to politicians.

In literature as in life, contenders for public office in New York City noshed knishes to profess their dedication to the Jewish vote. Susan Isaacs's 1980 thriller *Close Relations* depicts New Yorkers as diverse, middle-class survivors of grit, immersed in the melting-pot mentality and fluent in the knish. One knish, proffered by a Puerto Rican woman at a Queens shopping plaza, was tragic for a governor on the campaign trail. "He took it and held it aloft. It was a pale brown square, a knish, half wrapped in a rectangle of flimsy white paper."[51]

Well beyond the Lower East Side, the pastry pie still smacked of identity.

> "This is why I like campaigning in Queens," Gresham [the governor] enthused. "A knish. Real food!" The crowd beamed as the Ultimate WASP, their Beloved Non-Ethnic, smiled and inhaled, seeming to savor the greatness of the knish. The dignitaries seated behind him put smiles on their faces, showing that they too were enjoying this moment. . . . "Fantastic!" Gresham took a large bite. Too large, his nanny would have said. The clapping began again, the crowd expressing its pleasure at the communion of candidate and knish.

But that brief melding of politician and potato pie did not end well. Despite attempts at the Heimlich maneuver, the governor — he was wearing a corset — choked.

The novel's protagonist, a thirty-something Jewish woman from Queens — and the governor's speechwriter — witnesses the knish episode in person. Later on, she tunes in to television news, mid-broadcast:

> ". . . according to New York City Medical Examiner Irwin Robinson, the cause of death was a piece of liver knish. A knish" — and she [a newscaster with a Midwestern accent] blinked at the teleprompter — "is a fried or baked turnover of dough with a filling like potato or kasha or, in this case, liver. . . ." She pronounced "knish" with a silent k; I changed channels.[52]

So ingrained was the knish in New York life that its name doubled as a litmus test for authentic New Yorker status. Mispronunciation could trigger the same response as a cold knish: disappointment, revulsion, and a jabbing sense of missed opportunity. Or perhaps worse.

An icy knish can at least be reheated.

A Brief History of Competitive Knish Eating

In Coney Island, as per tradition, knishes are served hot or, worst case scenario, at ambient temperature. On July 7, 2009, thirty-six knishes, square ones, reclined in a rectangular foil tray. The tray sat balanced on the edge of a trash can. The trash can stood in a concrete passageway that led to a ball field. Keyspan Field, as it was called in the summer of 5768, was home to a ball club, minor league, named for a local roller-coaster.

The Cyclones were observing Jewish Heritage Night, which meant knishes. And, better yet, a contest. The crowds came from Bensonhurst. They came from Flatbush. They came from the Bronx and the Upper West Side of Manhattan. They trickled out of the Stillwell Avenue subway station onto Surf Avenue, past Nathan's, which no longer sells knishes; past Williams Candy, with rows of candy apples shiny enough to give passersby a glimpse of their soon-to-be loosened teeth. It was six o'clock. The sun stood high. The wind picked up. A cluster of people paused in front of the self-defined "Sausage Heros — Corn on the Cob — Hot Pizza" place. Six square packets of potato-stuffed dough reclined between paper boats filled with fried shrimp and corn on the cob. On the back wall, hand-painted letters proclaimed, *Our knishs are delicious.* The Ecuadorian-born guy behind the counter said they were good. *Real good.* That's what the customers said. He had never tried one. In his country, they did not have such a thing.

Two and half hours before the action was set to begin, Joel Podelsky purchased his ticket. One bleacher seat: eight dollars. Keyspan Field bore the name of the local utility and the reassigned adulation of a borough bereft of its team. The Brooklyn Cyclones were linked to the Mets. Podelsky preferred the Yankees. Still, he did not want to dillydally. It had been two years since he'd downed three and a half square knishes — in four minutes — for the title and the platter that read:

BROOKLYN CYCLONES 2007

CHAMPION • KNISH EATING CONTEST

Podelsky was not one to luxuriate in his success. Each competition was a blank slate, or rather, a full plate. Each competition demanded attention, skill, and focus. As he approached the stadium, Podelsky had resolve. He also had *shpilkes*.

Shpilkes sounds like something you have as a side dish with a schnitzel or a lean cut of brisket, something marginally delicious, decidedly lumpy, and not unlike what Podelsky was about to consume. *Shpilkes* is Yiddish for being on edge, having pins and needles, from the Polish *szpilki*, pins. The Italian-American equivalent is "to have *agita*"). The knish champ appeared calm; his thick black hair was slicked back, porcupine quills in repose. The previous contest lasted four minutes. This year it would go five. Podelsky was eager to get on with it — until he saw the red-haired guy.

The spectators poured forth. Some slowed for a beer; some stopped for shrimp (fried), a shish kebab on a stick, or a hot dog from the grill. There were no barkers on Surf Avenue, no bottleneck of bodies crammed the sidewalk or boardwalk. The bumper cars languished. The rain had rained. Nathan's Famous Hot Dog Eating Contest had left little trace. The spectators grabbed programs and pawed free decks of cards and shook hands with the upright seagull mascots: Sandy (named for the Brooklyn Dodgers' pitcher who refused to play in Game 1 of the 1965 World Series on Yom Kippur) and his propeller-beanied nephew, Pee Wee. Spectators nudged children under the wings of mascots and snapped photos of them waving Israeli flags, plastic and made in China. Israeli pop oozed through the loudspeakers. The crowd entered in rivulets. Sons of Abraham and daughters of Sarah had come to pray for the home team.

Next door at Peggy O'Neill's, Podelsky ordered a water and eyed the red-haired man. The guy looked like the eater who had nearly beat him in a hot dog–eating contest two weeks earlier. The red-head, if he was who Podelsky thought he was, had maintained a healthy two-dog lead over Podelsky with twelve dogs, buns and all. Then, with less than thirty seconds to go, he upchucked, immediate grounds for disqualification.

On the brink of the knish contest, Podelsky did not want the redhead in his vicinity. The champ's eyes shone like street chestnuts. His lips pursed like a nozzle on a mustard bottle. Then he realized the redheaded man was not *the* redhead of the hot dogs and thus not a threat.

Podelsky exuded a sigh and donned his competition regalia: on the temples, a terry cloth headband; around his neck, a plastic timer, digital. He wore a navy blue T-shirt from the Cheeburger Cheeburger franchise, knee-length camouflage shorts, and sockless loafers. He weighed in at 242 pounds, down from 270.

On the field, ten knish noshers were ready to go gnash-to-gnash. Each participant had to sign a waiver with a medical disclaimer and an indemnity clause. "They have to protect themselves," said Podelsky, "in case you choke."[1]

Mike Eagle of Bensonhurst sported a gold Star of David the size of his palm. Renee Kirsch of Canarsie came in a pinstriped baseball jersey from Jewish Heritage Night 5768. (Its Hebrew letters spelled "Cyclones.") Podelsky, who had grown up in a kosher home, was the sole competitor in gear that defied the dietary laws of his tradition. He had had his first encounter with *trayf* (nonkosher food) around age thirteen, with, as it so happened, a cheeseburger. The loss of his gastro-Judaic sanctity was brief and without fanfare. No guest list, no receiving line, no gifts, just hanging out with a friend. Unlike the religious rituals that mark a Jewish boy's passage to Jewish adulthood, the first inhalation of nonkosher food is generally received with neither ceremony nor blessing.

"It was good," said Podelsky, recalling that first melding of milk and meat in his molar region. "But you know, in respect to the Jewish heritage in which I was raised, it's not like I was happy about what I did." As soon as his mouth closed on that statement, he opened it up again: "I have to say I enjoyed it."

There weren't a ton of Jewish kids in Iselin, New Jersey, in the 1970s, said Podelsky, whose parents, forty years later, still kept a kosher home. Podelsky had migrated to the nearby town of Laurence Harbor. The synagogue where he had become a bar mitzvah had atrophied from lack of congregants. Podelsky did not attend services regularly, nor did he keep milk separate from meat: not at restaurants, not at home, and not in his stomach. But at bacon, he drew the line. For a decade and counting, the knish-eating champ had steered clear. "It's not that healthy," he said. "And it tastes too good." A similar distinction applied to the realm of professional eating. "I don't want to be hypocritical, but if I'm going to *not* eat

Podelsky at the plate: the reigning knish champion faced heated competition in 2009.

kosher [meat], I'd rather at least eat beef." The knish champ consumed seafood freely, but refused to "compete the shrimp," in the same way he would turn down an eating competition on Yom Kippur, should one present itself.

Born to Brooklyn parents and raised in suburban New Jersey, Podelsky had never inhabited the borough that breathed life into his mother and father, but from a young age, he came to visit. Kings County was in him. Soon the knishes would be, too. He stood behind a white plastic table lined with competitors ages eleven to sixty-two. An announcer invited those gathered to rise for the Israeli national anthem. Instead of *HaTikvah* (The Hope), he said "HaVitka" (which, for some members of the crowd, may have evoked the name Vitka Kempner Kovner, a partisan of the Vilna Ghetto).[2]

Stance of a Champion

In prayer, Jews face east: Jerusalem. For his inhalation, Podelsky faced north. For four years he had been shoveling stuff down his hatch: burgers, pizza, stinky French cheeses. With knishes, his birthright gave him the upper lip. "I know the food," said Podelsky, age forty-nine ("mental age, twenty-nine"). At the start of the contest he had three knishes on his plate. He had mauled more than that in less time. Podelsky scowled. Then he dove in.

His cheeks bulged, his hands moved mechanically. His jaw and jowl jiggled with the repeat motions of mastication. Five minutes later, Podelsky's mouth foamed with potato and his arms rose, in victory.

Such quick intakes of knishes were not new to the shoreline of Brooklyn. May 26, 1973, a Saturday, marked the first knish-eating competition on record. Contestants sated themselves with a cornucopia of knishes, some dairy, some meat. Word of the winner made headlines in Los Angeles, Chicago, and Boston. (The articles rarely took up as much space as an actual knish, but the Jewish food had inserted itself, not just in gullets, but also in the vernacular.) Under the headline, "Knishes Sweeter Than Wine," the *Sarasota Herald-Tribune* reported that Harris Schencher, a fifty-six-year-old garment cutter, set a world record: eleven knishes in eighteen minutes.[3] His intake: three meat, two blueberry, four

Peristalsis maximus: Podelsky defended his title and went home with a pair of tickets to a Mets game.

potato, and two cream-filled knishes, not necessarily in that order. According to contest organizers, Schencher's win marked Memorial Day weekend, the year Abe Beame would be elected the first Jewish mayor of New York City, and the seventy-fifth anniversary of the sale of the first knish at Coney Island.

A dozen years after that, the tradition resurfaced at the Brighton Beach Bath and Racquet Club. A man from Flatbush took the prize.[4] When the Earth had completed another revolution around the sun, Brighton Beach hosted another test of gastro-Judaic prowess that drew twenty-eight competitors (and not a single gastroenterologist). With three knishes down in five minutes and another one and a half in overtime, Ross Nathan, a teenager from Sheepshead Bay, seized the crown.[5]

Practice, Practice, Practice

The knish-eating contest embroiled itself in the zeitgeist of the time, and not just in Brooklyn. When, in 1988, the Carnegie Deli wanted to call attention to new ownership and a revamped menu that included one-pound knishes, it sponsored a competition to stir media fervor. Five eaters from three states brought their maws to the hallowed tables of the Seventh Avenue institution, a few blocks south of Central Park. The eaters included a coin collector from Michigan, a budding radio personality from New Jersey, and two sons of Brooklyn: Jay Resnick, champ of the Brighton Beach Baths, was up against Mark Littman, also of Brighton Beach.[6] The latter, a Pepsi distributor who arrived in brightly colored duds with a tie-dyed scarf around his forehead, took the title. Then Littman, who, with the exception of a year in Spain, had lived his whole life in Brooklyn, told the press he had "never seen a knish."[7]

Twenty years hence, when I met him, the knish champ of the Carnegie Deli had two quarters in a parking meter near the beach and crumbs of the fighting spirit in his heart. Mark Littman was waiting for his wife, who was having her nails done. He took a folding chair from his trunk and set it up on a Sheepshead Bay sidewalk. He was not happy to learn about Podelsky and the win at Keyspan Field. "You tell that knish-eating champ that I say he's not a champ," goaded Littman. "He's a chump."

Twenty-four hours later, reigning knish champ Joel Podelsky stood one hundred miles northwest of Littman's sunbathing spot, in Middlebury, Connecticut. Quassy Amusement Park vibrated with reggae music, and the aroma of jerk chicken and curry goat in aluminum pans, transported from Guyana and Jamaica by way of Long Island, the Bronx, and Yonkers. The potato pie-title holder had come "to compete the Jamaican beef patty" and would leave with a third-place medal. When he heard about Littman's threat, Podelsky got a glint in his eye and wanted to know where his rival lived.

"You tell him that I'll come to his turf," said the knish champ. "We'll do something for charity."

The Fine Art of Knish Making

Aromas of onions and potatoes ricocheted from kitchen cabinets and cinderblock walls. Empty wine bottles reclined, mucked with dough. Fifty of us milled around, raised our glasses, and congratulated ourselves. Soon there would be knishes.

"Let's say the *Shehecheyanu*," I blurted, to a room of non-Jews.

We were a group of artists, coders, and tech types in Tunnel Mountain Lounge, in the basement of Lloyd Hall, next to the laundry room. We were in the Rocky Mountains, home to more bears than people of Hebraic extraction. More stars graced the night sky than grains of kasha in a knish. More peaks than platters of whitefish. The mountains just stood there, impervious, supersized squeeze bottles dribbled in snow. Silence coated the environs. I had no reason to believe the knish had ever inscribed itself on that landscape. Or that it ever would.

A Prayer for First Times

THE BANFF CENTRE, ALBERTA,
CANADA, AUGUST 2009

Shehecheyanu is the name of a blessing that marks newness; it acknowledges fruition and arrival, and exudes gratitude. It is a celebration and a reminder that nothing is guaranteed. The arrival of Chanukah, Passover, and Rosh Hashanah are reasons to say the *Shehecheyanu*; so is a new home, a new suit, or meeting a friend after an absence of thirty days.[1]

"Let's say the *Shehecheyanu*," I blurted, then regretted it. Who was I to proselytize? Jews don't proselytize. We make it a point *not* to proselytize. And we're proud of that.

A few hours earlier I was ready to skulk away and leave the knish—and my new friends—in the lurch, and now I wanted them to bless the operation. These were people of technology and art, people of code and tweets, open rates and blips, beeps, and pings. Who was I kidding?

I was not against introducing the knish to the mountainous terrain. That had been my plan all along. I was in Banff for a five-day conference, a festival for artists and visionaries in video, television, and design from all over Canada and the world. I was there to talk knishes — what else? — and guessed that the audience just might not be familiar with my topic. I had planned to pick up some knishes en route. Before I left New York, I phoned My Marvin's Deli of Calgary. Three times. The phone rang and rang and rang. I figured Marvin (probably related to Finkelsztajn) had friends in town or bar mitzvahs to cater. I envisioned the store inundated with customers. I tried to place an order in advance, then decided to do it on the fly, but arrived to find the shop shuttered.

Plan B: Order in from New York. Yonah Schimmel's could ship them overnight. (Gabila's does mail order, too, but not with overnight turnaround.) Launching a dozen knishes across the country costs a hundred bucks, easy. I couldn't risk a delay at the border, and would need far more than a dozen to sate the curiosity of fifty newcomers to the food.

"What exactly is a knish?"

"Do you know how to make them?"

"Where can I try one?"

They asked, I sidestepped.

How to Act Out an Ethnic Food

It's not that I lacked experience in the realm of introducing friends to the ways of the Jews, which is to say, the foods of my family. My track record included ushering paramours to Ratner's for crash courses in the ways of my people and making matzoh ball soup for my peers in a Spanish-language immersion program in the Mexican town of Guanajuato. Even as a kid, I understood that foods familiar to my family would probably not make it to mainstream menus, palates, or mindsets. Exhibit A: charades, at a party for my eleventh birthday.

Sounds like (*I mimed doling out dollar bills*).

— Money? Dollars? Rich?

Cash.

Little word (*I mimed a pinch, with thumb and forefinger*).

— The? In? Of? On?

A (pronounced "uh")

New word (*My left hand chopped my right forearm, two times*).

Sounds like (*My hand cupped my ear, then moved up and down, from the wrist, as if painting a wall*).

— Paint? Color? Paintbrush? Pass.

Varnish.

Second word, second syllable (*two fingers in the air, one chop on the arm*).

Sounds like (*I mimed a steering wheel*).

— Drive? Steer?

Car.

Cash-uh Varnish-car.

My five guests, four and a half of them non-Jews, had no clue. No one complained (it was my house and my birthday), nor did they understand my explanation, even after I converted it from gestures to words and repeated, retooled, and restyled the definition. It wasn't fair, said my father. I didn't care; kasha varnishkes, buckwheat groats with bowtie pasta, notched us the win.

Varnishkes (say: 'varnish-kuhs) is considered a bastardization of *vareniki*, dumplings. (It didn't occur to me then, but "kasha" is also Yiddish for "question," as in the *fier kashas*, that quartet of inquiries recited by the youngest at the seder.)

Banff had neither rabbi nor synagogue, but the doorpost of the tattoo shop — owned by Israelis — sported a mezuzah. The nearest Jewish authority sat in Calgary, near the remains of My Marvin's, it should rest in peace. If anyone were going to lead a knish-baking session, it would have to be me.

I went for a walk.

> I turn my eyes to the mountains;
> from where will my help come?
> My help comes from the Lord,
> Maker of heaven and earth.[2]

Or, in my case, a plaque. I drifted toward Cave and Basin, a historic site where, in 1885, three railroad workers stumbled upon thermal springs that would give rise to Canada's national park system.[3] The trails bore modest signage, easy to miss, unless you are descended, as am I, from those obsessed with historic markers.

Banff, population 7,500, is known as a vacation wonderland, a mountain paradise, and Heaven on Earth. During the First World War, it was home to an internment camp. Six hundred prisoners — mostly Ukrainian immigrants — quarried rock, built a ski jump, and erected a palace made of ice.[4] I learned all that from a sign at the site that read:

The internees provided cheap labor to carry out park development projects. Life in the camps was often grim; working conditions were harsh, clothing was scarce and food was rationed. Desperation led to one suicide and more than sixty escape attempts.[5]

Now *there* was some history I could identify with.

On the walk back, I crossed the Spray River and a stone bridge — also built by inmates in Banff internment camps. I had not yet discovered the knish's Ukrainian side, but if Banff harbored such scars and hardship, then perhaps the Rocky Mountain playland *could* be hospitable to the knish.

There was also a question of kitchen credentials. My track record of collective cooking endeavors was, shall we say, a bit underdone.

1979 ● Heart-shaped cookies, at a Valentine's Day party at home. The downstairs neighbor complained about the noise.

1984 ● Gyoza, at Becky's. She turned out hundreds of perfectly puckered dumplings. Mine uncrimped themselves or fell to the floor, or both.

1985 ● Bagels, at the Junior High School 189 International Fair. My co-chefs — surnames Fitzpatrick and Christensen — and I donned red-and-white bibs that sang "Spaghetti." (I tell you this not to raise the question of what exactly constitutes an adult bib, nor to investigate how such an item found its way into my childhood home, but rather to underscore the unremarkable instance of kids of every extraction donning Italo-kitsch in service of bringing to life a food associated with the core of New York City.) The bagels were boiled, baked, and seeded to perfection — and displayed beneath the flag of a foreign land: Israel.

1998 ⊛ Latkes, at a Chanukah party at home. My co-chefs — friends of Italian and midwestern extraction — and I hosted a celebration with a holy trinity of pancake flavors: potato, sweet potato, and "from a mix." All that frying blew a fuse and made the building go dark.

By the time I arrived in Banff, baking seemed best left to those with know-how, lineage, or luck. My tradition hinged on buying, stockpiling, and reheating. I did not want to desecrate the good name of Mrs. Stahl.

The technorati beeped and chimed. They buzzed and clamored: "Knishes, knishes, knishes." My family tradition was to purchase them. *Didn't these people understand?*

They did. So well, in fact, that they repeated my own words back to me, with a flourish.

Mrs. Stahl's is gone. Move on.

They invoked the conference theme: The Makers. They reminded me I had promised to deliver a presentation that appealed to the senses. Sound and sight I could muster, but without actual food, my audience would miss out on the smell, the taste, and the essence of the knish.

And then there was the altitude. I imagined the words of my

tradition relayed from on high, which, at 4,800 feet, was not all that far away. The words of Rabbi Hillel came to me, slightly altered:

If I am not for the knish, who will be for it?
And when I am for the knish, what am "I"?
If not now, when?[6]

I had a set of directions, passed down to me via the Internet, where Sandy Loeffler had posted the recipe of her mother, Ida Zelkowitz Gardner, *zichrona l'vracha*, her memory should be for a blessing.[7]

Potatoes (russet), oil (vegetable), flour (three sacks), onions (yellow), mustard (deli-style), and dill (poetic license) were gathered, schlepped, unpacked, and prepped for service. I printed out the recipe in a thirty-point typeface. *The Makers should see what they were doing.*

I found a red apron, with "CUPE" emblazoned on it — and put it on. *I should look the part.* I had not heard of the Canadian Union for Public Employees, but liked the working-class vibe. The cotton scarf around my neck became a head covering, for sanitary precautions and Old World feel. Stations of the knish materialized: dough, filling, and assembly. Utensils were brandished. I had just the music to set the mood, a CD called *From Avenue A to the Great White Way: Yiddish-American Popular Songs, 1914–1950.*[8]

I went to fetch it and returned to find potatoes peeled, tables floured, and dough churned. Ingredients of the knish were chopped, diced, measured, and mixed. In a large pan, the onions drooped translucent: a good sign.

"Manischewitz!" squealed a woman from a neighboring town. No bottle of Extra Heavy Malaga had miraculously entered the premises or reached her bloodstream. But like "twenty-three skidoo," "rad," and "groovy," the name of the thick-enough-to-support-a-fork kosher wine was used, without sarcasm, to confer awe and approval. She had picked up the expression from her dad.

Laptops receded. Phones faded into the background. Androids inched into momentary refuge. With the absence of handhelds came face-to-face conversations. Devices became extraneous. So did I. The Makers stirred and conferred and invoked Talmudic reasoning to justify cooking instructions. I didn't know it at first, but in our midst stood an experienced knish maker: a woman (non-Jewish) who had worked at a nursing home in Winnipeg and once served as sous-chef to a resident who baked the Ashkenazi pockets to conjure her past.

A tendril of smell tugged at our nostrils. We, a handful of us, flocked to the narrow kitchen; some people peered over a tall counter, others remained entrenched in tête-à-têtes, oblivious to telltale aromas.

The knishes emerged and smiled up at us. One or two had the look of Mrs. Stahl's. Others exhibited different traits from different places. They came in shapes as diverse as their makers: samosa, pastel, empanada, calzone, knishing cousins, all huddled on the same baking sheet, all waiting to cool.

There were seconds, thirds, and leftovers, enough to serve at my presentation the following day. The knish dimpled the faces of its makers, occupied their guts and infiltrated the Rockies, which

was occasion for the *Shehecheyanu*. For a nano-moment, the room stopped noshing, then recited, after me:

Baruch ata adonai	Blessed are You,
eloheinu melech ha'olam	Our God, Creator of time and space
shehecheyanu v'kiy'manu	who has supported us, protected us
v' higi'anu la-z'man ha-zeh.[9]	and brought us to this moment.[10]

Amen.

Delicious Knishes by the Dozens

ST. PAUL, MINNESOTA, MAY 2011

By the time I landed at Lindbergh Terminal in the Twin Cities I had a half-dozen baking sessions under my thumbs. I had called on my father for homemade mustard and had been midwife to a batch of knishes of the gluten-free, vegan persuasion. Finally, I was ready to meet the Knish Ladies of the Sholom Home Auxiliary.

I had first learned of them four years earlier, in Slidell, Lousiana. In the extended wake of Hurricane Katrina, I was part of a team of volunteers who worked with a Twin Cities–based disaster-relief organization called NECHAMA, Hebrew for "comfort." We whacked at waterlogged floors, pried shower stalls from walls, and wrestled with sopping pink insulation. We carried couches, swatted carpets, and trudged through muck. We bowed our heads and snuck glances at curdled photographs.

By the time I arrived in New Orleans, Mrs. Stahl's was shuttered, Gabila's had gone to the 'burbs, and my potato pie consciousness was on the wane. The Big Easy was big on beignets, po'boys, and cryptic-sounding sandwiches ("muffaletta" made me blush). Gift shops sold Chanukah gelt that masqueraded as "doubloons." We were Jews and non-, volunteers from the Midwest and both coasts. We slept at Operation Blessing (more "Our Father" than *Baruch Ata*). I dined at a Waffle House franchise and was lured by potato chips in flavors like Cajun Dill and Voodoo.

Our last morning, at daybreak, a message came to me:

DELICIOUS KNISHES.

I dismissed it as a mirage.

Delicious Knishes, it persisted.

Towels dangled from upper berths. The room loomed cavernous and vast.

"Knishes?" I sputtered.

"Good morning," replied the woman in the sweatshirt that bore the holy message. "From Minnesota," she said.

I remembered a Duluth bed-and-breakfast where wall slats arranged themselves as crosses on every wall.

"Shalom," she said, with a twang.

Perhaps the Jews of Minnesota had a proclivity for Hebrew.

"Shalom!" I replied, in kind.

She was not dousing me with peaceful greetings, nor was she assessing my foreign language skills. The woman in the next bunk, I eventually discerned, was telling me about a Twin Cities residence for senior adults with a Ladies' Auxiliary that baked knishes.

In Minnesota? I blurted.

"They sell them at the State Fair."

That, I had to see.

I took notes, but made no promises. After a time, I dismissed those knishes as too far-flung to merit my attention. Then in May 2011, I landed smack-dab in the heart of Minnesota knish production.

Characters

LAURA SILVER: Wearing a green T-shirt that says *Year of the Knish*.[11]

HAZEL CHASE: Head of the knish ladies. Mid-eighties. Well coiffed, always.

DEDE SMITH: Hazel's daughter. Head of the dough-rolling crew.

RAE BERMAN: Hazel's daughter. Helps out in a pinch. Gluten-free.

LISA BERMAN: Hazel's granddaughter. Visiting from New York.

ADA RUBINSTEIN: Nineties. Resident of Sholom Home East. Past president of the Sholom Home Ladies' Auxiliary. Wearing a *Delicious Knishes* T-shirt.

ROZ JAFFEE: From Minneapolis. One of the "few people they let cross the river."

MURIEL LACHTER: Knish maker since her retirement, ten years earlier.

DEDE WOLFSON: Knish assembler, community leader, doting grandmother.

REENIE GITLIN: Forties. Looking for a job in health information management.

RENA GLAZER: Wearing a black baseball cap with glittery studs.

LISA HEILICHER: Boisterous. Treasurer of Sholom Foundation. Not a knish maker.

SOPHIE DUDOVITZ: Contagious smile. Advocate of the homemade potato knish.

BETTY SWEET: Eighties. Originally from Madison, Wisconsin. Enlisted her daughter to make knishes.

MICHELLE SHALLER: Sits on the Sholom Foundation board of directors.

LINDSAY BERG: Twenties. Teaches in a Jewish after-school program.

Time

Wednesday after Memorial Day weekend 2011, 9:30 a.m.

Setting

Lipschultz Family Office of the Shaller Campus of the Shirley Chapman Sholom Home East, St. Paul, Minnesota

Scene

Fluorescent lights cast a golden glow on a beige room. Framed copies of newspaper articles, and photographs of the Delicious Knishes booth at the Minnesota State Fair hang on the back wall, along with a framed print of stylized Hebrew letters that spell *dor l'dor*, from generation to generation. Two rows of tables extend across the room; one consists of tables of regular height, the other of waist-high tables. All tables are covered in plastic sheeting. On the taller tables, trays of mashed potatoes sit covered in plastic wrap next to a handful of ice cream scoopers. Women in full-length royal blue aprons greet one another. Those with walkers take seats at the lower tables. Three stations are set up: dough rolling, knish assembling, and *knipling*,[12] or sealing. Along the far wall, a pair of waist-high tables support long, flat cardboard boxes printed with the words "Pepperidge Farm."

HAZEL: Did anyone taste the potatoes? Kids, do the potatoes seem a little dry to you?

DEDE W.: She's in charge. She's the head honcho. Particular. (*Beat*) Very nice lady. (*Smiles*) And you know, you don't get a bunch of Jewish women together who listen to anybody. So you've got a whole roomful of bosses.

DEDE S.: (*Motions at flat squares of dough*) When they don't take it out early enough, we really work hard to put muscle into this. We're usually pretty tired by the time we're done. We do the rolling, they do the putting it together (*nods at women at standing-up table*), and they do the finishing (*nods at women at sitting-down table*). So, yes, we're specialists. But these ladies here (*motions to the sitting table*) have all been doing it twenty-plus years for sure. The dough has been defrosting, but it still needs to be flattened and cajoled and handled. When it's cold, sometimes it rips while you're trying to work with it. It tastes better if you've got a flaky knish.

HAZEL: (*To Laura*) Down in the kitchen, everything is according to weight. For these knishes I used the number-twelve scoop. That's what he told me to use for the amount of potatoes to be served as part of that meal. (*To room*) Girls, girls, let's watch how we're rolling. This is not good enough. (*Beat*) Gotta make sure we give them enough room for twisting so we can turn them off easily. . . . Be sure and cover the ends, kids. I don't like to waste any of the dough. Dough is expensive.

DEDE S.: Every Friday night when I was growing up my mother

would make chicken — and potato knishes. By hand. She made them for years; every Friday we had them. So it is a tradition.

HAZEL: My mother used to make them. My sister and I made them. At that time it was done a little differently. It was a stretch dough that went all over the table. You made the dough yourself. But things change and you go the modern way. It's just kind of a real specialty. My family loved them. (*Beat*) It's a lot of work. It made them happy, it made me happy. They'd eat them hot out of the oven.

SOPHIE: My mother made them all the time and I used to help her and we got the recipe to do it. I make them at home. They're wonderful to have in the freezer. You just take 'em out and bake them and that's it. Mustard? No, that's New York. We serve 'em with meat or poultry and it's a side dish. I know in New York, they eat them with mustard. It's different altogether.

HAZEL: It's an Eastern [European] dish. It's definitely a Jewish thing.

BETTY: Just today, I said to a man who's not Jewish, "I'm going to make knishes." He said, "What's a knish?" The answer? Dough with mashed potatoes that are baked and are delicious.

ROZ: I did not grow up in a home where there were knishes, so I have learned [to make them] and learned to love them.

DEDE W.: For years [at the Minnesota State Fair] non-Jewish people would come and want to get these potato knishes because they never had them before.

For twenty years, the Sholom Home Auxiliary sold their goods across the street from the State Fair.

RENA: There was a bus stop there. City bus drivers would get off the bus to come and buy them.

ADA: Many of us who worked to make the knishes also gave a few hours at the fair. We had a tent and tables and we had some kind of an oven on the table. . . . We had a built-in audience — people were going past our home — we developed a clientele. Sometimes they'd carry them away with a napkin. They never knew what to call it. "Those things," whatever . . . they always knew to come back to us.

LAURA: I saw a picture of the first booth that said, "fifty cents."

HAZEL: Really? That was before my time. When we sold them in the booth, they were one dollar. Remember, Ada?

LAURA: When was that? Nineteen ninety?

HAZEL: About.

LISA B.: One dollar. . . . That's when I worked there. They used to advertise it as being the cheapest thing at the fair.

LAURA: And not on a stick?

HAZEL: A lot of people talked about it. (*Beat*) A knish is a knish.

ADA: I can't imagine eating a knish on a stick.

HAZEL: Right.

RAE: It would have to be deep-fried and covered in chocolate.

HAZEL: You have to have *some* tradition.

ADA: It had to be baked right there. And served right away.

HAZEL: And not only that, Ada, the Hasidim that would come by . . . it had to be kosher enough for them to eat it, too. All these things have to be taken into consideration. It's interesting . . . the people from New York, when we would sell them at the booth, they would always put mustard on them. Remember that, Ada?

LAURA: I was looking for the mustard, but that's not your tradition, right?

HAZEL: Normally not. But when we had the booth, we had mustard and ketchup.

LAURA: (*In shock*) Ketchup? On a knish?

HAZEL: What can I say? (*Beat*) They're not all Jewish.

(*Laughter from those assembled*)

LAURA: I saw some people put mayonnaise on a knish.

HAZEL: (*Squeals*) Ugh! — Whoaaaa!

(*More laughter from those assembled, stronger than before*)

Ada Rubinstein, a former president of the Sholom Auxiliary, once gave a speech that began, "Women are very positive people."

HAZEL: But, umm . . . they told us that our knishes were better than the ones in New York. Remember, Ada? There was that fellow that was from New York who used to come by . . .

LAURA: Do you think there's any hope of bringing that booth back?

HAZEL: Well, the building has been sold. (*Beat*)

MICHELLE: We've all had relatives who've been residents. The building was old, and it just seemed like they deserved better.

HAZEL: We were there [at the fair] because it didn't cost us anything. We had the land right next to it. And we had the facility of the kitchen. We would just go down the hill and they would bring us hot knishes. We had an oven there. We'd have to have the knishes at a certain temperature for the health department. Everything has to be according to the rules.

LISA H.: We moved the recipe from the old home on Midway Parkway to the new home. They guard it. Every time we change the chefs in the kitchen here, who help us making the filling, we tell them, "It's a secret recipe." (*Beat*) Don't ask me how many I consume, it's how many my *grandchildren* consume. I just keep them in my freezer. They just know that they're there.

At the Jewish High Holidays, customers are encouraged to place their orders early and often.

REENIE: Eating knishes keeps you healthy. Making knishes makes you laugh all day on Wednesday and it keeps you laughing all week. I get Ada's wisdom — and most of these ladies are my mom's friends for years and years, so I've either known them or have heard about them or have taught their grandchildren. (*Beat*) Eventually it would be fun to do some evening knish making and learning from the elders. I think it's really hard, because in my generation, everybody works. You can't say to an employer, "I need to take Wednesday mornings off so I can go make knishes for an hour and a half." (*Beat*) Our synagogue does hamantaschen making, because that's a short season.[13] Knishes are year round, and that's Sholom's gig and we would never take it away. Every year at the fair we had different knish T-shirts and I have the whole collection: the Supreme Court one, the election one, we always had a theme.

HAZEL: (*Looking at trays of assembled, not-yet-baked knishes*) These are gorgeous.

LINDSAY: She likes them high up, not smooshed out. Nice and plump.

ROZ: And if they're not, the phrase is they "bake up."

MURIEL: We have a good time, it's for a good cause, and that's how it is.

HAZEL: Look at these: each one, perfect. These are the knishes that are going for the bas mitzvah dinner.

RENA: My granddaughter wanted them from Sholom because she thinks they make the best knishes. When she was in Washington a year ago with her dad, they went to the

Holocaust Museum. She bought a knish there and she said, "They're not like Sholom's." She wanted Sholom knishes.

DEDE S.: There are a lot of people in the community that depend on these, especially at the High Holidays. This is what they want to serve at High Holidays. So that's when we sell the most, right around Rosh Hashanah. From here on we gear up so they can fill up the freezers, and then they send out notices just before the High Holidays for orders. And that's the only time we do that. It's really a high holiday priority.

For thirty years, Minnesotans of many creeds have looked favorably on potato pies.

HAZEL: Most of the time, I have at least ten to fifteen women here every week. Sometimes, if everyone comes, we get a big crowd. . . . There's vacations in the summer, and in the wintertime. Ruthie leaves in October and Joanie leaves probably Thanksgiving time.

ADA: We usually stop around Thanksgiving.

HAZEL: I know we've sold over five hundred dozen for Rosh Hashanah. I think they made about eight thousand dollars.

BETTY: It's a *mitzvah*. That's why I do it.

(*Exeunt*)

HAZEL: (*On her way out the door*) Don't forget this, honey. (*Hands a new apron to Laura*) This one is for you.

An Ingathering of Granddaughters

SAN FRANCISCO, SEPTEMBER 2012

Mrs. Stahl's granddaughters were waiting for me on a stoop of a row house in the Mission. I turned the corner; they waved. This was the home of Toby Engelberg and the site of daylong knish parties that generally coincided with December 25th. ("What else am I going to do?" said Toby.) But this year she would bake knishes and host a party on the night before Erev Rosh Hashanah. I had come to watch and to work, to learn, and to take stock of stories. I flew across the country because this was the closest I could get to the spirit — and the recipe — of Mrs. Stahl, may she rest in peace.

I dropped my bags and bowed at the portrait of Mrs. Stahl in the sitting room. We had to shop and prep, but first, we would need to eat. Toby picked a place in her neighborhood, Wise Sons ("since 5771"), a delicatessen in the nouveau, local, and milk-and-meat-together tradition.

We ate: Pickles (from cucumbers, carrots, and garlic), a sandwich (we shared it), and babka ("better than on the Upper West Side," said a cousin). There were other delicacies, too, later overshadowed by the sheer weight of the occasion. The moment we walked in, I ran into someone I knew. Fermentation guru Sandor Katz was in town on a book tour.[14] (A year earlier, on Governors Island, just south of Manhattan, I had struck up a conversation with his cousin in front of a vending machine in the Jewish tradition.)

We ate. Leo Beckerman, one half of Wise Sons' "combined management," came to our table. The ancestors on the wall were his ancestors; the Yiddish record albums and literary magazines that dappled the walls, his purchases, from eBay. Beckerman had dreadlocks, a Los Angeles pedigree, and, when it came to a certain stuffed pastry, a conflict.

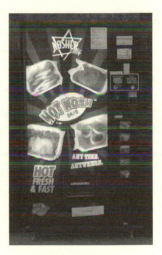

"Do you know how much *tsuris* I get for not having knishes?" asked Beckerman.

One could imagine.

"Just yesterday I was accosted by a fifty-year-old New Yorker," he lamented.

This machine doesn't vend on Shabbes.

"It is *curious* that you don't have knishes." I said.

"It is also curious that there aren't twenty-six hours in the day," retorted Beckerman.

"The only way to make knishes is: Have children," said Toby, who did not.

"Knishes, I think, are seen as unhealthy," said Sara, the elder granddaughter.

"We use schmaltz in dough and schmaltz in the filling," said Beckerman. "We make them; they're just not a regular item."

"Just tell people that, outside of the schmaltz, it's fat free," quipped Toby, who didn't use chicken fat in her knishes.

We ate and, as is the custom, we sat. Sandor, who grew up on the Upper West Side of Manhattan, not far from Sara's apartment, pulled up a chair. I refilled our coffees.

"Mrs. Stahl's is still a brand that exists," said/asked Sandor. Before he could insert the slight uptick in intonation that would nudge his statement into a question, the granddaughters and I emitted a sound akin to that of the Staten Island Ferry pulling out of the harbor, a low-drone warning that goes on far longer than expected — or reasonable: "*Noooooooooooooooooooooo.*"

I showed him photos, or rather photos of photos of, Mrs. Stahl. The originals I had seen and photographed at Sara's house a few weeks earlier: Mrs. Stahl in a white dress and white apron next to her shop, on Brighton Beach Avenue. Mrs. Stahl at the beach, feet plunged into the sand. Mrs. Stahl with a cue stick in hand, during the occasional game of pool at the home of relatives in Queens.

"Isn't she cute?" gushed Toby, who is the daughter of Mrs. Stahl's youngest, Dora (née Dvorah).

Fannie Stahl on Brighton Beach Avenue,
around the corner from her shop, circa 1950s.

Anna Spatz, Mrs. Stahl's daughter
and a co-owner, circa 1960s.

Sandor left. The granddaughters (average age sixty-two) and I (nearly forty-two) nudged the babka back and forth, like family, and recapped how we found each other.

"One time I let slip something about Mrs. Stahl's," said Sara, who is the daughter of Mrs. Stahl's eldest, Anna (née Chaneh).

Sara had been speaking to her friend Audrey at the pool of the JCC, the Jewish Community Center on the Upper West Side of

Manhattan. Audrey had lived in Brooklyn; she knew Mrs. Stahl's. Later on, when Sara heard about a lecture on knishes at the New York Public library, she mentioned it to her friend. "That's impossible," said Audrey. "That must be Jill's friend Laura."

⊛ ⊛ ⊛ *We slid the remains of the babka* toward each other, like family.

"It's funny that you connected with Toby at the same time," said Sara.

A few days before the talk at the library, I stared at a file folder labeled "Mrs. Stahl's Research" and frowned. The folder was covered in coffee stains but the checklist written on the outside of it remained pristine:

☐ death certificate   ☐ marriage certificate
☐ burial info   ☐ surviving family
☐ Mrs. Stahl's business info

How dare I stand up to discuss knishes in front of a New York crowd without any notion of the real Mrs. Stahl?

I had cozied up to clerks at the Department of Health, stood on serpentine lines, and bowed my head before scores of official forms.

APPLICATION FOR A DEATH CERTIFICATE

Question 18 "Why do you need this certificate?"
             Genealogical research.
Question 19 "What is your relationship to deceased?"
             Great-grandniece.

Ahem.

Even that hadn't helped. I'd looked up marriage records, death records, building records. Nothing had panned out. In a last-ditch effort, I addressed my supplications to the Internet.

I registered my wish in a browser window, typing gingerly, as if whispering into the tiny plastic window of a Magic 8 Ball: "Mrs. Stahl's found."

"Mrs. Stahl's FOUND," the Internet responded, with a post by "bruklinboy":

> My mother, who grew up in Brighton eating Mrs. Stahl's . . . has news! She and my father . . . happened to stop in a deli in Mill Basin . . . that is selling Mrs. Stahl's knishes.[15]

Discussion board discussions waxed practical — and Talmudic: Was "bruklinboy" sure the establishment in question wasn't the Mill Basin Deli? (He was.) Did this fabled place really hold The Recipe for Mrs. Stahl's? (It didn't, not anymore.) Were Stahl's on par with Hirsch's and Shatzkin's? Or vice versa? (Inconclusive.) Near the end of the thread huddled a comment by "pianist355":

> Bless you. Mrs. Stahl (1885–1961) was my mother's oldest sister. To me she was just "Aunt Fannie" — a very wonderful person who kept me in free knishes when I was a little kid. She was also a "hands on" business woman and made the knishes right alongside the other workers (including children, cousins, etc.).[16]

Fannie?

My folder was stuffed with leads for *Lena*. (Later, I retraced that first name to a competing knish dynasty. Oy.)

Fannie Stahl. I cross-referenced and doubled back and scavenged and quadruple-cross-referenced. The next morning my phone rang.

"Hello, this is Marietta Axler. We received a call from this number, but no one left a message."

Marietta Axler was married to Andrew Axler, a piano teacher, retired, on Staten Island. He read to me from a booklet of family history compiled by his cousin Toby in San Francisco.

I texted Jill: "I found Mrs. Stahl's granddaughter."

The next day, Jill e-mailed me: "My mom's friend Sara . . . is the granddaughter of Mrs. Stahl and used to work in the store in Brighton. Sara will be there [at the knish presentation] tonight and will come up to talk to you after the talk."[17]

At the Mid-Manhattan Library, across the street from the one with the lions, I asked Mrs. Stahl's descendants to rise. (Sara was there, as was her cousin Arthur, Toby's brother.) The audience applauded. Soon after that, I visited Sara on the Upper West Side, met her brother and sister-in-law, and through photos, stock certificates, and aerograms written in Yiddish, became acquainted with her grandmother.

Forty days after that, we sat in San Francisco, Sara and Toby and I. We pushed the babka at each other and eventually took two buses to the city's Russian neighborhood. En route to the Richmond, Toby recounted great moments in knish making. There

From left: Anna, Rae, Abie, Dora, Mrs. Fannie Stahl, and Bella, circa 1920s.

was the time — at Sara's daughter's wedding — that she arrived in Baltimore with several dozen, in a suitcase.

TOBY: I hand them to the caterer. They put them on a platter. Our immediate relatives *hurl* themselves at the table.

SARA: Knishes!

TOBY: The WASPS are sitting there primly, waiting for salvation, probably.

SARA: (*with suspicion*) "What are these, dumplings?"

TOBY: If there were any left by the time they got there.

SARA: (*in reverie*) They were perfect. They tasted like Gramma's knishes.

Remembrances were good; but to re-create the knish of my youth, I would also need tips on technique, a recipe, insider information.

TOBY: To my mind, [the secret is] getting a lot of oil — more oil than you think is possible to be absorbed by a food substance. And you have to nail the salt.

SARA: They take an unbelievable amount of oil. I remember my mother: "More oil, more oil." *What are you doing?* "In the dough and in the filling and when you're rolling them out, put a little more oil on the dough, use your baster, even."

Toby had tried to revive her grandmother's business. She had baked at home and then moved to a commercial kitchen. Toby transported the knishes on BART, from the Mission to Oakland, about a half hour, in a shopping cart. She dropped off her goods — twelve dozen a week — at Saul's Deli.

"We did that for not that long," said Toby. "Just a few months."

Then her deli connection called it off. He was freezing them and by the end of the week the knishes were "not that good." He needed them two or three times a week.

"The economics weren't there for me to do it," said Toby. You need a half day beforehand. And a full day. And the delivery."

"Well, you need a staff," said Sara, "so all those things are happening at the same time."

"But they're all relatives," said Toby.

"Well . . . ," said Sara.

"I couldn't even ramp up that much. There wasn't a market to do it consistently. And to do it consistently was so many hours for the return."

After the deal with Saul's dried up, Toby made knishes for

friends. On Christmas, as an alternative to Chinese food. "Why not?" she said. "It was such a good excuse to spend the day doing that."

After our round-trip expedition to the Richmond, we settled into Toby's kitchen to prep cabbage and potatoes. Toby told of her knish overtures to Michael Tilson Thomas. The director of the San Francisco Symphony — and grandson of Yiddish theater stars Boris and Bessie Thomashefsky — had a thing for knishes, as mentioned in an interview in the *New York Times:*

> Anytime I'm in New York in the fall, I go to Yonah Schimmel's knishes, which has been a fixture on East Houston Street since the 1890s. Sometimes I head to Yonah's straight from the airport. Nothing warms you up as the weather starts getting cool like a fresh potato or kasha knish.[18]

Through a friend of a friend, Toby arranged to have a box of knishes delivered to the maestro, who thanked her, but never requested an encore.

I ran out for more onions. Toby donned an apron from Katz's, Sara donned an apron from Ratner's. I put on one from Minnesota, *Sholom Home Delicious Knishes*.

A reporter knocked at the door.

TOBY: Sara's here to really say, "Should the rolls be thinner or fatter?" or "Roll more times through the dough" or . . .

SARA: Or, "We did it this way . . . "

TOBY: It's all recovered memories.

SARA: I'm older, that's why.

TOBY: I've made it the most at this point.

SARA: Toby changed some things. Toby modified. I'm probably the closest to my grandmother and my mother, who were the big knish makers.

TOBY: She's more of the direct line.

SARA: My mother ran the store — while my grandmother was alive and after she died. She worked in the store from the beginning.

Sara reminisced about the cocktail knishes, thousands of them, prepared for New Year's Eve.

I rolled and rerolled dough until it was thin as a tablecloth. In the slanted light of late afternoon, under the tutelage of the granddaughters, I spooned on farmer's cheese and sour cherries and coaxed the package into a thin log with see-through skin.

Mrs. Stahl's granddaughters: Sara Spatz and Toby Engelberg.

Then again, with cabbage. Then I ducked into the sitting room for another look at the young Fannie Stahl: hair swept-back, eyes soft, face placid. The portrait reminded me of a youthful image of the woman whose love of knishes sparked so many pilgrimages to Mrs. Stahl's: my grandma, Fritzie.

Fritzie who was born in Riga, Latvia, in 1898

Fritizie who swore her grandfather was head of the Jewish
     something-or-other

Fritizie who said her Yiddish was different from everyone else's

Fritizie who arrived, with her brothers and mother, in New York, at
     age six

Fritzie who was born Freyda Rifke, but wrote "Ruth" on official papers

Fritzie who, single, took the last name Reidell (like Rydell, the high
     school in Grease)

Fritzie who eloped to Elkton, Maryland

Fritzie who differentiated between "lonely" and "lonesome"

Fritzie who hitchhiked with her friends to Florida

Fritzie who landed a beachside apartment in senior housing

Fritizie who insisted on correct grammar

Fritzie who gifted me stationery and postage stamps

Fritzie who made batches of applesauce pinked with skins

Fritzie who was known for stuffed cabbage, sweet, and delivered
     in jars

Fritzie who, on the 1940 census, took ten years off her age

Fritzie who listed her place of birth as Massachusetts

Fritzie who, three days before her daughter, was buried at Beth Moses

"*Tobeleh,* is it time to take these out of the oven?" crooned the reporter, peeking at a tray of cabbage knishes.[19]

The guests, many of them ex–New Yorkers, *hurled* themselves at the knishes. They mingled and conversed and hurled and re-hurled themselves. I forgot about the *Shehecheyanu,* but persuaded one guest — the man who dubbed Toby a "knish heiress" — to belt out the fight song of his alma mater.

Proudly we cry
"There can be no fairer Alma Mater than Tilden High."

The hulking school in the East Flatbush section of Brooklyn had been decommissioned two years earlier. We didn't discuss that, and I forgot to ask if he knew Ruby the Knish Man, who counted Tilden as his territory.

There were no leftovers, but the granddaughters of Mrs. Stahl had an offering for me: a T-shirt, white, with red cursive letters. Preshrunk, but still too big. I packed it to take back to where the story began.

DELICIOUS
Mrs. Stahl's
EST. 1935
HANDMADE KNISHES
BRIGHTON BEACH, BROOKLYN

Epilogue

I had one more pilgrimage to make: Vineland, New Jersey. In a place once known as the land of Jewish chicken farmers, in a borough called Buena, on a road called Wheat, Conte's Pasta awaited me. Its mascarpone-colored façade masked a wall of metal siding, corrugated, like manicotti. The brim of the building rose in strips of brick: red and redder, a cross-section of lasagna, thick with sauce.

Mike Conte was open to a visit, on the condition that I coordinate with the knishes. Production had turned sparse. Knishes emerged from Conte's ovens less often than the full moon rose over Jersey. Conte made knishes according to orders received. The orders came from distributors, who shuttled knishes to delis and bagel stores. When Conte first took over Mrs. Stahl's Knishes, he had a handful of distributors. Seven years later, he was down to one.

Steve Rapillo, the owner of Tufo's Foods, a wholesaler in the Bronx, had been hawking Mrs. Stahl's knishes since the 1990s. He remembered the green Plexiglas panels his customers displayed to lure clients. "People know your stuff because they see the sign and they remember their childhood," said Rapillo. "'You have Mrs. Stahl's? I used to go to the boardwalk all the time . . .'"[1]

Without the sign, the knish risked anonymity. "If you're standing there and you looked at the knish, it might not come to mind right away," said Rapillo.

He remembered when he would place orders by the caseload, every other week, back in the day. By 2012, the green signs with the Mrs. Stahl's name were long gone, his customer base had dwindled, and the lineage was, at best, eclipsed. The lack of advertising was one obstacle of many. "The next generation, they don't know from it," said Rapillo. "Unless they grew up in that tradition."

Did he mean the Jewish tradition, the middle-class New Yorker tradition, or the tradition of eating cheap food off the street? Regardless, the majority of knishes on his order form fell under the category of Mrs. Stahl's.

Assorted Cocktail Knishes

Blueberry Cheese Knishes

Broccoli Knishes

Cherry Cheese Knishes

Kasha Knishes

Mixed Veg. Knishes

Mushroom Potato Knishes

Onion Cheese Knishes

Pineapple Cheese Knishes

Potato Cocktail Knishes

Potato Knishes

Spinach Cheese Knishes

Spinach Knishes

Strawberry Cheese Knishes

Sweet Potato Knishes

Not that all of them were in circulation. (Who still speaks of the Onion Cheese or the Pineapple Cheese?) "When it went down to Conte, there were some growing pains," said Rapillo. "Now there are shrinking pains. I used to buy a hundred cases from Mrs. Stahl's every other week; now I order thirty or forty from Conte every other *month*." Distribution had shrunk by 90 percent.

"He's not crying over it," said Rapillo. Conte had done well with his line of gluten-free pasta — so well, he built a million-dollar gluten-free outpost of Casa Manicotti.[2]

Every knish that came out of Conte's factory, however, contained gluten. And every knish went through Rapillo, who sold them to "a scant few bagel stores." He was getting more and more orders for "thaw and serve."

It sounded like a botched experiment in cryogenics.

"They're fully baked and fresh," said Rapillo. "You just take them out of the freezer. They come to room temperature. You can serve it the way it is." (I would lobby to heat it up, but that was for another time.) The downside of thaw and serve was that defrosting made for a limited shelf life. After three days, the knish "started to break down."

Another industry trend was delivering items "par-baked."

It sounded like a golf tournament, heavy on the cannabis.

"Factories bake it off seventy or eighty percent," explained Rapillo. "That way it's actually a fresh-baked item. You put it in the oven for five minutes. . . . You can have them nice and fresh all day long."

The next time he called Conte to place an order, he'd call me, too. Rapillo took down my number and clipped it to his knish file. I plotted my route and kept my schedule loose.

I imagined Mrs. Stahl's derivative knishes on trays, conveyor belts, the shelves of tall rolling carts, in boxes. That was June, then July. Paper clips failed. Memory slipped. I called Conte. I called Rapillo. In August, I missed the shipment. In October, ditto. (By then I had met Mrs. Stahl's granddaughters, who were also curious about the knishes that bore their grandmother's name.)

In November, I called Conte. Brittany, who answered the phone, said I would be notified when the knishes were put on the schedule. Two weeks later, she put me on hold.

"Be sure to check Acme, Shoprite, Murphy's, and Supervalue Supermarkets for Conte's pasta products, as well as specialty stores that insist on carrying only the best," said the hold message.

Finally, I was on the verge of finding Mrs. Stahl's in exile. Now, if only the hold message would hint at knishes.

"For a delightful blend of crunchy and chewy textures and an explosion of traditional Italian flavor, you have to try Conte's gourmet cheese pizza. A traditional pizza shell cradles Angela Conte's . . ."

"Hello?"

"Hi."

"What was the name, again?"

"Laura."

"Laura, at this time, the company Mrs. Stahl's Knishes is up for sale."

Gulp.

"So, right now, because of the sale, we don't have the intention of making any more. If you have any other questions, you can talk to the new owner once he contacts you."

Huh? Casa Manicotti was destined to be a knish mausoleum.

I told Rapillo.

"What's he gonna get for it?" he said, about Conte. "Who's he going to sell it to? It's really just the name."

Wake of the Storm

Two weeks after Superstorm Sandy, the boardwalks of Brooklyn were mired in sand. Damp, thick, ubiquitous sand. From all over, people came to tame it. We swept and shoveled and shoveled and swept. I snuck glimpses at the horizon.

To Riga!

To Bialystok!

To Knyszyn!

In Coney Island, groups of strangers coaxed clumps of displaced beach into sloppy pyramids. Afterward, I ate onion rings. I walked to Brighton, nodded at the window of apartment 12A, and made a beeline for the site of Mrs. Stahl's. Banners bragged about a TUSCAN CHICKEN MELT and MELTY MOUTHWATERING GOODNESS. A neon sign abided: COFFEE. But just past dusk at Subway store number 37526, the java had already evaporated.

Around the corner at Brighton Bazaar, customers vied for borscht, blintzes, and blini at steam tables that rivaled top-of-the-line bar mitzvah buffets. A tray of cheese knishes sat adorned with granules of sugar. Above it crouched a shellacked, apple-mouthed piglet, petrified.

That made two of us.

⊛ ⊛ ⊛ **When I told Toby about** the possible sale of the Stahl's name, she wanted to know how much.

A few weeks later, I received an e-mail:

Mrs. Stahl's knishes brought back such great memories that I contacted Conte's Pasta last week and negotiated an option to purchase Mrs. Stahl's. I plan on conducting a casual focus group . . . to determine public interest in having Mrs. Stahl's handmade knishes return to the marketplace in some form (maybe a retail store or website with mail order etc.).[3]

It was signed Don Marton. I phoned immediately. He was a serial entrepreneur in real estate and mulch who had first encountered Mrs. Stahl's knishes in the Catskills. *Was he sure they were Mrs. Stahl's?* I interrupted. *After all, the Catskills were Ruby the Knish Man territory.*

Yes, Mrs. Stahl's. Friends from Brooklyn brought them to the mountains. The would-be owner, born on Long Island, had consecrated the bulk of his adulthood to Boca Raton. He was not of Brooklyn, but at least he knew the Festival Flea Market Mall in Pompano, where Aunt Jean, native of Knyszyn, may she rest in peace, went for knishes.

"I'm located in South Florida. I'm Jewish, from New York," said the prospective heir to the Mrs. Stahl's name. "A lot of our tribe has retired to Florida," he offered. "Why not have Mrs. Stahl's retire here, too?"[4]

Made sense. Except the real Mrs. Stahl *never* retired.

Mrs. Stahl, born Feige Goldenberg in Kulikov, Galicia, in 1887[5]
Mrs. Stahl, whose father who was a shochet, a mohel, and a cantor[6]
Mrs. Stahl who married a man nearly twenty years her senior

Mrs. Stahl who, on Valentine's Day 1914, arrived in New York on the S.S. Noordam

Mrs. Stahl who, on the ship's manifest, listed as her last name the maiden name of her husband's mother

Mrs. Stahl who came with twenty dollars, two of four children, and one on the way

Mrs. Stahl who went to work as a domestic, with a baby in tow

Mrs. Stahl who went by the name Fannie

Mrs. Stahl who worked at the first kosher cafeteria on the Lower East Side[7]

Mrs. Stahl who made knishes at a basement restaurant on Rivington Street[8]

Mrs. Stahl who, when her youngest fell ill, moved to Yonkers to work at the Home for Polio[9]

Mrs. Stahl who, in Brooklyn, made challah and pastries to sell to neighbors[10]

Mrs. Stahl who, at the suggestion of her daughter Rae, sold, on the beach, knishes

Mrs. Stahl who, as not to arouse suspicion, sat with a basket on the sand[11]

Mrs. Stahl who didn't work Saturdays[12]

Mrs. Stahl who, two hours after meat, wouldn't eat ice cream but offered it to the grandkids[13]

Mrs. Stahl who, on the 1940 census, listed herself as head of household[14]

Mrs. Stahl who was "a queen and a delightful person and a very hard worker"[15]

Mrs. Stahl who, when a counter boy wanted to bring home a knish, said, "Take, take"[16]

Mrs. Stahl who, with her eldest daughter, knit sweaters for the Jews of Palestine[17]

Mrs. Stahl who, at the Brooklyn Hadassah Luncheon, was listed as Star Patroness[18]

Mrs. Stahl who, at age sixty-nine, boarded her first plane on "pilgrimage" to Israel

Mrs. Stahl who stood up from the shiva for her daughter Rae and had a heart attack

Mrs. Stahl who was buried at Wellwood, next door to my Gramma Fritzie

Mrs. Stahl who, in her will, remembered each of the eight
    grandchildren

Mrs. Stahl whose death certificate listed her occupation as "H.W.":
    housewife

"She was *never* a housewife," said Sara, her granddaughter.

The man with the option to buy Mrs. Stahl's Knishes had time. He couldn't say how much time, and he wouldn't say how much cash he'd plunked down. What he could say was that in a month's time, the Mrs. Stahl's Facebook page he'd set up had garnered a thousand "likes."

Reprise, Reconsidered

If and when Mrs. Stahl's returns as a dedicated knish business, the opinions will be heated. There will be those who gravitate toward it and those who steer clear. There will be those who praise it and those who deem it a poor rendition of what came before. If and when Mrs. Stahl's gains a foothold in Florida, it will — at least at first — do little to change the knish situation in Brooklyn, which still is not at all what it once was.

And thank goodness.

Nostalgia can freeze you, but it can also set you free. The truth is, you *can* get a good knish in Brooklyn — or anywhere. You just have to know where to look, or be willing to take matters into your own hands. From Williamsburg to Kings Highway, from San Francisco to St. Paul, the knish isn't giving up anytime soon. It's experiencing a renaissance on food trucks, at Jewish nosh festivals, and in private homes.

And on the Lower East Side of Manhattan, a guy originally from Staten Island has started his own knish concern. Noah Wildman, "owner, operator, chef, and garbage man of Knishery NYC," grew up on Mrs. Stahl's; his mother worked in Brighton and brought them home by the armload. "As a kid, I thought everyone had a box of knishes in their freezer," said Wildman. "Why wouldn't anybody have that?"[19]

Fast-forward to age forty. After careers in the music industry and graphic design, Wildman went to culinary school and started making his then-favorite food, from the Italian tradition. He produced "neo-Neapolitan" pizza at several restaurants in Brooklyn, but something wasn't quite right. A few years later he stumbled on expansive outdoor fairs filled with "people taking foods from their heritage and doing something new with it." Then his wife saw a listing for a course called Knish History 101 — at a place called the Brooklyn Brainery.[20] It got Wildman thinking. "I didn't see a knish stand [at any of the newfangled food fairs]. . . . If there was something from my youth that there needed to be a stand for, of course it would be a knish."

In class, Wildman asked about the signature inner membrane of Mrs. Stahl's output. I sketched a cross-section in chalk on the blackboard and suggested that a knish should only be served warm. "If it's fresh and good," countered Wildman, "just like with cold pizza, you can eat a cold knish." Then things got heated. Wildman took it as a good sign that "we could actually have an argument like two Jewish people and enjoy it, rather than get angry with each other."

He asked for a recipe. I suggested the one I had used in Banff. He arrived at the second session with a box of knishes, homemade. Since 2011, Wildman has single-handedly rolled, stuffed, and baked thousands of knishes. He has appeared on ABC News and has garnered accolades from *New York Times* food critic Florence Fabricant.[21]

In October 2012, at the Hester Street Fair, right off Essex Street (not far from the fictitious knish stand run, according to Sholem Aleichem, by Motl's relative Yoneh), Knishery NYC set up shop under a pop-up tent. Wildman sold a selection of kosher-style knishes to a clientele of "half locals and Jews, half tourists and foodies, and a small mix of senior citizens."

Potato & Onion

Spinach & Roasted Garlic

Pastrami

Kasha & Pumpkin

His knishes aren't cooked under strict certification, but they don't include pork or shrimp, which wasn't always the case.

"I need to take the foundation and the walls — which are based on kosher — and build upwards," said the knish chef, who, early on, tried traditional recipes like lung and brisket. He also dabbled in ham-and-cheese and shellfish, but has since dismissed *trayf*

Noah Wildman sells his handmade pies on the Lower East Side.

flavors as unsound. "You can't slap pork and shrimp on a kosher foundation. It's disrespectful to the people who came before," said Wildman, foreman of a business designed to link his young children — and his customers — to their ancestors.

"The people who have come before me made the brand — the word 'knish' — mean something," he said. "I don't want to dilute that, I want to make it stronger."

The next challenge is to perfect a knish with distinct inner chambers, à la Mrs. Stahl's. "If you're going into the future," said Wildman, "you have to know where you came from."

Longtime knish distributor Steve Rapillo echoed that sentiment. He was talking about bigger establishments, but the same principle applied to home cooks.

"If you have a kitchen," he said, "you make your own."

Recipe: Mrs. Stahl's Potato Knishes

Fannie Stahl's granddaughters summoned recovered memories to bring this recipe to life. Toby Engelberg, who sold her knishes in the Bay Area for a while, enlisted the help of her elder cousin from New York, Sara Spatz, who, as a young woman, worked in her grandmother's shop in Brighton Beach. I was there to learn. What struck me most was the aroma. It filled the kitchen as soon the skins were peeled from the first onions, and lingered long after the last tray of knishes had cooled.

Dough:
3¼ cups flour
1 Tbs. sugar
1 tsp. salt
½ cup vegetable oil
1 cup lukewarm water

Turn on oven on low until dough is ready. Mix flour, sugar, and salt. Add oil and water. Mix with a spoon until the dough pulls together, or use a food processor or stand mixer (with a dough hook). Turn out the dough on board and knead it, incorporating all pieces. Knead until dough is one piece, smooth and glossy. Turn off the oven. Oil the dough and place it in oiled, covered bowl. Place in oven until you are ready to use it. Let the dough rest at least 2 hours; the dough should barely rise, if at all. Keeping the dough overnight in the refrigerator is fine. Bring it back to room temperature before use.

Potato filling:
6 lbs. russet or new potatoes
1 cup oil
¼ cup salt, or to taste
1½ tsp. pepper
8 cups thinly sliced raw onions

Scrub potatoes and peel them, unless the new potatoes have very thin, unblemished skins. Boil potatoes for about 20 minutes until knife tender, then drain. Mash with a potato masher. Add oil, salt, and pepper to taste. Mix. Stir in the onion.

ASSEMBLING AND BAKING

Vegetable oil and flour as needed

Preheat oven to 450 degrees. Roll out about half the dough on a lightly floured counter or tabletop. Roll with handle-less rod-style rolling pin out from the center until dough is thin enough to see through, about $\frac{1}{16}$-inch thick.

Oil top edge of dough with a pastry brush. Place a 2-inch-diameter line of filling about 2 inches from the top edge of the dough. Pick up top edge and drape over filling. Brush oil on dough in a 2-inch strip on the bottom edge of the filling. Pick up the dough with filling and roll again onto the oiled dough, compressing the filled dough as you turn it. Repeat until the dough covers the filling three to four times, being sure always to brush oil on the dough first. Use a knife to separate the filled potato knish log from the remaining dough. Cut off edges of filled dough. Cut the filled roll into pieces about 6 inches long and coil each piece like a snail. Tuck the remaining end into the bottom of the coil. Alternatively, place stuffed roll of dough onto ungreased cookie sheet and slash with a knife crosswise every 2 inches. Leave an inch of space between each roll or coil of dough.

Bake 20–25 minutes until the knish skin is browned and knishes are cooked through. Start knishes on lowest rack of the over and raise them to top rack after about 10–12 minutes. Let the knishes cool in pan. If you cooked the knishes in long rolls, cut them into individual pieces.

Knishes can be reheated in the oven or in a skillet on the stove top.

Makes about 18 knishes.[1]

Where to Get a Good Knish

You *can* get a good knish, you just have to know where to look. Here are eighteen places I recommend, for starters.

NEW YORK CITY AND ENVIRONS

Gabila's
www.gabilas.com

Gottlieb's Restaurant
(718) 384-6612

Knish Nosh
www.knishnosh.com

Knishery NYC
www.knisherynyc.blogspot.com

Liebman's Bronx Delicatessen
www.liebmansdeli.com

Mile End Deli
www.mileenddeli.com

Oceanside Knish Factory
www.knishfactory.com

Pastrami Queen
www.pastramiqueen.com

Yonah Schimmel Knish Bakery
www.knishery.com

Zabar's
www.zabars.com

ANN ARBOR, MICHIGAN

Zingerman's Delicatessen
www.zingermansdeli.com

BALTIMORE

The Knish Shop
www.knishshop.com

BOSTON AREA

Zaftigs Delicatessen
www.zaftigs.com

CLEARWATER, FLORIDA

Brooklyn Knish
www.brooklynknish.biz

LOS ANGELES

Factor's Famous Deli
www.factorsdeli.com

SAN FRANCISCO

Knish King
www.knishking.com

Old World Food Truck
www.oldworldfoodtruck.com

TWIN CITIES, MINNESOTA

Sholom Home Knishes
(651) 328-2000

Acknowledgments

Like a batch of knishes, a book benefits from many hands. Throughout this process, I have been bolstered and humbled by the support of family and friends, colleagues and strangers. I have received servings of kindness and generosity that I hope to repay, and not just in knishes.

My first dispatch on the humble pie appeared in the anthology *Jews of Brooklyn* (2002). After the demise of Mrs. Stahl's, then-editor in chief of *Brooklyn Papers* Gersh Kuntzman pushed me to issue a "clarion call" for the pastry and dubbed me the Knish Lady. Sharon Ashley published my ode to the disappearing pastry pie in the *Jerusalem Report*. I thought I was done with it.

Susan Shapiro encouraged me to write a book. Ryan Fischer-Harbage helped me develop a proposal. The Women's National Book Association gave me a chance to pitch. Pamela Druckerman and Lauren Weber provided full-bodied, generous feedback. Harriet Bell took me under her wing and reminded me that a knish, at its core, is a pillow. Diane Jacobs, Lea Beresford, and Joe Veltre contributed editing and ideas. Temim Fruchter imposed order on a half decade of research. Hallie Newman refined the morass of early drafts and images, with heart.

Jill Slater kept listening and kept telling me to keep going. Nina Frenkel kept me company and reminded me, many times, why it mattered. David Sauvage diagramed the story. Alisa Algava stayed up late so I could submit something. Gabrielle Maisels edited on screen. Lindsay Packer listened, many times. Jesse Tisch offered expert editing advice. Kelly Waggoner applied an eagle eye to early drafts. Jeff Hoover read and reread the manuscript and provided astute suggestions on structure, wording, and style. The book is better for his input, and I am better for his guidance and friendship.

Kathleen Doyle kept me on track. Ian Hodder contributed crosswords, ultimatums, and top-of-the-line proofreading skills. Joan Larkin sent a poem, an article, and reassurance. Deb Goldstein insisted on a Kickstarter campaign.

Peter Hamlin donated a beautiful video. Bertha Lowitt wanted to know where the book was. Daniel Cainer cracked me up. Gloria Aroffo offered gifts of every ilk. Ilana Abramovitch did everything, including reconnaissance on the "Pizza/Knish" aisle. Liz Kazmier demanded a definition of the word *plotz*. Sara Michael drove me to Zingerman's. Boris Fishman offered support and Ukrainian contacts. Doug Rosenberg told me to finish it, already. David Rakoff invited me for lunch on the steps of the library. The Jewish Meditation Center offered calm.

The story of the potato pie doesn't belong to any one person, but descendants of distinguished knish lineages bear a special claim. I am grateful for Andrew Axler's post, which led me to the family of Fannie Stahl, who welcomed me with open arms, and a pinch of disbelief. Toby Engelberg immediately suggested I come to San Francisco to make knishes. Sara Spatz had me to her home, several times. Jonas and Lois Spatz laid out their recollections. Three generations of the Colby family—Madeleine, Helen, Danielle—shared memories and mementos. Cori Kesler put me in contact with the Weingasts, who were generous with their memories and mementos. Marvin Hirsch entertained endless requests for information. Larry Hirsch shared notes on his knish-making technique. Pamela Hirsch let me borrow a prized image of her grandfather. Mort Shatzkin doled out recollections. Jerry Oshinsky, may his memory be for a blessing, dished out pure *joie de knish* and love of Jewish ritual. Bonnie Abrams delivered a live performance of "Ruby's Knishes" at the New York Public Library. Noah Wildman, at every opportunity, plied me and those around me with you know what. To everyone who shared time, reminiscences, recipes for knishes and good living, I extend a special, heartfelt thanks. You are the true heroes of the ever-evolving history of the knish.

A small army of intercontinental translators made it possible for me to insert myself, literally and vicariously, into other places and time periods. Il'il Paz-el translated from Hebrew; Chana Pollack and Myra Mniewski from Yiddish; Mateusz Zurawik and Gosha Zaremba from Polish; Paula Teitelbaum, beloved Yiddish teacher, from *mamaloshen*, Polish, and Russian. Ostap Kin translated from Ukrainian. Lubow Wolynetz explained everything I could possibly want to know, but had no idea how to ask, about the Ukrainian *knysh*.

Barbara Henry, Jay Dubb, and Julia Verkholantsev translated handfuls of documents from the archives in Bialystok. At the New School, super-librarian Brita Servaes sleuthed out German-language etymological connections to the knish. Maxim Piz provided context and camaraderie.

In Poland, Agnieszka Kręglicka came to meet me early on a Saturday morning, scoured Warsaw for knish connections and, again and again, extended the warmest possible welcome. Katarina Piechocki and her family offered extraordinary hospitality. Karol Kempnerski ran across the city in record time to look for a fabled street fair knish, then helped me make sense of goings on in Bialystok and Knyszyn. Barbara Kirshenblatt-Gimblett, director of the core exhibition at the Museum of the History of Polish Jews, provided detailed, thoughtful, and very generous answers, every time. Anna Kraus unearthed essential ancient sources at the University of Warsaw Library. Marcin Bartosiewicz of the Foundation for the Preservation of Jewish Heritage in Poland became a relentless ally, valued colleague, and repeated source of good humor. Tomek Wiśniewski not only translated but also shepherded—and chauffeured— genealogical wanderings. In Knyszyn, Krysztof Bagiński gave me an official welcome. Henryk Stasiewicz, may he rest in peace, pedaled over on a moment's notice and made sure I saw the Jewish names on the centuries-old plaque that listed members of the city council. Friends of the Forum for Dialogue Among Nations invited me on a once-in-a-lifetime trip filled with important conversations and new perspectives. Jonathan Ornstein and the entire JCC of Kraków team made me feel at home *and* in the right place.

In Paris, I benefited from the hospitality and longstanding friendship of Laurent Dureuil and Ni Liang. Andreas Simma lent me his apartment and his ear. Yitskhok Niborski was a welcome guide to Yiddish sources. In Israel, the Hazon Sustainable Food Tour, co-sponsored by the Heschel Center for Environmental Learning and Leadership, gave me a chance to contextualize the knish.

In Kiryat Bialystok, my family indulged me with food and drink reminiscent of my first visit, when Cohava, may her memory be for a blessing, shuttled homemade salads to the balcony, and Simcha asked after every person in our extended clan. In Tel Aviv, Tova Dickstein and Susan Weingarten opened windows on foodways of Talmudic times. Janna Gur initiated a boureka-tasting extravaganza. November Wanderin filmed my Tel Aviv knish expeditions, shared footage of her quest for Ashkenazi food, and became a good friend right off the bat.

In Minnesota, I was fortunate to come into contact with a tight-knit community, new friends, and exceptional support for the arts. The Tofte Lake Center, Jerome Foundation, and Rimon, the Minnesota Jewish Arts Council, offered unflagging support, as did the Howard B. & Ruth F. Brin Jewish Arts Endowment Fund, a designated fund of the Jewish Community Foundation of the Minneapolis Jewish Federation. I am grateful for the generosity and warmth of David Jordan Harris, Dede Smith, Rae Berman, the Sholom Home, and the Jewish Historical Society of the Upper Midwest. John Page Corrigan drove me to the archives and found an article on happy hour at the senior home ("Free drinks for everyone over 90 when accompanied by parents"). Carla Vogel, another descendant of Knyszyn, became family on our first meeting. Ditto Judith Brin Ingber, who offered presence and presents of every stripe. Under the leadership of Hazel Chase, the Knish Ladies of Sholom Home (at this writing, Dede Wolfson and Rina Glaser are at the helm) introduced me to Minnesota Yiddishkeit. Beneath the fluorescent lights of their headquarters, I learned how to seal a pocket of dough and pry open my myopia. It's difficult to admit, but it just might be okay to consume a knish sans mustard.

In New York, the YIVO Zumerprogram turned my smidgens of Yiddish into sentences and let me share preliminary knish findings in the language of my grandmothers. Samuel Freedman's Writers' Seminar on the Jewish People provided an opportunity to hone my knish theories in the company of thoughtful colleagues. Heidi Boisvert tipped me off to the magic of the New York Public Library's Wertheim Study. Jay Barksdale granted me access to the room—a shelf of my own—and extended good cheer at every opportunity. My hometown may be the epicenter of North American knish history, but it would be nothing without its libraries.

Each archives and manuscript collection mentioned in the bibliography provided opportunities to glimpse new worlds and gather valuable knish-related tidbits. Special thanks to Katherine Tane and Andrea Klein Bergman at the Jewish Historical Society of the Upper Midwest, Leonora Gilgund and Kenn Cobb at the Municipal Archives of the City of New York, and Bob Freedman of the Robert and Molly Freedman Jewish Music Archive at the University of Pennsylvania. I was ably assisted by Heather Halliday of the American Jewish Historical Society and Melanie Meyers and the indefatigable Zachary Loeb at the Center for Jewish History. Leo Greenbaum and Yeshaya Metal at the YIVO Archives and Library provided repeated assistance. Cynthia Harris of Kansas State University retrieved and relayed important materials from the Clementine Paddleford Collection.

At the New York Public Library, Amanda (Miryem-Khaye) Siegel went out of her way to suggest and retrieve sources. Jeremy Megraw and Steve Massa identified a rogue photo as a publicity still for *The Night They Raided Minsky's*. Joy Holland, Ivy Marvel, and June Koffi at the Brooklyn Public Library's Brooklyn Collection responded to my relentless inquiries with poise and smiles. At New York University's Bobst Library, Evelyn Ehrlich offered a crash course in Jewish sources; Timothy Johnson fielded questions about food history. At the Jewish Theological Society of America, Rena Borow, Ina Cohen, and Rina Krautwirth distilled centuries of Jewish sources. Chana Pollack, archivist at the *Forward*, unearthed the front-page article on Gussie Schwebel and spurred the section on the knish queen of Houston Street. Sara Malcolm of the FDR Presidential Library and Museum located Mrs. Schwebel's correspondence with the first lady. If you come across any descendants of Gussie Schwebel, please send them my way.

I have been fortunate to receive generous grants, residencies, and fellowships from the Tofte Lake Center, the Jerome Foundation, and the Lilly Foundation. The Millay Colony for the Arts, Religion Newswriters Association, and the Wellspring House opened doors for me. Asylum Arts, CEC Artslink, and YIVO afforded me access to new — and old — worlds. The Hadassah-Brandeis Institute gave me my first award, then another (thank you, Debbie Olins and Shula Reinharz, for years of support), anointed me as a Research Associate, and shared my book idea with Brandeis University Press. Through several iterations and many seasons, with tough love and an outstretched arm, my editor, Phyllis Deutsch, guided me away from gobbledygook and toward the heart of my story. Phyllis ushered this book to fruition with generosity and patience and reminded me that heavy foods are generally easier to digest with levity. I did my best. (Also, try Alka-Seltzer.) Jessica Stevens ushered this book into production with poise and precision. Amanda Heller weeded out inconsistences and polished my prose with the utmost care.

Food writing greats Matthew Goodman, Joan Nathan, and Andrew F. Smith shared time, served up guidance, and helped me find a place at the table. Ditto Gil Marks, Molly O'Neill, and especially Arthur Schwartz, who, like Mark Kurlansky, cordially agreed to an interview when I was just getting started. Jenny Coffey, Laura Mass, and Allen Salkin were there at the beginning. Norman Stiles helped with story and structure. Joanne Lehman welcomed me and memories of Deena. Aunt Jeanette and Uncle Paul, may they rest in peace, informed my explorations. Shawn Shafner offered levity. Suzan Sherman, Helene Silver, and Cheryl Smith reminded me of the life force. Wendy Palitz, Sam Lorber, Heidi Szpek, and Andreas Kahrs each provided assistance right when I needed it. Allan Appel was a role model; Belinda Plutz, unfailing in her encouragement. Colleagues and friends at UJA-Federation, the Tenement Museum, and Transportation Alternatives egged me on. David Kestin, Erin Healy, Sarah Whiteside, and Jen Ziegler provided practical help and joie de vivre.

I have received much help from many people along the Knish Route, but any omissions, oversights, and errors are mine alone. This book belongs, really, to my parents, who might regret ever taking me to Mrs. Stahl's. Nonetheless, they have ladled on support of every flavor, year after year, and have done their best to conceal skepticism under their placemats. Let it be known that Barbara (Babs) Silver served as a persistent and gifted senior research associate on special assignments and that Michael (Mickey) Silver is a master mustard maker and lover of literature of the highest order. I offer these knish chronicles to them and, as Simcha says, *to each and every* member of our extended family, in loving memory of my grandmothers and *each and every* one who came before. Their stories are dense, wrapped in hardship, and worth telling.

Heartfelt thanks. Before there was a book, there was you.

Mitchel Agoos
Alisa Algava
Gloria Aroffo
Nathalie Bachand
Frank E. Bell
Amir Bennatan
Zackary Sholem Berger
Joel Berkowitz
Olaf Bertram-
    Nothnagel
Rachel Blake
Mike Blum
Daniel Canty
Eliot Caroom
Christopher Chafe
Patricia Clark
Kathleen Doyle
Jonathan Farbowitz
Joel Farbstein
Ken Farbstein
Jeffrey P. Feinman
Ida Feuer
Laura and Martin
    Forsberg
Nina Frenkel
Marie Galati
Faith Gertner
Jeanine and Steve
    Goldman

Daniel Goldstein
David Goldstein
Deborah Goldstein
Tamara Greenfield
Alex Halperin
Peter Hamlin
Kate Hartman
Madeline Snow
    Hayden
Tom Hayden
Erin Healy and
    Sarah Whiteside
Barbara Henry
Anne Hillam
Ian Hodder
Ben Jacobs
Elise Jakabhazy
Micki Josi
Joan Jubett
Joan and Brian Kaplan
Celia Keenholtz
    (in loving memory)
Astri Kingstone
Laura Kwerel
Gabe Landes
Maxine Levaren
Zack Logan
Gloria Lomuscio
Sam Lorber

Warren MacMillan
Sara Marcus
Judy and Bill Mays
Marcia Michael
Kate Mondloch
Rachel Natelson and
    Seth Fogelman
Frances Ohanenye
Maria Petulla
Jordan Rosenblum
Nola Safro
Mark Sandiford
Shawn Shafner
Joel Shatzky and
    Ilana Abramovitch
Pamela Shaw
Nancy Siesel
Barbara and
    Michael Silver
Franny Silverman
Audrey Slater
Elaine Spital
June Thomas
Kelly Waggoner and
    Chris Simpson
Jeffrey Yoskowitz

World Famous

KNISH NOSH ™
SINCE 1952

www.Knishnosh.com

CATERING SPECIALISTS

ALL NATURAL
FREE DELIVERY

Hand-Rolled Large KNISH

POTATO	3.00
KASHA	3.25
SPINACH	3.25
BROCCOLI	3.25
MUSHROOM	3.25
CARROT MUSHROOM	3.25
CABBAGE	3.50
SWEET POTATO	3.50
MEAT	3.50
1 DOZ. ASST KNISHES	38.00

WORLD FAMOUS

FRANKS IN A BLANKET
KNISHES
100% BEEF FRANKS

REG. SIZE	3.00
FOOT LONG	4.00
CABBAGE DOG	4.50

KNISH NOSH

KNISH WRAPS

PASTRAMI	5.00
CORNED BEEF	5.00
TURKEY	5.00

COCKTAIL KNISHES

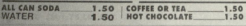

	DOZEN	2 DOZEN	100 PCS
POTATO	4.50	8.50	30.00
KASHA	4.75	9.00	32.00
SPINACH	4.75	9.00	32.00
BROCCOLI	4.75	9.00	32.00
CABBAGE	6.00	11.50	44.00
SWEET POTATO	6.50	11.50	44.00
MEAT	6.50	12.00	46.00
PASTRAMI	6.50	12.00	46.00
CORNED BEEF	6.50	12.00	46.00
TURKEY	6.50	12.00	46.00
Cocktail FRANKS	4.50	8.50	32.00

HOUSE SPECIALTIES

SHEPARD'S PIE	5.00
SWEET POT. PIE	5.00
POTATO KUGEL	4.00

POTATO LATKAS	1/ 1.25
VEG. LATKAS	1/ 1.25

POTATO LATKAS
SMALL 4.50   LARGE 9.00

DESSERTS

RAISIN RUGALLECH 1.25 Ea.
PKG. 9.50

KIDS MEAL

4 MINI KNISHES
4 MINI HOT DOGS
4.50

We Send our LOVE
AND KNISHES
ANYWHERE IN U.S.

ALL CAN SODA	1.50
WATER	1.50

COFFEE OR TEA	1.50
HOT CHOCOLATE	1.50

Notes

PREFACE

1. Henryk Stasiewicz, *Knyszyn i Ziemia knyszyńska,* trans. Gosha Zaremba (Knyszyn: Knyszyn Regional Association of King Sigismund Augustus in Knyszyn, 2008), 205.

2. Krzysztof Bagiński, "Meeting with Multicultural Knyszyn," pamphlet, Municipality of Knyszyn, 2008, 2, 21.

AU REVOIR, MRS. STAHL'S

1. The holy ark in Hebrew is called *aron hakodesh*. In modern Hebrew, *aron* means "closet."

2. Fist to chest: During Yom Kippur prayers, it is customary to hit oneself in admission of sins that are recited by the congregation.

3. Sitting *shiva* refers to observing the ritual mourning period after a death in the family by receiving visitors at home. By extension, it means to go into mourning for someone or something.

4. *Kaddish,* related to the Hebrew word for holy (*kadosh),* is the mourner's prayer, recited in Aramaic.

5. Pat Singer (founder and executive director, Brighton Neighborhood Association), interview by the author, November 2, 2005.

6. Street games. Potsy is akin to hopscotch, and ring-a-levio is a form of tag played in groups.

7. Marty Markowitz, Brooklyn Borough President, letter to the author on the occasion of "Knish History 101" course, July 1, 2011. "It's my hope that you'll spark an interest in the new renaissance of the knish . . . that Brooklyn enjoyed many years ago—from the Boardwalk to almost every community in which Jews resided."

8. Palestinian Talmud (Tractate Taanit, 1:1)

9. Les Green (former owner of Mrs. Stahl's Knishes), interview by the author, November 5, 2005.

10. Mike Conte (owner of Conte's Pasta), interview by the author, November 21, 2005.

11. Steve Cuozzo, "Knish Plant Bites Dust," *New York Post*, November 22, 2005.

12. Elliott Gabay (president, Gabila's Knishes), interview by the author, January 16, 2006.

13. Israel Shenker, "Taste for Business Builds Brooklyn Knish Empire," *New York Times*, May 9, 1971.

14. Ilia Gabay, Petition for Naturalization, August 4, 1925, *Petitions for Naturalization from the U.S. District Court for the Southern District of New York, 1897–1944*, ser. M1972, roll 317, National Archives, Washington, D.C.

15. Shenker, "Taste for Business Builds Brooklyn Knish Empire."

16. Ilia Gabey, Petition for Naturalization, December 29, 1925, *Petitions for Naturalization from the U.S. District Court for the Southern District of New York, 1897–1944*, ser. M1972; roll 347, National Archives, Washington, D.C

17. Shenker, "Taste for Business Builds Brooklyn Knish Empire."

18. Ibid.

19. Elliott Gabay, interview.

20. A *hecksher* is a symbol of *kashrut*, or kosherness. KOF-K is a *hecksher* indicating that a product was prepared under strictly Orthodox supervision.

21. Joseph Heller, *Now and Then: From Coney Island to Here* (New York: Knopf, 1998), 51.

22. Mort Shatzkin (formerly of Shatzkin's Knishes), interview by the author, December 10, 2009.

23. Julie Wheelock, "Taste of New York: Store Flies in East Coast Knishes to Whet West Coast Appetites," *Los Angeles Times*, October 3, 1991.

24. Weegee was born Usher Fellig in 1910, in the town of Zolochiv, then Austria, now Ukraine. "Weegee's World: Weegee Chronology by International Center of Photography," from the exhibition *Weegee's World: Life, Death, and the Human Drama*, International Center for Photography, New York, November 2, 1997–March 8, 1998; see http://museum.icp.org/museum /collections/special/weegee/.

25. Marvin Hirsch (formerly of Hirsch's Knishes), interview by the author, June 7, 2009.

26. Richard Reeves, "This Is the Battle of the Titans?" *New York Times Magazine,* November 1, 1970, 224.

27. Rob Edelman, "Mano Hirsch's: A Coney Island Institution," *Flatbush Life,* July 21, 1975, clipping in private collection.

28. Bonnie Abrams (songwriter, "Ruby's Knishes"), interview by author, March 5, 2009.

29. Pamela Gray (screenwriter of the film *A Walk on the Moon*), e-mail message to Bruce Brodinsky, updated April 1999, http://www.brucebrodinsky.com/ruby2.html.

30. Jerry Oshinsky (son of Ruby the Knish Man), interview by the author, March 6, 2009.

31. Bruce Brodinsky (webmaster of Ruby's Knishes website), e-mail message to the author, April 30, 2013.

32. Ibid.

33. Babylonian Talmud, Berachot 40a. See also *Shulchan Aruch* (Oruch Chayim, 167:5).

34. Steve Oshinsky (nephew of Ruby the Knish Man), "Ruby before Knishes," http://www.brucebrodinsky.com/ruby4.html (accessed August 31, 2012).

35. Jerry Oshinsky (son of Ruby the Knish Man), interview by the author, March 6, 2009.

36. Ed Litvak, "101-Year Old Yonah Schimmel Endangered by East Houston Reconstruction," *The Lo-Down: News from the Lower East Side,* posted February 20, 2012; http://www.thelodownny.com.

37. Ed Litvak, "Follow-Up: Temporary Solution to Yonah Schimmel Parking Woes," *The Lo-Down: News From the Lower East Side,* posted February 21, 2012, http://www.thelodownny.com.

38. Susan Caruso Green (project director, "Jewish Heritage Mural"), interview by the author, August 30, 2012.

39. Hedy Pagremanski (artist), interview by the author, August 10, 2012.

40. Hedy Pagremanski, letter to Steven Miller, curator, Museum of the City of New York, n.d. (circa 1979).

41. Ibid.

42. Ibid.

43. Nathan Ausubel, "Hold Up the Sun! Kaleidoscope: The Jews of New York," first draft, Works Progress Administration Historical Records Survey: Federal Writers' Project, Jews of New York, New York Municipal Archives, microfilm no. 176, box 7, folder 243, 21–25.

44. Molly Picon. "Di (Ganze) Velt Is a Te'atr" on *Di Groyse Schlagers Fun Kine Un Te'atr,* CD (Israel Music, 2005).

45. "Rivington Street Sees War," *New York Times,* January 27, 1916.

46. "'Knishe' Founder Cheers East Siders," *New York Sun,* December 11, 1916. "H. C. O'Living" stands for "high cost of living."

47. "'K' in Knisch as in Pigs' Knuckles," *The Mediator,* no. 4, August 8, 1919, 12. Thank you to Barry Popik for leading me to this article with his "Knish" post of July 16, 2004, http://www.barrypopik.com/index.php/new_york_city /entry/knish/.

48. Ibid.

49. Milton Glaser and Jerome Snyder, "Yonah Schimmel's Knishes Bakery," in *The Underground Gourmet: Where to Find Great Meals in New York for Less Than $3.00 and as Little as 50¢* (1966), rev. 2nd ed. (New York: Simon and Schuster, 1970), 239–241.

50. New York City Health Code, Article 81, Food Preparation and Food Establishments, §81.03(q), July 14, 2004, 4, http://www.nyc.gov/html/doh /downloads/pdf/camp/camp-article81-healthcode.pdf (accessed August 3, 2013).

51. Sam Grobart, "Where Are the Knishes of Yesteryear?" *New York Times, February 2, 2003.* See also: New York City Health Code, Article 89, Mobile Food Vending, §89.01(d): "A mobile food processing unit is a mobile food unit on or in which foods are prepared or processed, or on or in which potentially hazardous foods are handled. . . . Foods typically sold from processing units include kebab, gyros, falafel, baked potatoes, soft ice cream, and roasted

nuts," as cited in http://www.nyc.gov/html/doh/downloads/pdf/rats/article
_81.pdf (accessed August 3, 2013).

52. Aby Schwebel and Gussy Sussman, Certificate and Record of Marriage, no. 20575, October 15, 1904, New York City Department of Health, Lafayette Hall.

53. Hyman Goldberg, "She Puts in Things, Out Come Knishes: Mrs. Schwebel Founded an East Side Dynasty on Them." *New York Post*, September 3, 1941.

54. Hyman Goldberg, "She Puts in Things, Out Come Knishes: Mrs. Schwebel Founded an East Side Dynasty on Them," *New York Post*, September 3, 1941.

55. Ibid.

56. Clementine Paddleford, "The 'Knische Queen' in an Expansive Mood," *New York Herald Tribune*, August 11, 1942.

57. Glaser and Snyder, "Yonah Schimmel's Knishes Bakery," 241.

58. Paddleford, "The 'Knische Queen' in an Expansive Mood."

59. "Now It's Giving 'Knishes,' She Is!" *Eugene Register-Guard* (Ore.), August 24, 1942.

60. Paddleford, "The 'Knische Queen' in an Expansive Mood."

61. "Wars or No Wars the Knish Queen Carries On: Mrs. Schwebel Turns Out Her Special Delicacies Golden Brown and the Big Shiny Cars Pull Up to Get Them," *New York Sun*, undated clipping (ca. 1941), Papers of Eleanor Roosevelt, Franklin D. Roosevelt Library, Hyde Park, N.Y.

62. Gussie Schwebel to Eleanor Roosevelt, January 6, 1942, folder S 1942, ser. Gifts: Miscellaneous, Papers of Eleanor Roosevelt.

63. "The History of University Settlement," updated July 13, 2012, http://usadultliteracy.wordpress.com/2012/07/13/the-history-of-university-settlement/ (accessed January 10, 2013).

64. Malvina C. Thompson to Gussie Schwebel, January 12, 1942, folder S 1942, ser. Gifts: Miscellaneous, Papers of Eleanor Roosevelt.

65. Gussie Schwebel to Malvina C. Thompson, January 18, 1942, folder 1942–45 R–W, ser. Gifts: Food, ibid.

66. Malvina C. Thompson to Gussie Schwebel, January 21, 1942, ibid.

67. "First Lady to Get a Taste of Knishe: Read about Mrs. Schwebel in the *New York Sun*," *New York Sun*, January 27, 1942.

68. "Knishes for Mrs. Roosevelt," *Forward*, January 28, 1942. Translated by Myra Mniewski.

69. Ibid.

70. Mary Harrington, "Romanian Chef Describes Plan for Peace—Built around Food," *Washington Post*, May 13, 1945.

IN SEARCH OF THE FIRST KNISH

1. For their immigration records, see EllisIsland.com.

2. Crown Heights and Borough Park are Brooklyn neighborhoods with large Hasidic populations. Ditto Monsey in Rockland County, New York.

3. Bob Cohen, "Moldova: The Hidden Gardens of Knish," in *Dumnezau: Ethnomusicological Eating East of Everywhere*, modified February 12, 2009, http://horinca.blogspot.com/2009/02/moldova-hidden-gardens-of-knish.html (accessed May 5, 2010).

4. "The dead number 120 and the injured about 500. . . . Babes were literally torn to pieces by the frenzied and bloodthirsty mob. At sunset the streets were piled with corpses and wounded. Those who could make their escape fled in terror, and the city is now practically deserted of Jews." From "Jewish Massacre Denounced," *New York Times*, April 28, 1903.

5. C. N. Bialik, "In the City of Slaughter," in *C. N. Bialik: Selected Poems*, ed. and trans. David Auerbach (New York: Overlook Duckworth, Peter Mayer Publishers, 2004), 80.

6. Lag B'Omer, literally the thirty-third day of the Omer, or period between Passover and Shavuot, is a joyous day during an otherwise solemn period.

7. Lenny Karpman (food and restaurant blogger, Costa Rica), e-mail to the author, June 29, 2009.

8. Andrew Simmons, "A Kare Pan Is a Pretty Good Start," *Gastronomica* 12, no. 1 (Spring 2012): 89.

9. Anthony T. Cacace, Steven M. Silver, and Martha Farber, "Rapid Recovery from Acoustic Trauma: Chicken Soup, Potato Knish, or Drug Interaction?" *American Journal of Otolaryngology* 24, no. 3 (2003): 200.

10. Nathan Ausubel, "Hold Up the Sun! Kaleidoscope: The Jews of New York," first draft, Works Progress Administration Historical Records Survey: Federal Writers' Project, Jews of New York, New York Municipal Archives, microfilm no. 176, box 7, folder 243, 21–25.

11. Alden Oreck, "The Pale of Settlement," Jewish Virtual Library, http://www.jewishvirtuallibrary.org/jsource/History/pale.html (accessed March 1, 2013).

12. Martin Gilbert, *The Atlas of Jewish History,* 8th ed. (London: Routledge, 2010), 72.

13. Erica Marcus, "A Knish Is Still a Knish," *Long Island Newsday,* October 30, 2001. Eve Jochnowitz (Yiddish food expert), e-mail to author, January 22, 2013.

14. Babylonian Talmud, Kiddushin, 40b. "Our Rabbis taught: He who eats in the marketplace is like a dog; and some say that he is unfit to testify." See also Epstein, Rabbi Dr. I. *The Babylonian Talmud.* London: Soncino Press, 1935–1948.

15. Janna Gur (Israeli food expert), e-mail to the author, October 29, 2009.

16. Elders of Sheinkin Street, interviewed by Iris Bar, Tel Aviv, ca. 2008, filmed and provided courtesy of November Wanderin.

17. Bella Sherman (knish maker at Café Batya, Tel Aviv), interview by the author, November 21, 2009. Translation and transcription by Il'il Paz-El.

18. Batya Yom Tov (founder of Café Batya, Tel Aviv), interview by the author, December 1, 2010.

19. Shmil Holland (chef and restaurant owner, Jerusalem), interview by the author, November 16, 2009.

20. *Schmaltz,* literally, chicken fat. In American Judeo-English slang, "schmaltzy" has come to mean cheesy or corny.

21. Babylonian Talmud, Berakhot 42a.

22. Tosefta Berakhot, iv. This comes from the Mishnah, or the Oral law of

Judaism, written in approximately the third century CE, specifically from a tractate Berakhot or Blessings.

23. From a book of Geonic responsa, found in the Cairo *Genizah*. Susan Weingarten (food historian), interview by author, November 11, 2009.

24. "Kisan/kisnin" in Nathan ben Jehiel, *Arukh Ha-Shalem*, edited by Alexander Kohut (New York: Pardes, 1955) vol. 4, 275–276.

25. E-mail from Tova Dickstein and Susan Weingarten (food historians), March 8, 2010.

26. Jean Zilberman (owner of Pitchi Poï restaurant, Paris), interview by the author, September 9, 2009.

27. Regina Frishwasser, *Jewish-American Cookbook: 1,600 Selected Recipes* (New York: Forward Association, 1946). With thanks to Matthew Goodman for the extended loan of the book.

28. Yitskhok Niborski (chairman of Medem Bibliothèque at the Centre for Yiddish Culture, Paris), interview by author, September 12, 2009.

29. Every seventh year, the Jewish leap year, *Vayakhel* and *Pikudei* are read on separate weeks; all other years they are read on the same week.

30. Mordecai Kosover and YIVO Institute for Jewish Research, *Yidishe Makholim: A Shṭudye in Kulṭur-Geshikhṭe; Un Shprakh-Forshung* (New York: YIVO, 1958), s.v. "knish," citing Pinchas Dov Goldenshtein, "My Life Story." Translated by Paula Teitelbaum.

31. Dora Engelberg (daughter of Fannie Stahl) written recollections, ca. 1980s, collection of Tony Engelberg.

32. "The word 'Holocaust' is commonly used in English-speaking countries, whereas the Hebrew word *Shoah*, which means 'catastrophe,' is used in France." See http://www.memorialdelashoah.org/index.php/en/.

33. "Sacha Finkelsztajn/La Boutique Jaune: Historique," http://finkelsztajn.com/htfr/0002.htm (accessed September 9, 2009).

34. Grzegorz Piątek. "Fake Palm Tree" (attraction 38) in *Warsaw: Tourist Map for Young Travelers*. (Warsaw: Bęc Zmiana Foundation/USE-IT, 2010). The "Greetings from Jerusalem Avenue" installation is by artist Joanna Rajkowska.

35. Ibid.

36. Mrs. Stahl didn't work on the Sabbath. Sara Spatz (granddaughter of Fannie Stahl), interview by the author, January 18, 2013.

37. *Tekiah gedola* is the longest blast of the *shofar*, sounded at the conclusion of prayers on Yom Kippur.

38. *Yizkor*, Hebrew for "he will remember," is the prayer of remembrance for departed relatives.

39. Anna Spatz (daughter of Fannie Stahl) and Bella Member (daughter of Fannie Stahl), interview by Abby Cohen (great-granddaughter of Fannie Stahl), personal audio recording, ca. 1988.

40. Hasia Diner (professor of American Jewish History, New York University), interview by the author, April 7, 2010.

41. Leo Rosten, *The New Joys of Yiddish* (New York: Random House Digital, 2010), 183–184.

42. Barbara and Dorota Szczepanowicz, *Kuchnia Żydowska: Święta, Obyczaje i Potrawy Świąteczne* (Kraków: Wydawnictwo Petrus, 2011), 199.

43. Lubow Wolynetz, (Ukrainian food expert), interview by author, January 26, 2013.

44. Lubow Wolynetz, "Christmas Knysh," *Nashe Zhyttia* (Our Life) (November 1974): 29. Translated by Ostap Kin and Lubow Wolynetz.

45. Ibid.

46. Kazimierz Feleszko, *Bukovina My Love: Polish Language in Carpathian Bukovina through 1945*, vol. 2 (Warsaw: Instytut Slawistyki Polskiej Akademii Nauk/Slawistyczny Ośrodek Wydawniczy, 2003), 115–116.

47. Maria Ochorowicz-Monatowa, *Uniwersalna Książka Kucharska: z ilustracjami i kolorowymi tablicami odznaczona na wystawach hygjenicznych w Warszawie w roku 1910 i 1926* (Poznań: Kurpisz, 2002), 527. *Gribenes*, Yiddish for "scraps," are the cracklings of chicken or goose skin. Translation by Paula Teitelbaum.

48. Michał Grabowski, ed., *The Diary of Mr. Karol Mincowski: Home Diaries* (Warsaw: S. Olgebrand, 1845), 152–154.

49. Lubow Wolynetz, "Christmas Knysh."

50. Hanna Szymanderska, *Polska Wigilia* (Warsaw: Wydawnictwo WATRA, 1989), 5–8.

51. Ivan Kotliarevsky, *Eneïda*, trans. Melnyk Bohdan (Toronto: Basilian Press, 2004), 45.

52. Matthias Kramer and Adam Abrahamsz van Moerbeek, *Neues Deutsch-Holländisches Wörterbuch: worinnen alle Wörter und Redensarten, nebst vorkommenden Kunst- und Handelswörtern fleißig Zusammengetragen, und dem Gebrauche der besten Schriftsteller gemäß erkläret worden* (Leipzig: Junius, 1768), s.v. "knitschen," http://www.mdz-nbn-resolving.de/urn/resolver.pl?urn=urn:nbn:de:bvb:12-bsb10796761-9 (accessed January 24, 2013). Thank you to Brita Servaes for this lead.

53. Jan from Kijany, *Fraszki Sowirzała Nowego* (1614), in *Polska Fraszka Mieszczańska: Minucje Sowiźrzalskie*, ed. Karol Badecki (Kraków: Polish Academy of Sciences, 1948), 178–179. Translation by Paula Teitelbaum.

54. Tova Dickstein, "Food in Roman-Byzantine Palestine" (Ph.D. diss., Bar-Ilan University, 2011), 140–143.

55. Tova Dickstein (food historian), e-mail to the author, January 3, 2012. See also Tova Dickstein, "Food in Roman-Byzantine Palestine." Ph.D. diss., Bar-Ilan University, 2011: 144–145.

56. Yona Sabar (Aramaic expert), e-mail to the author, January 18, 2013; Yona Sabar, *A Jewish Neo-Aramaic Dictionary: Dialects of Amidya, Dihok, Nerwa, and Zakho, Northwestern Iraq; Based on Old and New Manuscripts, Oral and Written Bible Translations, Folkloric Texts, and Diverse Spoken Registers, with an Introduction to Grammar and Semantics, and an Index of Talmudic Words Which Have Reflexes in Jewish Neo-Aramaic* (Wiesbaden: Harrassowitz, 2002), 187.

MRS. GOLDBERG TO GANGSTA RAP

1. *Wise Guys,* directed by Brian DePalma, DVD (1986; Burbank: Turner Entertainment, 2006); "41 Down. Jewish deli order: KNISH," Peter Muller, "My Treat" (crossword puzzle), ed. Will Shortz. *New York Times Magazine*, July 3, 2011, 48. "Answer to Puzzles of 7.3.11," *New York Times Magazine*, July 10, 2011, 49.

2. Gertrude Berg and Myra Waldo, *The Molly Goldberg Jewish Cookbook* (1955; New Hope, Pa.: Ivyland Books, 1999), 184–185.

3. Timothy McNulty, "Obituary: Henry 'Hank' Stohl, Puppeteer from TV's Early Days," *Pittsburgh Post-Gazette,* December 17, 2008.

4. Mitzi McCall (former children's television host), interview by the author, March 11, 2013.

5. Timothy McNulty, "Obituary: Henry 'Hank' Stohl, Puppeteer from TV's Early Days."

6. Ibid.

7. Hank Stohl, *When We Were Kids* (Bloomington, Ind.: AuthorHouse, 2005), 30.

8. Knish Big League card, Hank Stohl Photographs and Videotapes, ca. 1950–ca. 1990, MSS 726, Thomas and Katherine Detre Library and Archives, Senator John Heinz History Center, Pittsburgh, Pa.

9. Knish Good Kid Club membership card, ibid.

10. "Sweathog Clinic for the Cure of Smoking," *Welcome Back, Kotter,* season 2, episode 11 (1976 ABC), permanent collection, Paley Center for Media, New York.

11. "Sophia's Wedding, Parts 1 and 2," *The Golden Girls,* season 4, DVD (1988; Burbank: Touchstone Television/Buena Vista Home Entertainment, 2006).

12. "Sid Knishes and His Mosh Pit-tatoes," *Muppets Tonight,* season 1, episode 108 (ABC, June 23, 1996), http://www.youtube.com.

13. Kirk Thatcher (writer of "Sid Knishes" script), response relayed via e-mail by Karen Falk, archivist of the Jim Henson Company, to the author, March 7, 2012.

14. "That's Somebody's Knish," *Less Than Kind,* season 2, episode 7 (HBO Canada, 2010), distributed by Breakthrough Entertainment, Toronto.

15. Poster, *The Night They Raided Minsky's,* MoviePoster.com. The film is based on a novel of the same name by Rowland Barber (New York: Simon & Schuster, 1960).

16. *Whatever Works,* directed by Woody Allen, DVD (Culver City, Calif.: Sony Pictures, 2009).

17. The Maven's Deli Menu, subgroup 11, ser. 11.3, box 1, Papers of Alan Dershowitz, Brooklyn College Special Collections, Brooklyn College Library.

18. Heather Quinlan, interview by the author, December 11, 2012.

19. Fyvush Finkel (performer), interview by the author, January 20, 2013.

20. Ian Finkel, "Reuben the Knish Man," skit in *Fyvush Finkel Live* at the National Yiddish Theater–Folksbeine, New York, October 17–November 7, 2010.

21. Ian Finkel (performer, author of "Reuben the Knish Man" skit), interview by the author, August 18, 2012. Another Heifetz-knish connection: Musician Vladimir Heifetz (1910–1979) sketched out a song, "Ballad of Knish," whose last line is "Un di levone mit a shmeichl" (And the moon with a smile). "Balade Fun Knish" (handwritten musical score), undated, RG 1259, 62, YIVO Archives, New York.

22. Max Gross, "Meet David Wise, the Grandma You Never Knew," *Forward,* March 19, 2004.

23. David Wise (writer and performer of *Momma's Knishes*), interview by the author, December 20, 2012.

24. Michele Lea Biaso, "'Mamma's Knishes' Tells Saga of Polish Jews' Lives," *News-Times* (Danbury, Conn.), April 13, 2003. http://www.danbury.org /lfs/etc/newstimes.htm (accessed December 8, 2012).

25. David Wise, interview by the author, December 20, 2012.

26. Mickey Katz, "Knish Doctor," on *Most Mishige,* Capitol Records, 1958. © 1958 Haimish Music (BMI).

27. Ross Bagdasarian (as David Seville), "Witch Doctor," Liberty Records, 1958.

28. Katz, "Knish Doctor." Translation by Myra Mniewski.

29. Josh Kun, "The Yiddish Are Coming: Mickey Katz, Antic-Semitism, and the Sound of Jewish Difference," *American Jewish History* 87, no. 4 (December 1999): 345.

30. Mickey Katz, "Little White Knish That Cried," Capitol Records, ca. 1940. 45 rpm. Available at UCLA Ethnomusicology Archive.

31. Henry Roth, *Call It Sleep,* reprint ed. (New York: Picador, 2005), 37.

32. Yaacov Shapiro, "Ich Hob Leib a Knish," on *Geshmakene* [Dirty] *Yiddish*

Songs, CD (1987; Haifa: Hataklit, 2005). (*Petzel* is a diminutive form of *putz*, which is Yiddish slang for men's private parts.) Shapiro added avuncular libido to earlier incarnations of this tune. Mickey Katz's non-incestuous rendition of "Kiss of Meyer," was a parody of "Kiss of Fire" (lyrics by Lester Allen, recorded by Georgia Gibbs in 1952), set to the tune of "El Choclo" (Spanish for "The Corn Cob"), written by Argentine composer Ángel Villoldo and first presented in Buenos Aires in 1903.

33. Pearl Williams, *A Trip around the World Is Not a Cruise*, After Hours Records, ca. 1960, Rodgers and Hammerstein Archives of Recorded Sound, New York Public Library for the Performing Arts, Astor, Lenox and Tilden Foundations.

34. Ibid. Also available at "Pearl Williams: For This You'll Need a Glusenshpiegelbaster," on WFMU's Beware of the Blog, updated August 10, 2005, http://blogfiles.wfmu.org (accessed December 5, 2012).

35. Judy Batalion (founder of the Knish Collective along with Claire Berliner, Mekella Broomberg, and Rachel Mars), interview by the author, November 29, 2012.

36. Lyrics by the Knish Collective, the title track of the film *I Am Ruthie Segal, Hear Me Roar*, Minkie Spiro, dir. (UK: Third Man Films, 2009). © The Knish Collective. As heard during the Knish Collective's interview by Jason Solomons, host of the "Sounds Jewish" podcast of the *Guardian* and the JCC of London, November 10, 2009, http://www.guardian.co.uk (accessed December 1, 2012).

37. Knish Collective, interview by Jason Solomons, host of the "Sounds Jewish" podcast of the *Guardian* and the JCC of London, November 11, 2009, http://www.guardian.co.uk.

38. Sarah Silverman, Twitter feed (@SarahKSilverman), posted December 29, 2010, https://twitter.com/SarahKSilverman/.

39. Amy Silverman (granddaughter of knish aficionado), interview by the author, May 24, 2011.

40. Derek Brantley (SD3), "1 Potato, 2 Potato, 3 Knish" video clip, http://www.youtube.com (accessed December 1, 2012).

41. Derek Brantley (performer known as SD3), interview by the author, December 13, 2012.

42. Sholem Aleichem, "The Roof Falls In" (1899), in *Tevye the Dairyman and Motl the Cantor's Son*, trans. Aliza Shevrin, intro. Dan Miron (New York: Penguin, 2009), 25.

43. Sholem Aleichem, "Motl the Cantor's Son: Writings of an Orphan Boy" (1916), ibid., 319–320.

44. Leib Kvitko, *Der Groyser Knish* (Kovno: Kultur-lige, 1921), 3. Translation by Myra Mniewski.

45. Ibid, 5.

46. Isaac Bashevis Singer, *Meshugah,* trans. Nili Wachtel (New York: Farrar, Straus and Giroux, 2003), 8.

47. Isaac Bashevis Singer, *Love and Exile: An Autobiographical Trilogy* (New York: Farrar, Straus and Giroux, 1996), 259–260.

48. Wallace Markfield, *Teitelbaum's Window* (New York: Knopf, 1970), 130.

49. Ibid., 269.

50. Ibid., 379.

51. Susan Issacs, *Close Relations.* (New York: Lippincott & Crowell, 1980), 12.

52. Ibid., 24.

A BRIEF HISTORY OF COMPETITIVE KNISH EATING

1. Joel Podelsky (knish-eating champion), interview by the author, July 7, 2009.

2. Itzik Gottesman, "Vitka Kempner Kovner, Vilna Partisan, Dies: Credited with First Act of Sabotage against Nazis in Ghetto," *Forward,* February 24, 2012.

3. "Knishes Sweeter Than Wine," *Sarasota Herald-Tribune*, May 27, 1973.

4. Gregory Jaynes, "Thrill of Gluttony Beats the Agony of Indigestion," *New York Times,* March 26, 1988.

5. "Fourteen-year-old Ross Nathan walked off as the full-bellied winner of the annual Knish-Eating Contest at the Brighton Beach Bath and Racquet Club. Nathan, who is 5-foot-7 and weights 130 pounds, took the top prize, and his friends, David Micucci and Evan Wiskoff, split the second prize, each

getting $25." "'Knish Nosh' in Brooklyn Neighborhoods," *Long Island Newsday,* September 4, 1986.

6. Through repetitive interactions with the Internet, cold calls to medical professionals named Resnick, and sheer luck, I located the knish-eating champion of the Brighton Beach Baths, who saw some of my early knish writings and said they reminded him of *his* grandmother, who had also lived near Mrs. Stahls's. Jay Resnick (knish-eating champion of Brighton Beach Baths), e-mail to the author, July 8, 2009.

7. Mark Finston, "Munchers Vie to Become King of the Knishes," *Newark Star-Ledger,* March 25, 1988.

THE FINE ART OF KNISH MAKING

1. Talmud Berachot 58b.

2. Psalm 121.

3. "Cave and Basin: Discovery," Parks Canada, http://www.pc.gc.ca/ (accessed May 24, 2013).

4. *House of Commons Debates,* no. 074 (March 24, 2005), at 1630 (Hon. Stephen Harper), cited in Jonathan Maryniuk, "Ukrainian Internment," Centre for Constitutional Studies, citation 12, http://www.law.ualberta.ca /centres/ccs/issues/ukrainianinternment.php (accessed February 18, 2013).

5. "Internment Camps," historic plaque at Cave and Basin Historic Site, Banff National Park, Banff, Alberta, Canada, (visit by author, August 2009).

6. Hillel: "If I am not for myself, who will be for me? But if I am only for myself, who am I? If not now, when?" Ethics of the Fathers *(Pirkei Avot)* 1:14.

7. Sandy Loeffler, "Knishes, Ida Gardner's," Jewish Food Mailing List Archive, http://www.jewishfood-list.com/recipes/ (accessed November 12, 2008).

8. *From Avenue A to the Great White Way: Yiddish-American Popular Songs, 1914–1950,* CD, Columbia/Legacy, 2002.

9. Rabbi Jules Harlow, ed. and trans., *Siddur Sim Shalom: A Prayerbook for Shabbat, Festivals and Weekdays* (New York: The Rabbinical Assembly and United Synagogue of America, 1985).

10. Rabbi Nina Beth Cardin, *The Tapestry of Jewish Time* (Springfield, N.J.: Behrman House, 2000).

11. "Flaky on the surface, you're actually a person of depth and substance. Consider Medical or Law School but don't get too wrapped up in yourself. Compatible with Pickle. Avoid Lox, who's out of your league. Year of the Knish: 1941, 1953, 1965, 1977, 1989, 2001, 2013." Seth Front. Wording on *Year of the Knish* T-shirt from Jewish Zodiac, http://www.jewzo.com/Knish-T-shirt -Women-p/jz-607.htm.

12. "Kniple: 1. Noun: a button. 2. Noun: money tied in a knot in the corner of a handkerchief; any money stashed away; a nest egg. 3. (Vulgar) [and not what the Knish Ladies were referring to] noun: hymen; virginity." Paul Hoffman and Matt Freedman, *Dictionary Schmictionary! A Yiddish and Yinglish Dictionary* (New York: Quill, 1983), 74. See also Sissy Carpey, *Piece of Her Heart: The True Story of a Mother and Daughter Separated by the Russian Revolution* (Bloomington, Ind.: iUniverse, 2009), 175: "'Every woman needs her own *knipple*,' she [Mema Yetta, her great-aunt] told me. A *knipple* is a small piece you break off. When you are baking, you take a *knipple* of dough from the larger mound to roll out your cookies. I knew that Mema Yetta wasn't talking about cookies. She was teaching me that I had to have money of my own, my *knipple*."

13. Hamantaschen: triangular pastries filled with poppy seeds, prune, and other fillings, made for the holiday of Purim; named for their supposed resemblance to the villain Haman's three-cornered hat.

14. See Sandor Ellix Katz, *The Art of Fermentation: An In-Depth Exploration of Essential Concepts and Processes from around the World* (White River Junction, Vt.: Chelsea Green, 2012).

15. Bruklinboy, "Mrs. Stahl's FOUND," Chowhound discussion board, updated October 12, 2005 (Erev Yom Kippur), http://chowhound.chow.com /topics/247574 (accessed August 6, 2012).

16. Pianist355, response to "Mrs. Stahl's FOUND," Chowhound discussion board, posted December 3, 2007, http://chowhound.chow.com/topics /247574#3176916 (accessed August 6, 2012).

17. Jill Slater, e-mail to the author, August 7, 2012.

18. Steven McElroy, "My New York," *New York Times,* October 12, 2008.

19. Faith Kramer, "Mrs. Stahl's Famous Knish Recipe Finally Found—in San Francisco," *j. The Jewish news weekly of Northern California,* September 28, 2012: 6, 32.

EPILOGUE

1. Steve Rapillo (owner, Tufo's Foods), interview by the author, July 13, 2012.

2. Edward Van Embden. "Gluten-Free Specialty Helps Buena's Conte Pasta Grow Profits, Expand Facilities and Create Jobs," *Press of Atlantic City,* April 30, 2010.

3. Don Marton, (entrepreneur), e-mail to the author, December 4, 2012.

4. Don Marton (entrepreneur), interview by the author, December 4, 2012.

5. Kulokov is a town north of modern-day Lviv, Ukraine.

6. A *shochet* is a ritual slaughterer; a *mohel* performs ritual circumcisions.

7. Barbara Hewitt (daughter of restaurant owners Anshel and Lilly Greenberg), interview by the author, December 11, 2012.

8. Anna Spatz (daughter of Fannie Stahl), interview by Abby Cohen (great-granddaughter of Fannie Stahl), personal audio recording, ca. 1985.

9. Ibid.

10. Dora Engelberg (daughter of Fannie Stahl), written remembrances about Fannie Stahl, ca. 1970–1980s, collection of Toby Engelberg.

11. Madeleine Colby (niece of Fannie Stahl), interview by the author, December 11, 2012.

12. Sara Spatz (granddaughter of Fannie Stahl), interview by the author, January 18, 2013.

13. Ibid.

14. *1940 United States Federal Census: New York,* Kings, roll T627_2557, page 11A, Enumeration District 24-429A, National Archives, Washington, D.C.

15. Jack Birnbaum (employee of Mrs. Stahl's Knishes, summer 1943), interview by the author, May 22, 2013.

16. Ibid.

17. "Palestine Supplies: It is very encouraging to see the warm response of our 'knitters and sewers.' Thanks so much to Mrs. Stahl and her daughter, Mrs. Spatz . . . for the lovely sweaters they knitted," in "The Bulletin," Brighton Beach Group of Hadassah, February 1945, Hadassah Archives at the American Jewish Historical Society housed at the Center for Jewish History, New York. RG15, Operations and Functions/Series 1/ Chapters Box 52: Brooklyn/ Folder Brighton Beach Newsletters.

18. Program, Annual Donor Luncheon, Brooklyn Chapter of Hadassah, April 1949, Hadassah Archives, ibid.

19. Noah Wildman (founder, Knishery NYC), interview with the author, October 20, 2012.

20. "Knish History 101" taught by author at the Brooklyn Brainery, Brooklyn, New York. July 6 and 13, 2011. http://brooklynbrainery.com /courses/knish-history-101.

21. Florence Fabricant, "Brews and Bites Off the Usual Track," *New York Times*, May 29, 2012.

RECIPE: MRS. STAHL'S POTATO KNISHES

1. From: Faith Kramer, "Mrs. Stahl's Famous Knish Recipe Finally Found—in San Francisco," *j. the Jewish News Weekly of Northern California*, September 27, 2012.

Selected Bibliography

ARCHIVAL AND MANUSCRIPT COLLECTIONS

Nathan and Theresa Berman Upper Midwest Jewish Archives, University of
    Minnesota, Minneapolis

Brooklyn Collection, Brooklyn Public Library

Brooklyn College Special Collections, Brooklyn College Library

Bureau of the Census, *Fifteenth Census of the United States, 1930*. Washington,
    D.C.: National Archives and Records Administration, 1930. T626, 2,667 rolls

Bureau of the Census, *Sixteenth Census of the United States, 1940*. Washington,
    D.C.: National Archives and Records Administration, 1940. T627, 4,643
    rolls.

Canadian Jewish Congress Charities Committee National Archives, Montreal,
    Québec

Central Archives for the History of the Jewish People, Jerusalem

Dartmouth Jewish Sound Archives, New Lebanon, N.H.

Department of Buildings, 1866–1975, New York Municipal Archives

Thomas and Katherine Detre Library and Archives, Senator John Heinz
    History Center, Pittsburgh, Pa.

Dorot Jewish Division, New York Public Library

Robert & Molly Freedman Jewish Sound Archive, University of Pennsylvania,
    University Libraries

General Research Division, New York Public Library

Hadassah Archives at the American Jewish Historical Society, housed at the
    Center for Jewish History, New York, N.Y.

Jewish Historical Society of the Upper Midwest, Minneapolis, Minn.

Judaica Sound Archives at Florida Atlantic University Libraries, Boca Raton,
    Fla.

Manhattan Marriage Certificates, 1853–1937, New York City Municipal
    Archives

Manhattan Death Certificates, 1949–present, New York City Department of Health

Irma and Paul Milstein Division of United States History, Local History and Genealogy, New York Public Library

Music Division, Library of Congress, Washington, D.C.

Clementine Paddleford Papers, Morse Department of Special Collections, Kansas State University, Manhattan, Kans.

Paley Center for Media, Permanent Collection, New York, N.Y.

Passenger and Crew Lists of Vessels Arriving at New York, New York, 1897–1957, National Archives, Microfilm Publication T715, 8892 rolls, Records of the Immigration and Naturalization Service, National Archives, Washington, D.C.

Petitions for Naturalization from the U.S. District Court for the Southern District of New York, 1897–1944, NARA Microfilm Publication M1972, 1457 rolls, Records of District Courts of the United States, Record Group 21, National Archives, Washington, D.C.

Prints & Photographs Division, Library of Congress, Washington, D.C.

Rhode Island Jewish Historical Association, Providence, R.I.

Rodgers and Hammerstein Archives of Recorded Sound, New York Public Library for the Performing Arts, Astor, Lenox and Tilden Foundations

Eleanor Roosevelt Collection, Franklin D. Roosevelt Presidential Library and Museum, Hyde Park, N.Y.

Billy Rose Theatre Division, New York Public Library for the Performing Arts, Astor, Lenox and Tilden Foundations

State Population Census Schedules, 1925. Albany: New York State Archives

Works Progress Administration Historical Records Survey: Federal Writers' Project, Jews of New York, New York Municipal Archives

YIVO Archives, New York, N.Y.

INTERVIEWS

Bonnie Abrams, songwriter, "Ruby's Knishes," March 5, 2009

Judy Batalion, a founder of the Knish Collective, November 29, 2012

Jack Birnbaum, former employee of Mrs. Stahl's Knishes, May 22, 2013

Lois Brand, board member of Sholom Home, February 25, 2009

Derek Brantley, performer known as SD3, December 13, 2012

Miri Chacham, owner, Café Batya, Tel Aviv, December 25, 2010

Hazel Chase, head of the Knish Ladies, December 20, 2010; June 1, 2011;
    November 28, 2012

Madeleine Colby, niece of Fannie Stahl, December 11, 2012

Mike Conte, owner of Conte's Pasta, November 21, 2005; July 5, 2012

Mildred Covet, Cajun-Jewish cooking expert, August 1, 2009

Tova Dickstein, biblical food expert, March 8, 2010; January 3, 2012

Hasia Diner, professor of American Jewish History, New York University,
    April 7 and 26, 2010

Jarosław Dumanowski, Polish food historian, October 22, 2012

Mike Eagle, knish-eating contestant, July 7, 2009

Toby Engelberg, granddaughter of Fannie Stahl, August 6, 2012; September 14
    and 15, 2012

Fyvush Finkel, performer, January 20, 2013

Ian Finkel, performer and author of "Reuben the Knish Man" script, August
    18, 2012

Andrew Gabay, vice president/CEO, Gabila's Knishes, October 17, 2012

Elliott Gabay, president, Gabila's Knishes, January 16, 2006; October 17, 2012

Susan Caruso Green, project director, "Jewish Heritage Mural," August 30,
    2012

Scott Gilbert, member of KNISH Klezmer band, December 26, 2012

Les Green, former owner of Mrs. Stahl's, November 5, 2005; December 5, 2012

Janna Gur, Israeli food expert, October 29, 2009; January 6, 2012

Lisa Heilicher, treasurer, Sholom Home Foundation, May 23, 2011

Barbara Hewitt, daughter of restaurant owners Anshel and Lilly Greenberg,
    December 11, 2012

Marvin Hirsch, formerly of Hirsch's Knishes, June 7, 2009; May 23, 2013

Larry Hirsch, knish maker at Hirsch's, May 23, 2013

Shmil Holland, chef and restaurant owner, Jerusalem, November 16, 2009;
    January 12, 2012

Eve Jochnowitz, Yiddish food scholar, January 22, 2013

Lenny Karpman, food and restaurant blogger, June 29, 2009

Kathy Kaye, knish maker, Petah Tikvah, Israel, November 13, 2009

Knish Ladies of the Sholom Home, June 1, 2011; April 25, 2012

Agnieszka Kręglicka, food writer and restaurant owner, September 5, 2009.

Don Lesser, former knish salesman, Rockaway Beach, N.Y., February 12, 2010

Mark Litmann, knish-eating champion, July 11, 2009

Sandy Loeffler, daughter of Ida Zelkowitz Gardner, May 13, 2010

Don Marton, entrepreneur, December 4, 2012; January 9, 2013

Mitzi McCall, former children's television host, March 11, 2013

Yitskhok Niborski, chairman of Medem Bibliothèque, Centre for Yiddish Culture, Paris, September 12, 2009

Maciej Novak, restaurant critic, September 5, 2009

Hedy Pagremanski, artist, August 10, 2012; September 6, 2012

Jerry Oshinsky, son of Ruby the Knish Man, March 6, 2009.

Joel Podelsky, knish-eating champion, June 24, 2009; July 7, 2009; July 12, 2009

Heather Quinlan, film director, December 11, 2012

Steve Rapillo, owner, Tufo's Foods, July 13, 2012; November 16, 2012

Jay Resnick, knish-eating champion of Brighton Beach Baths, July 8, 2009

Yona Sabar, Aramaic scholar, January 18, 2013

Howard Schack, longtime resident of Spring Valley, N.Y., January 16, 2013

Anita Schetzen, daughter of Morris Weingast, former owner of Mrs. Stahl's, August 1, 2011

Mort Shatzkin, formerly of Shatzkin's Knishes, December 10, 2009

Bella Sherman, knish maker at Café Batya, Tel Aviv, November 21, 2009

Amy Silverman, granddaughter of knish aficionado, May 24, 2011

Pat Singer, founder and executive director, Brighton Neighborhood Association, November 2, 2005; August 23, 2012

Jonas Spatz, grandson of Fannie Stahl, August 15, 2013

Sara Spatz, granddaughter of Fannie Stahl, August 15, 2012; September 14 and 15, 2012; and January 18, 2013

Henryk Stasiewicz, historian, Knyszyn, Poland, September 7, 2009

Jerry Stiller, comedian, September 25, 2009

Jack Szwergold, former employee at Mrs. Stahl's, June 5, 2009

Dina Wasserman, knish maker, Petah Tikvah, Israel, November 13, 2009

Susan Weingarten, food historian, November 11, 2009, March 8, 2010

Noah Wildman, founder, Knishery NYC, October 20, 2012

David Wise, writer and performer, December 20, 2012

Martha Wise, knish maker, Oklahoma City, April 22, 2009

Lubow Wolynetz, Ukrainian food expert, January 4 and 26, 2013

Kobi Yizraelovich, co-owner of Café Batya, Tel Aviv, January 6, 2012

Batya Yom Tov, founder of Café Batya, Tel Aviv, December 1, 2010; January 6, 2012

Jean Zilberman, owner of Pitchi Poï restaurant, Paris, September 9, 2009; December 5, 2012

BOOKS, ARTICLES, VIDEOS, AND RECORDINGS

Abramovitch, Ilana, and Seán Galvin. *Jews of Brooklyn*. Hanover, N.H.: University Press of New England/Brandeis University Press, 2002.

Abrams, Bonnie. "Ruby's Knishes." On *Welcome to My Mid-Life Crisis*. CD. Rochester, N.Y.: Dynamic Recording Studios, 2007.

Ackerman, Diane. *The Zookeeper's Wife: A War Story*. New York: W.W. Norton, 2007.

Aleichem, Sholem. *Tevye the Dairyman and Motl the Cantor's Son*. Translated by Aliza Shevrin. Introduction by Dan Miron. New York: Penguin, 2009.

Allen, Woody, dir. *Whatever Works*. DVD. Culver City, Calif.: Sony Pictures Classics, 2009.

Apfelbaum, David. "Jewish Cuisine." *Ethnology* 40, no. 2 (2001): 165–169.

Arad, Dafna. "A Big Serving of Israeli History." *Haaretz*. February 22, 2013.

———. "Ten Israeli Restaurants, Six Hundred Years in the Kitchen." *Haaretz*. December 2, 2011.

Auerbach, David, ed. and trans. *C. N. Bialik: Selected Poems*. New York: Overlook Duckworth, Peter Mayer Publishers, 2004.

Ausubel, Nathan. *Pictorial History of the Jewish People, from Bible Times to Our Own Day throughout the World*. New York: Crown Publishers, 1953.

Bagiński, Krzysztof. "Meeting with Multicultural Knyszyn." Pamphlet, Municipality of Knyszyn, 2008.

Balinska, Maria. *The Bagel: The Surprising History of a Modest Bread*. New Haven: Yale University Press, 2008.

Berg, Gertrude, and Myra Waldo. *The Molly Goldberg Jewish Cookbook*. New Hope, Pa.: Ivyland Books, 1999.

Berg, Jennifer Schiff. "From Pushcart Peddlers to Gourmet Take-Out: New York City's Iconic Foods of Jewish Origin, 1920 to 2005." (Ph.D. diss., New York University, 2006.)

Berger, Joseph. "Trendiness among the Tenements." *New York Times*, September 2, 2004.

———. "Yesterday's Borscht and Knishes Return as Today's Reading List; Alumni of Faded Catskill Hotels and Bungalow Analyze Summer Experience, Reborn as Writers' Shtick." *New York Times*. August 31, 2000.

Bialystoker Memorial Book, The. New York: Bialystoker Center, 1982.

Biaso, Michele Lea. "'Mamma's Knishes' Tells Saga of Polish Jews' Lives." *News-Times* (Danbury, Conn.), April 13, 2013.

Bleier, Mel, as told to Ed Eisenberg. "A Brooklyn Landmark: Mrs Stahl's Has Sold 15 Million Knishes." *Township* (Brooklyn, N.Y.), July 28, 1972. Collection of Barry Weingast.

"Blessings Sheet." Falls Village, Conn.: Isabella Freedman Retreat Center, in cooperation with Adamah, Elat Chayim, and the Open Siddur Project, 2011.

Bohlen, Celestine. "Dinkins and Koch Vie for Jews' Votes." *New York Times*, September 10, 1989.

Brooks, Mel, and Carl Reiner. *The 2000 Year Old Man*. New York: Warner Books, 1981.

Cacace Anthony T., Steven M. Silver, and Martha Farber. "Rapid Recovery from Acoustic Trauma: Chicken Soup, Potato Knish, or Drug Interaction?" *American Journal of Otolaryngology* 24, no. 3 (2003): 198–203.

Carpey, Sissy. *Piece of Her Heart: The True Story of a Mother and Daughter Separated by the Russian Revolution*. Bloomington, Ind.: iUniverse, 2009.

Cashman, Greer Fay. "The Tel Aviv Skyline Is Increasingly Resembling that of Manhattan as the City's Landmarks Disappear." *Jerusalem Post*, September 13, 2012.

Coates, Paul. "Here's to the Knish—Real Whiz of a Dish Fit for a King's Wish." *Los Angeles Times*, April 2, 1963.

Cohen, Abby. Oral history interviews with Anna Spatz and Bella Member. Personal audio recording. Ca. 1988.

Cohen, Bob. "Moldova: The Hidden Gardens of Knish." Modified February 12, 2009. http://horinca.blogspot.com/2009/02/moldova-hidden-gardens-of-knish.html.

Coleman, Leo. *Food: Ethnographic Encounters*. New York: Berg, 2011.

Cook, Blanche Wiesen. *Eleanor Roosevelt*. New York: Viking, 1992.

Cooper, John. *Eat and Be Satisfied: A Social History of Jewish Food.* Northvale, N.J.: Jason Aronson, 1993.

Cowan, Matthew. "Knish Knack." *Village Voice,* May 25, 1999.

Cuozzo, Steve. "Knish Plant Bites Dust." *New York Post,* November 22, 2005.

De Pomiane, Edouard. The Jews of Poland: Recollections and Recipes. Garden Grove, Calif.: Pholiota Press, 1985.

Decter, Avi Y., Juliana Ochs Dweck, and Jewish Museum of Maryland. *Chosen Food: Cuisine, Culture, and American Jewish Identity*. Baltimore: Jewish Museum of Maryland, 2011.

Denker, Joel. *The World on a Plate: A Tour through the History of America's Ethnic Cuisines*. Boulder, Colo.: Westview Press, 2003.

DePalma, Brian, dir. *Wise Guys*. 1986. DVD. Burbank: Turner Entertainment, 2006.

Dickstein, Tova. "Food in Roman-Byzantine Palestine." Ph.D. diss., Bar-Ilan University, 2011.

Didner, Motl. *Fyvush Finkel Live!* New York: Yiddish National Theater-Folksbeine, November 7, 2010.

Dim, Joan Marans. "Remembrance of Things Pastrami." *New York Times,* January 3, 1982.

Diner, Hasia R. *Lower East Side Memories: A Jewish Place in America*. Princeton, N.J.: Princeton University Press, 2000.

———, Jeffrey Shandler, and Beth S. Wenger. *Remembering the Lower East Side: American Jewish Reflections*. Bloomington: Indiana University Press, 2000.

Edelman, Rob. "Mano Hirsch's: A Coney Island Institution." *Flatbush Life*, July 21, 1975.

Esbenshade, Claudia W. "The Knish—Filled with Seasoned, Mashed Potatoes—Makes Its Way Here, to the Delight of Some Native New Yorkers." *McClatchy-Tribune Business News*, July 11, 2012.

Fabricant, Florence. "O Brave New Knish, That Has Such Filling in it!" *New York Times*, January 13, 1999.

———. "Brews and Bites Off the Usual Track." *New York Times*, May 29, 2012.

Facing History and Ourselves. *The Jews of Poland*. Brookline, Mass.: Facing History and Ourselves National Foundation, 1998.

Federman, Mark Russ. *Russ and Daughters: Reflections and Recipes from the House that Herring Built*. New York: Schocken Books, 2013.

Feldberg, Michael, editor, with the American Jewish Historical Society in cooperation with Yeshiva University Museum and the American Sephardi Federation. *Greetings from Home: 350 Years of American Jewish Life*. New York: American Jewish Historical Society, 2005.

Feleszko, Kazimierz. *Bukovina My Love: Polish Language in Carpathian Bukovina through 1945*, vol. 2. Warsaw: Instytut Slawistyki Polskiej Akademii Nauk/Slawistyczny Ośrodek Wydawniczy, 2003.

Finkel, Ian. "Reuben the Knish Man." New York: The National Yiddish Theater–Folksbeine, 2010.

Finston, Mark. "Munchers Vie to Become King of the Knishes." *Newark Star-Ledger*, March 25, 1988.

"First Lady to Get a Taste of Knishe: Read about Mrs. Schwebel in the *New York Sun*." *New York Sun*, January 27, 1942.

Frishwasser, Regina. *Jewish-American Cookbook: 1,600 Selected Recipes*. New York: Forward Association, 1946.

Fuchs, Leo, and Sholom Secunda. *Hop Along Knish*. Sound recording. Victor, 1900.

Gilbert, Martin. *The Routledge Atlas of Jewish History*. 8th ed. London: Routledge, 2010.

Glaser, Milton, and Jerome Snyder. "Yonah Schimmel's Knishes Bakery," in *The Underground Gourmet: Where to Find Great Meals in New York for Less than $3.00 and as Little as 50¢.* (1966), rev. 2nd ed. New York: Simon and Schuster, 1970. 239–241.

Gold, Allan R. "Mixing Law and Kosher Salami for the Cambridge Crowd." *New York Times*, April 6, 1988.

Goldberg, Hyman. "She Puts in Things, Out Come Knishes: Mrs. Schwebel Founded an East Side Dynasty on Them." *New York Post*, September 3, 1941.

The Golden Girls: The Complete Fourth Season. DVD. Burbank, Calif.: Buena Vista Home Entertainment, 2006.

Goldman, Judy Lael. "A Moveable Feast: The Art of a Knish Maker." *Western Folklore* 40, no. 1 (1981): 11–18.

Goldwyn, Tony, dir. *A Walk on the Moon.* DVD. Burbank, Calif.: Miramax, 1998.

Goodman, Walter. "Screen: 'Wise Guys.'" *New York Times*, April 18, 1986.

Goodwin, Doris Kearns. *No Ordinary Time: Franklin and Eleanor Roosevelt; The Home Front in World War II.* New York: Simon & Schuster, 1994.

Grabowski, Michał, ed. *The Diary of Mr. Karol Mincowski: Home Diaries.* Warsaw: S. Olgebrand, 1845.

Grobart. Sam. "Where Are the Knishes of Yesteryear?" *New York Times*, February 2, 2003.

Gross, Max. "Meet David Wise, the Grandma You Never Knew." *Forward*, March 19, 2004.

Gruber, Ruth Ellen. *Virtually Jewish: Reinventing Jewish Culture in Europe.* Berkeley: University of California Press, 2002.

Guillemoles, Alain. *Sur les traces du Yiddishland: Un pays sans frontières.* Paris: Petits Matins, 2010.

Gur, Janna. *The Book of New Israeli Food: A Culinary Journey.* New York: Shocken, 2008.

Hahn, Barbara. "Gone Knishin': Mama Knish Has Turned the Garage into a Bakery That Soon Will Be Blow-Torched Clean and Kosher." *Grants Pass (Ore.) Daily Courier*, August 1, 1995.

Harrington, Mary. "Romanian Chef Describes Plan for Peace — Built Around Food." *Washington Post*, May 13, 1945.

Harris, Mark. "Twilight of the Tummlers." *New York Magazine,* June 1, 2009.

Hauck-Lawson, Annie, and Jonathan Deutsch. *Gastropolis: Food and New York City.* New York: Columbia University Press, 2009.

Heller, Joseph. *Now and Then: From Coney Island to Here.* New York: Knopf, 1998.

Hellman, Geoffrey T. "Incidental Intelligence." *New Yorker,* November 12, 1949, 26.

Hoffman, Paul, and Matt Freedman. *Dictionary Schmictionary! A Yiddish and Yinglish Dictionary.* New York: Quill, 1983.

Holden, Stephen. "A Sentimental Journey." *New York Times,* October 12, 2012.

Holland, Shmil. *Schmaltz.* Moshav Ben-Shemen: Toad Publishing and Modan Publishing House, 2011.

Howe, Irving, and Ruth R. Wisse, and Khone Shmeruk. *The Penguin Book of Modern Yiddish Verse.* New York: Penguin Books, 1987.

Isaacs, Susan. *Close Relations.* New York: Lippincott & Crowell, 1980.

Jan from Kijany. *Fraszki Sowirzała Nowego.* 1614. In *Polska Fraszka Mieszczańska: Minucje Sowiźralskie,* ed. Karol Badecki. Kraków: Polish Academy of Sciences, 1948. 178–179.

Jaynes, Gregory. "Thrill of Gluttony Beats the Agony of Indigestion." *New York Times,* March 26, 1988.

Jim Henson Productions. "Sid Knishes and His Mosh Pit-tatoes." *Muppets Tonight.* Season 1, episode 108. ABC. June 23, 1996.

"'K' in Knisch as in Pigs' Knuckles." *The Mediator,* no. 4, August 8, 1919, 12. Microfilmed from 1917–1919, on the same reel as *The Jewish Bakers' Voice.* New York Public Library Schwartzman Building, Dorot Jewish Division.

Katz, David. "The View from New York," *Jewish Quarterly,* no. 203 (Autumn 2006).

Katz, Dovid. *Lithuanian Jewish Culture.* Vilnius: Central European University Press, 2010.

Katz, Mickey. *Greatest Shticks.* CD. KOCH Records, 2000.

———. "The Kiss of Meyer" (parody of "Kiss of Fire" by Lester Allen, Robert Hill), 78 rpm. Capitol Records, ca. 1940.

———. "The Little White Knish That Cried" (parody of Johnny Ray's "The Little White Cloud That Cried"), 45 rpm. Capitol Records, ca. 1940.

———. *The Most Mishige.* LP. Capitol Records, 1958. © Haimish Music (BMI).

Kaufman, Jonathan. *A Hole in the Heart of the World: Being Jewish in Eastern Europe.* New York: Viking, 1997.

Kirshenblatt-Gimblett, Barbara. "Food and Drink." *YIVO Encyclopedia of Jews in Eastern Europe.* http://www.yivoencyclopedia.org/article.aspx/Food_and_Drink (accessed May 25, 2012).

Kirshenblatt-Gimblett, Barbara, and Jonathan Karp, editors. *The Art of Being Jewish in Modern Times.* Philadelphia: University of Pennsylvania Press, 2007.

"Knish Nosh." *Long Island Newsday,* September 4, 1986.

"'Knishe' Founder Cheers East Siders." *New York Sun,* December 11, 1916.

"Knishes Sweeter Than Wine." *Sarasota Herald-Tribune,* May 27, 1973.

Kobrin, Rebecca. *Jewish Bialystok and Its Diaspora.* Bloomington: Indiana University Press, 2010.

Kosover, Mordecai, and YIVO Institute for Jewish Research. *Yidishe Makholim: A Shṭudye in Ḳulṭur-Geshikhṭe: Un Shprakh-Forshung.* New York: YIVO, 1958.

Kotliarevsky, Ivan. *Eneïda.* Translated by Melnyk Bohdan. Toronto: Basilian Press, 2004.

Kozłowski, Maciej, Andrzej Folwarczny, Michał Bilewicz, Forum Dialogu Między Narodami, and American Jewish Committee. Translated by Erica Lehrer. *Difficult Questions in Polish-Jewish Dialogue: How Poles and Jews See Each Other; A Dialogue on Key Issues in Polish-Jewish Relations.* Warsaw: Jacek Santorski & Co., Agencja Wydawnicza, 2006.

Krajewska, Monika. *Tribe of Stones: Jewish Cemeteries in Poland.* Warsaw: Polish Scientific Publishers, 1993.

Kramer, Faith. "Mrs. Stahl's Famous Knish Recipe Finally Found—in San Francisco." *j, the Jewish Newsweekly of Northern California,* September 27, 2012.

Krawczuk, Tomasz Piotr. *Knysze Jak Knyszyn: Legendy i gawędy.* Knyszyn: Knyszyńskie Towarzystwo Regionalne im. Zygmunta Augusta, 2006.

Krawczuk, Tomasz Piotr, and Mieczysław Piasecki. *Knysze knyszyńskie.* Knyszyn: Knyszyńskie Towarzystwo Regionalne im. Zygmunta Augusta, Urząd Miejski, 2010.

Kreiger, Rosalin. "A Knish on a Plate of Scones: How to Become Canadian." *Canadian Ethnic Studies* 35 (2003): 177–180.

Kun, Josh. "The Yiddish Are Coming: Mickey Katz, Antic-Semitism, and the Sound of Jewish Difference." *American Jewish History* 87, no. 4 (December 1999): 345.

Kvitko, Leib. *Der Groyser Knish.* Kovno: Kultur-lige, 1921.

Lear, Norman, dir. *The Night They Raided Minsky's.* DVD. Beverly Hills, Calif.: MGM/UA, 2008 (originally released on film in 1968).

Lebedeff, Aaron. "Hot Dogs and Knishes." On *Aaron Lebedeff on 2nd Avenue.* Record Collectors Guild. 1968. Judaica Sound Archives of Florida Atlantic University. https://faujsa.fau.edu/lebedeff/.

Lewis, Stephen. "Outdoor Dining à La Cart: New York Loves Its Food Vendors." *Chicago Tribune,* January 13, 1985.

Litvak, Ed. "101-Year-Old Yonah Schimmel Endangered by East Houston Reconstruction." *The Lo-Down: News from the Lower East Side,* posted February 20, 2012; http://www.thelodownny.com.

———. "Follow-Up: Temporary Solution to Yonah Schimmel Parking Woes." *The Lo-Down: News from the Lower East Side,* February 21, 2012.

Marcus, Erica. "A Knish Is Still a Knish: Though How It's Made Is a Bakers' Secret, This New York Staple Has Changed Little in the Past 100 Years." *Long Island Newsday,* October 30, 2001.

Markfield, Wallace. *Teitelbaum's Window.* New York: Knopf, 1970.

Marks, Gil. *Encyclopedia of Jewish Food.* Hoboken: John Wiley & Sons, 2010.

Marriott, Michel. "Midtown Pushcart Plans Disgust Many Vendors." *New York Times,* November 1, 1988.

McElroy, Steven. "My New York." *New York Times,* October 12, 2008.

McNulty, Timothy. "Obituary: Henry 'Hank' Stohl, Puppeteer from TV's Early Days." *Pittsburgh Post-Gazette,* December 17, 2008.

Moskin, Julia, and Kim Severson. "Jamaica Passions." *New York Times,* July 20, 2005.

Nadell, Pamela S., ed. *American Jewish Women's History: A Reader.* New York: New York University Press, 2003.

Nagourney, Adam. "In Politics, Ethnic Posturing Isn't Simple Anymore." *New York Times,* October 31, 1999.

Nathan, Joan. *Quiches, Kugels, and Couscous: My Search for Jewish Cooking in France.* New York: Alfred A. Knopf, 2010.

"Now It's Giving 'Knishes,' She Is." *Eugene Register-Guard* (Ore.), August 24, 1942.

Ochorowicz-Monatowa, Maria. *Uniwersalna Książka Kucharska.* Poznań: Kurpisz, 2002.

O'Neill, Molly. *New York Cookbook: From Pelham Bay to Park Avenue, Firehouse to Four-Star Restaurants.* New York: Workman Publishing, 1992.

Overbeke, Grace Kessler, "America's Madwomen: Jewish Female Comedians in the Twentieth Century." Honors thesis, Wesleyan University, 2008.

Owen, June. "Size and Filling May Vary, but a Knish It Is." *New York Times,* August 17, 1961.

Paddleford, Clementine. "The 'Knische Queen' in an Expansive Mood." *New York Herald Tribune,* August 11, 1942.

Parker, Milton, and Allyn Freeman. *How to Feed Friends and Influence People: The Carnegie Deli; A Giant Sandwich, a Little Deli, a Huge Success.* Hoboken, N.J.: Wiley, 2005.

Picon, Molly. "Di (Ganze) Velt Is a Te'atr." *Di Groyse Shlagers Fun Kine Un Te'atr.* CD. Tel Aviv: Israel Music, 2005.

Prince, Todd. "Brooklyn Deli Leaves Russians Cold." *Russia Journal,* January 18, 2002.

Quinlan, Heather, dir. *If These Knishes Could Talk: The Story of the New York Accent.* New York: Canvasback Kid Productions, 2013.

Ray, Johnny. "The Little White Cloud That Cried." 78 rpm recording. Decca Records, 1951.

Reeves, Richard. "This Is the Battle of the Titans?" *New York Times Magazine,* November 1, 1970.

"Rivington St. Sees War." *New York Times,* January 27, 1916.

Robbins, Michael W., and Wendy Palitz. *Brooklyn: A State of Mind.* New York: Workman Publishing Company, 2000.

Robinson, Murray. "Coney Island: Which Way's the Ocean?" *Collier's*, September 1951, 30–31, 47–48.

Roden, Claudia. *The Book of Jewish Food: An Odyssey from Samarkand to New York*. New York: Knopf, 1996.

Rosten, Leo. *Hooray for Yiddish! A Book about English*. New York: Simon and Schuster, 1982.

———. *The Joys of Yiddish: A Relaxed Lexicon of Yiddish, Hebrew, and Yinglish Words Often Encountered in English . . . from the Days of the Bible to Those of the Beatnik*. New York: McGraw-Hill, 1968.

———. *The New Joys of Yiddish*. New York: RandomHouse Digital, 2010.

Roth, Henry. *Call It Sleep*. New York: Picador, 2005.

Rybal, Izaak. "A Mission of Joy and Sorrow." *Bialytoker Stimme*, April 1986, 1–2.

Sabar, Yona. *A Jewish Neo-Aramaic Dictionary: Dialects of Amidya, Dihok, Nerwa, and Zakho, Northwestern Iraq; Based on Old and New Manuscripts, Oral and Written Bible Translations, Folkloric Texts, and Diverse Spoken Registers, with an Introduction to Grammar and Semantics, and an Index of Talmudic Words Which Have Reflexes in Jewish Neo-Aramaic*. Wiesbaden: Harrassowitz, 2002.

Sax, David. *Save the Deli: In Search of Perfect Pastrami, Crusty Rye, and the Heart of Jewish Delicatessen*. Boston: Houghton Mifflin Harcourt, 2009.

Schluger, James. "Warm Memories and Hot Knishes." *New York Times*, February 9, 2003.

Schwartz, Arthur. *Arthur Schwartz's Jewish Home Cooking: Yiddish Recipes Revisited*. Berkeley, Calif.: Ten Speed Press, 2008.

Seville, David. *The Witch Doctor Presents David Seville and His Friends*. LP. Liberty, 1958.

Shandler, Jeffrey. *Adventures in Yiddishland: Postvernacular Language & Culture*. Berkeley: University of California Press, 2006.

Shapiro, Yaacov. *Geshmakene Yiddish Songs*. 1987. CD. Haifa: Hataklit, 2005.

Shenker, Israel. "Taste for Business Builds Brooklyn Knish Empire." *New York Times*, May 9, 1971.

Shepard, Richard F. "A New York Era Dies with a Deli Man." *New York Times*, March 6, 1996.

———. "Stage: Yiddish Revival." *New York Times,* November 6, 1979.

Sheraton, Mimi. *The Bialy Eaters: The Story of a Bread and a Lost World.* New York: Bantam, 2000.

Shulman, Abraham. *The Old Country.* New York: Scribner, 1974.

Sillen, Peter, dir. *Grand Luncheonette.* 2005. New York: WNET Channel 13, Reel New York Series, 2006.

Silver, Laura. "From under the Subway to 'Subway': Mrs. Stahl's Now Made in Jersey." *Brooklyn Papers,* January 21, 2006.

Simmons, Andrew. "A Kare Pan Is a Pretty Good Start." *Gastronomica* 12, no. 1 (Spring 2012): 87–90.

Singer, Isaac Bashevis. *Love and Exile: An Autobiographical Trilogy.* New York: Farrar, Straus and Giroux, 1986.

———. *Meshugah.* Translated by Nili Wachtel. New York: Farrar, Straus and Giroux, 2003.

Sokolsky, George. "These Days . . ." *Washington Post and Times Herald,* November 5, 1958.

"Sounds Jewish." Podcast. November 11, 2009. http://www.guardian.co.uk/.

Stasiewicz, Henryk. *Knyszyn i Ziemia Knyszyńska.* Knyszyn: Wydawnictwo AMANITA, 1997.

Steinberg, Ellen F., and Jack Prost. *From the Jewish Heartland: Two Centuries of Midwest Foodways.* Urbana: University of Illinois Press, 2011.

Stern, Jane, and Michael Stern. "Knish Nosh Builds Its Business on Cornerstone of Jewish Cuisine." *Orlando Sentinel,* April 17, 1986.

Stohl, Hank. *When We Were Kids.* Bloomington, Ind.: Author House, 2005.

Sunder, Madhavi. "Mavens' Deli Shuts Its Doors." *Harvard Crimson,* January 18, 1989, 1.

"Sweathog Clinic for the Cure of Smoking." *Welcome Back, Kotter.* Season 2, episode 11. ABC. 1976. Paley Center for Media, New York.

Szczepanowicz, Barbara, and Dorota Szczepanowicz. *Kuchnia żydowska: święta, obyczaje i potrawy świąteczne.* Kraków: Wydawnictwo Petrus, 2011.

Szpek, Heidi M. "Jewish Epitaphs from Białystok, 1905–6: Towards Mending the Torn Thread of Memory." *East European Jewish Affairs* 41, no. 1–2 (August 1, 2011): 1–23.

Szymanderska, Hanna. *Polska Wigilia*. Warsaw: Wydawnictwo WATRA, 1989.

Trillin, Calvin. "U.S. Journal: The Lower East Side," *New Yorker*, February 24, 1973, 112.

Van Embden, Edward. "Gluten-Free Specialty Helps Buena's Conte Pasta Grow Profits, Expand Facilities and Create Jobs." *Press of Atlantic City*. Updated April 30, 2010.

Weinreich, Beatrice, and Uriel Weinreich. "Der Repertuar fun Teyg-Maykholim fun a Yiddisher Balebosteh." *Yidisher Folklor* 1, no. 3 (March 1962): 58–59, 66–67, 69.

Wenger, Beth S. "Memory as Identity: The Invention of the Lower East Side." *American Jewish History* 85, no. 1 (March 1997): 3–27.

West, Melanie Grayce, and Monica Williams. "City News—Lunchbox: Yonah Schimmel Knish Bakery; Old Flavors of the Lower East Side." *Wall Street Journal*, October 19, 2010.

Wex, Michael. *Born to Kvetch: Yiddish Language and Culture in All of Its Moods*. New York: St. Martin's Press, 2005.

Wheelock, Julie. "Taste of New York: Store Flies in East Coast Knishes to Whet West Coast Appetites." *Los Angeles Times*, October 3, 1991.

Williams, Pearl. *A Trip around the World Is Not a Cruise*. After Hours Records. Ca. 1960. Rodgers and Hammerstein Archives of Recorded Sound, New York Public Library for the Performing Arts, Astor, Lenox and Tilden Foundations.

Wiśniewski, Tomasz. *Jewish Bialystok and Surroundings in Eastern Poland: A Guide for Yesterday and Today*. Ipswich, Mass.: Ipswich Press, 1998.

Wolynetz, Lubow. "Christmas Knysh." *Nashe Zhyttia*, November 1974, 29. Translated by Ostap Kin and Lubow Wolynetz.

Zborowski, Mark, and Elizabeth Herzog. *Life Is with People: The Culture of the Shtetl*. New York: Schocken Books, 1995, 11–48.

Ziegelman, Jane. *97 Orchard: An Edible History of Five Immigrant Families in One New York Tenement*. New York: HarperCollins, 2010.

Zuckerman: Larry. *The Potato: How the Humble Spud Rescued the Western World*. North Point Press, 1999.

Illustration Credits

3   Courtesy of Sara Spatz

7   Michael Kamber

17   Photo by Mark Sherman. Courtesy of Enid Sherman

21   Courtesy of Enid Sherman

22   Barbara Pfeffer Collection, Museum of Jewish Heritage, New York

24   Courtesy of Enid Sherman

26   Craig Matthews/CM Works Photography

33   Courtesy of Gabila's Knishes

33   Courtesy of Gabila's Knishes

37   Brian Merlis/Brooklynpix.com

41   Courtesy of Pamela Hirsch

47   Brooklyn Public Library, Brooklyn Division

51   Library of Congress, Prints & Photographs Division, LC-USZ62-72444

57   Hedy Pagremanski/Museum of the City of New York

58   Library of Congress, Prints & Photographs Division, LC-DIG-ggbain-22928

60   Rebecca Lepkoff

66   Clementine Paddleford, "'Knishe Queen' in an Expansive Mood," *New York Herald Tribune*, August 11, 1942. Photo credit: *Herald Tribune*, Zerbe

76   Library of Congress, Music Division (DCM 1490: Pamela Chamberlin; glaze by Dudley Smith/Double Ocarina, ca. 1979)

108   Forward Association

110   Courtesy of an anonymous collection

114   Courtesy of Yad Vashem Photo Archive. Origin: Normann Heine

117   (*Bottom*) Tomek Wiśniewski

121   Forward Association

123   (*Bottom*) Foundation for the Preservation of Jewish Heritage in Poland, www.fodz.pl

Illustrations Credits

127   (*Top*) *Knysh* or "bread with soul." 2011. Village of Honcharivka, Vinnytsia Province, Ukraine. Made by Oksana Motorna and Mariya Ivanyshyna. From the exhibition "Baking, Baking Bread . . ." at the Ivan Honchar Museum, December 2011. Photograph by Bohdan Poshyvailo. Courtesy of the Ivan Honchar Museum, Kiev, Ukraine

127   (*Bottom*) *Knysh.* 2011. Village of Zozuli, Lviv Province, Ukraine. Made by Olha Nalyvaiko. From the exhibition "Baking, Baking Bread . . ." at the Ivan Honchar Museum, December 2011. Photograph by Bohdan Poshyvailo. Courtesy of the Ivan Honchar Museum, Kiev, Ukraine.

140   Thomas and Katherine Detre Library and Archives, Senator John Heinz History Center

145   Billy Rose Theatre Division, The New York Public Library for the Performing Arts, Astor, Lenox and Tilden Foundations. Tandem Productions, distributed by United Artists

148   Dayle Vander Sande

151   Wendy Carlson

186   By permission of Sholom Home/graphic design by Phil Higley at Diversified Imprints

191   By permission of Sholom Home

192   Photo by David Sherman

193   By permission of Sholom Home/graphic design by Phil Higley at Diversified Imprints

195   (*Top*) By permission of Sholom Home/graphic design by Phil Higley at Diversified Imprints

195   (*Bottom*) Photo by David Sherman

199   Courtesy of Sara Spatz

199   Courtesy of Sara Spatz

203   Courtesy of Toby Engelberg

206   Photo by Faith Kramer

217   Courtesy of Toby Engelberg

226   Photo by Faith Kramer, first appeared in *j, the Jewish news weekly of Northern California,* www.jweekly.com

All other photos are by the author or from her collection.

Index

Note: Page numbers in *italics* indicate photographs; "n" in a page number indicates location in the notes section followed by the note number.

Abrams, Bonnie, 42–45, 49
Africa, 74, 152
Agoos, Mitch, 5
aknish (assembly), 95–96
Aleichem, Sholem, 158–59
Allen, Woody, 146
All Saints' Day, 107, 129
ancestor hunts in Poland, 109–22
ancestors, knish as tribute to, 39, 107, 127–28, 129, 130–32, 221
Anistratov, Ellen, 52–53
antiquity, seeking knish predecessor in, 88–91, 133
anti-Semitism and persecution, 75–76, 77, 109, 110, 240. *See also* Holocaust
Aramaic language, 95–96, 133–34
art of making knishes: author's tribulations over, 175–81; cross-cultural education in Banff, 175–84, *184*; as devotional act, 139; Mrs. Stahl's granddaughters, 196–208; Sholom Home Auxiliary ladies, 185–96, *191*, *192*, *195*
Ashkenazi Jews, Paris, 92–93. *See also* Eastern European origins

Ausubel, Nathan, 58, 77
Axler, Andrew, 202
Axler, Marietta, 202

baba ghanoush, 80–81
bagel stores, 26, 42, 152, 180–81, 210, 212
Bagiński, Krzysztof, 115
Banff Centre, 175–84, *184*
Batalion, Judy, 155–56
Beckerman, Leo, 197–98
Berg, Gertrude, 138
Berg, Lindsay, 188
Berger, Arthur, 56
Berger, Harold, 56
Berger, Joseph, 56
Berger, Lillian, 55
Berger, Rose (née Schimmel), 56
Berman, Lisa, 187, 192
Berman, Rae, 187, 192
Bialik, Chaim Nachman, 76
Bialystok, Poland, *108*, 108–13, *110*, 122–23
biblical underpinnings, knish's lack of, 133–35
Bibliothèque Medem, 94–95

blintzes, 10, 19, 28, 79, 129, 161

Bnei Brak, 81–82

Book of New Israeli Food: A Culinary Journey, The (Gur), 81

Borscht Belt, 36

bourekas, 79, *81*, 81–82

Boutique Jaune, La (The Yellow Boutique), 91–92, 97

Brantley, Derek "SD3," 157–58

Brighton Beach, 3–7, 11–12, 13–20, 22, 40–41, 172, 214. *See also* Mrs. Stahl's Knishes

Brodinsky, Bruce, 46

Bronx, NY, 8, 14, 35, 80, 106, 210

Brooklyn, NY: and author's childhood, 1–10; Brighton Beach, 3–7, 11–12, 13–20, 22, 40–41, 172, 214; connective role in social fabric, 34–36; and Fritzie Silver, 10–14; Marvin Hirsch's knishes, 39–41; and Ruby the Knish Man, 43, 46–48, 47, 49–50. *See also* Coney Island; Mrs. Stahl's Knishes

Brooklyn Dodgers, 16, 18, 167

Broward Stage Door Theater, 147–48

bryndzia, 129

buckwheat (kasha), 10, 26, 38, 129–30

Bulgaria, and bourekas origins, 82

Café Batya, 83, *84*, 85–88

Call It Sleep (Roth), 153–54

Carmel Market, Tel Aviv, 79

Carnarsie section of Brooklyn, 47

Carnegie Deli, 173

Catherine the Great, 77

Catskills, 42, 50, 215

cebularze, 106

cemeteries: Bukovina, 129; Farmingdale, Long Island, 4–5; Poland, 96, 109–10, 110, 113, 116, 123; Washington Cemetery in Brooklyn, 111

Chase, Hazel, 187, 189–90, 191–92, 193, 194, 196

chausson aux pommes, 91, 94

Chianti (restaurant), 107

Chișinău (Kishinev), Moldova, 75–76

cholent, 108

Christian knishes in Ukraine, 129–30, 131

Close Relations (Isaacs), 163–64

cocktail knishes, 24, 206

comedy and humor, knish in. *See* culture

community and connection, 2, 34–36, 75, 95–96, 177–84

competitive knish eating, 165–74

Concord Hotel, 36

Coney Island: eating contests, 165–68; Gabila's knishes, 27–34, *33*, 37; heyday of knishes in, 16; Shatzkin's knishes, 36–39; square fried knish, 21, 31, 33, 34; Superstorm Sandy aftermath, 214 connection and community, 2, 34–36, 75, 95–96, 177–84

Conte, Mike, 25–27, 210, 213

Conte's Pasta, 25–27, 26, 209–13

Copiague, Long Island, 28, 31

culture, knish in: connection role of knish, 2, 34–36, 75, 95–96, 177–84; cross-cultural education in Banff, 175–84, *184*; fiction, 153–54, 158–64; film, *145*, 145–47; Knish Collective, 155–56; *Momma's Knishes*, 150–52; music, 44–45, 152–53, 155–58, 157–58; and Sholom Home Auxiliary ladies, 185–96, 191, 192, 195; television, 138–45, *140*; vulgar meaning of knish, 153–57, 246–47n32; Yiddish, 94–95, 125–26, 147–49, 152–53, 152–56, 155–56, 159–60. *See also* Jewish cultural and religious traditions

Czapnik, Riva "Nana" (Mrs. Eva Farbstein), 8, 80, 104, 105–6, 113, 116, 123

Czapnik, Szejna "Aunt Jean" (Mrs. Jean Haren), 112–13, 115–16, 215

Czapnik family name, 111, 115, 116

David, Larry, 146

Day of the Dead, knish association with, 131

Delancey Street, Gabay's pushcart knishes on, 29

Delicious Knishes, 185–96, 191, 192, 195

"Der Groyser Knish" (story in verse), 159–60

Dershowitz, Alan, 146–47

Diner, Hasia, 124, 125, 130

Dudovitz, Sophie, 188, 190

Dumile, Daniel, 157

Eastern European origins: etymology, 96; and mixtures of foods in Israel, 87; Moldovan connection, 75–76; Pale of Settlement, 35, 77, 125; 20th-century literary references, 159–60; Ukraine (*knysh*), 44, 46, 126–30, 127, 131, 132. *See also* Poland

Ekland, Britt, 145–46

Ellis Island, 74

Engelberg, Dora (née Dvorah), 198

Engelberg, Toby, 196, 198, 200, 202–6, 207, 214

Escazú, Costa Rica, 76

etymology of *knish*, 96, 125–35

falafel, 79

family history, knishes in author's, 2–10

Farbstein, Eva Levy "Nana" (née Riva Czapnik), 8, 80, 104, 105–6, 113, 116, 123

fatayer (Senegal), 74

Federal Writers' Project, 58

female genitalia, knish as term for, 153–57, 246–47n32

fiction, knish in, 153–54, 158–64
film references, 145, 145–47
Finkel, Fyvush, 148–49
Finkel, Ian, 149
Finkelstein, Izzy, 63, 66
Finkelsztajn, Dora, 97
Finkelsztajn, Henri, 97
Finkelsztajn, Itzik, 97
Finkelsztajn, Sacha, 91
Finstrom, Tony, 147
fish, 74, 85, 93
Flamhaft Levy Kamins & Hirsch, 40
Florida, 48–49, 112–13, 214–15, 218
foods, maintaining traditional,
    93–94. *See also* kosher food
France, knishes in, 91–99
fruit filling for knish, 10, 48, 162
frum, 49
Fyvush Finkel Live! (variety show),
    148–49

Gabay, Andrew, 34
Gabay, Bella, 28–29
Gabay, Elias, 28–30, 64
Gabay, Elliott, 30, 31–34
Gabila's, 27–34, 33, 37
Gandhi, Mahatma, 162
Gardner, Ida (née Zelkowitz), 182
gefilte fish, 85
Germany *(knitschen)*, 131–32
Getty, Estelle, 143–44
Gitlin, Reenie, 187, 194
Glaser, Milton, 63

Glazer, Rena, 187, 191, 194–95
gołampki, 78
Goldbergs, The (TV show), 138–39
Golden Girls (TV show), 143–44
Green, Les, 20–25
Green, Max, 61–64
Green, Susan Caruso, 54
Gur, Janna, 81, 82

Hadassah, 113, 115, 117, 217
hamantaschen, 98, 250n13
Haren, Jean "Aunt Jean" (née Szejna
    Czapnik), 112–13, 115–16, 215
Hasidic Jews, 30, 192
hatzilim, 80–81
Hebrew, 101–3, 116, 122 , 133–34, 148,
    168, 188
Heilicher, Lisa, 187, 193
Heller, Joseph, 36–37
Helsinki, Finland, 99
hip-hop references, 157–58
Hirsch, Mano, 40, 41
Hirsch, Marvin, 39–41
Hirsch's, 39–41, 40
holidays, knish's association with, 4,
    5, 8, 76, 94, 107–8, 129, 131, 193, 195.
    See also Rosh Hashanah
Holland, Shmil, 87
Holocaust: Auschwitz, 78; and loss
    of food traditions, 93–94; loss of
    heritage in, 78, 90, 93, 99, 101–2,
    111, 115; Paris memorial, 97; as
    term, 242n32

Houston Street, Lower East Side:
Gussie Schwebel, 64–71, 66, 132;
Yonah Schimmel Knish Bakery,
26, 50–61, 57, 60, 62–63, 149, 205
Hurricane Katrina, 185

I Am Ruthie Segal, Hear Me Roar
(musical), 155–56
"Ich Hob Leib a Knish" (Shapiro,
song), 154
If These Knishes Could Talk (film),
146–47
immigrant experience: Conte family,
26–27; Fannie Stahl, 206–7;
Fannie Svendlick, 56–57; Fritzie
Silver, 10–11; Gabay family, 28–29;
Jean Haren, 112–13; knish as part
of, 73–74, 150; and loss of ties to
origins, 144; Manhattan at turn of
20th century, 50, 51
Isaacs, Susan, 163–64
Israel, 74, 78–91
Italian immigrants (Conte's story),
25–27
Izzy's Knishes, 43

Jaffee, Roz, 187, 190, 194
Jerusalem Avenue, Warsaw, 100
Jewish Association for Services to
the Aged (JASA), 12
Jewish cultural and religious
traditions: author's ambivalence,
8–9, 101–2; finding knish's
evolution within, 52–61, 124–25;
kaddish, 93, 95, 235n4; knish as
tribute to ancestors, 39, 107,
127–28, 129, 130–32, 221; knish's
role in, 6–10, 19–20; kosher food,
33–34, 49, 104, 168–70, 220–21;
salt in, 47–48; Shabbat, 82, 84,
104–5; *Shehecheyanu*, 175–77,
184; synagogue, 8–9, 95, 134; and
unreliability of portable food, 79;
Yom Kippur, 4, 5. *See also* culture;
mourning rituals
"Jewish Heritage Mural," 54
Jewish intellectuals and ancestral
foods, 94
Jewish neighborhood, Paris (Marais),
91–92
Jewish Neo-Aramaic Dictionary, A
(Sabar), 134

kaddish, 93, 95, 235n4
Kamińska State Jewish Theater, 103
karjalanpiirakka, 99
kasha knish, 10, 26, 38, 129–30
Katz, Mickey, 152, 247n32
Katz, Sandor, 197–99
Kempnerski, Karol, 117, 123
Key Largo, Jerry Oshinsky's knishes
in, 48–49
Kiev, Ukraine, origins of Ruby's
knish, 44, 46
King David Knishes, 33–34
Kiryat Bialystok, Israel, 80

kisanin/kisnin, 88–89, 133
Kishinev, Moldova, 75–76
kniple, 188, 250n12
knish: in art, 54–58, 57; author's family lineage of, 35–36; competitive eating of, 165–74; cousins of, 74, 187; etymology of, 96, 125–35; food and word, 25; Gabila's square knish lineage, 34; importance for author's family, 1–2; ingredients and cooking methods, 2; and Israel, 74, 78–91; vs. latke/*leviva memulet*, 85–86, 86; need for revival of, 19–20; Parisian leg of search, 91–99; as pastry pocket, 88–89; persistence of, 218–19; in Poland, 100–107; shrinking distribution of, 26, 210–13; as signifier, 25, 128; simple sensuality of, 9–10; as subject and muse for writers, 58–59; as tribute to ancestors, 39, 107, 127–28, 129, 130–32, 221. *See also* art of making knishes; Brooklyn; culture; Eastern European origins; Lower East Side
Knish (puppet), 139–41
Knish Alley, 147–48, 148
Knish Alley (play), 147–48
Knish Collective, 155–56
"Knish Doctor, The" (Katz, song), 152–53
Knishery NYC, 219–21, 221

Knish Nosh, 26, 52
knishta (synagogue), 95, 134
knyszyk, 129
Knyszyn, Poland, xi, 113–24, 114, 117, 121, 123
kosher food, 33–34, 49, 104, 168–70, 220–21
Kotliarevsky, Ivan, 131
Kovel, Poland, 83
Kraków, Poland, 122
Krakowiec, Ukraine (formerly Poland), 132
Kręglicka, Agnieszka, 106–7

Lachter, Muriel, 187, 194
latke, 1, 85–86, 86, 140, 181
Leon Bakery, 81
Less Than Kind (TV show), 144–45
Levy, Celia and Max, 109, 111
Levy, Jean "Aunt Jean" (née Szejna Czapnik), 112–13, 115–16, 215
linguistic approach to knish ancestry, 96, 125–35 ·
literary references to knish, 58–59, 125, 153–54, 158–64
"Little White Knish That Cried, The" (Katz, song), 153
Littman, Mark, 173
Loch Sheldrake, NY, 43
Loeffler, Sandy, 182
London, Morris, 61–64
London, Simcha, 80, 89–91
Long Island: Gabila's migration to

Copiague, 27–28, 31; Hirsch's in Mineola, 40–41. *See also* Brooklyn
Los Angeles, CA, 38–39
Love and Exile: An Autobiographical Trilogy (Singer), 161
"Love and Knishes" trio, 41
Lower East Side: Gabay grandparents in, 28–29, 64; Gussie Schwebel, 64–71, 66, 132; Knishery NYC, 219–21, 221; persistence of knish in, 26; politics and knishes in, 63, 68–71, 163; Ratner's (Delancey Street), 98, 104, 131, 177, 205; Rivington Street, 51, 61–64; Yonah Schimmel, 26, 50–61, 57, 60, 62–63, 149, 205
Lviv, Ukraine, 132

makheteneste, 64
Markfield, Wallace, 161–62
Marton, Don, 215
matzoh, 1, 11, 97, 103, 113
matzoh balls, 33, 116, 177
Mavens Kosher Court, 146–47
McCall, Mitzie (née Steiner), 139–40
melamed, 55
Mémorial de la Shoah, 97
Mémorial des Martyrs de la Déportation, 97
Memorial to the Sacrifices of the Bialystok Pogrom, 109, 110
Meshugah (Singer), 160–61
Middle Eastern food, and knish, 87

Mineola, Long Island, 40–41
Minneapolis, MN (Delicious Knishes), 185–96, 191, 192, 195
Minnesota (Delicious Knishes), 185–96, 191, 192, 195
Mitzi's Kiddie Castle (TV show), 139–41, 140
Mm . . . Food (Dumile, album), 157
Moldova, 75–76
Molly Goldberg Jewish Cookbook, The (Berg), 138
Momma's Knishes (Wise, live solo performance), 150–52
Mordkowna, Riwa, 122
mourning rituals: bourekas in, 82; knish in, 4–5, 116, 131; sitting shiva, 13, 53, 82, 235n3
Mrs. Stahl's Knishes: in author's family culture, 2, 5–8, 12–13; author's search for, 14–27; as brand, 198; Conte as owner of, 25–27, 210–12; finding family and tradition, 196–208; Florida revival of, 214–15, 218; Heller on, 37; kosher operations, 104; legacy of, 214–15, 218–20, 221–22; Les Green as owner, 20–25; in Los Angeles, 39; photos, 3, 7, 14, 17, 24; searching for, 14–27, 200–202; in Spring Valley, NY, 97
Muppets Tonight (TV show), 144
Museum of the City of New York, 55–57

musical references, 44–45, 152–53,
155–58
mustard, 4, 6, 12, 46, 78, 190, 192

Nathan's, 166–67
NECHAMA, 185
New Orleans, LA, 185
New York tradition, knish as, 53. *See
also* Brooklyn; Lower East Side
Niborski, Yitskhok, 94–95, 96
Night They Raided Minsky's, The
(film), 145–46
nikudim vs. knish, 133
nostalgia factor, 16, 22–25, 38–39, 52,
103–6, 141, 218
*Now and Then: From Coney Island to
Here* (Heller), 36–37

Oshinsky, Hershel, 43
Oshinsky, Jerry, 43, 46, 48–50
Oshinsky, Ruby, 43–50, 47

Paddleford, Clementine, 66
pagan origins of knish, 130–33
Pagremanski, Hedy, 55–57
Pale of Settlement, 35, 77, 125
Paris, France, 91–99
parsha, 95
Pas Yisroel, 34
persecution, 75–76, 77, 109, 110, 240.
See also Holocaust
Picon, Molly, 61
pierogi, 96, 97

Pikudei, 95, 96, 242n29
pilgrimages, 1, 3, 12, 31, 80, 96, 206,
209, 217
Pitchi Poï, 92–94, 98–99
place-names reminiscent of knish,
Poland, 133
placinta/pateu (Moldova), 75
pocket food, knish in family of,
88–89
Podelsky, Joel, 166–71, 170, 172, 173–74
Podlasie, Poland, 109
pogroms, 75–76, 109, 110, 240
Poland: and author's origins, 78;
and Batya's lack of knishes,
87; Bialystok, 108, 108–13, 110,
122–23; kasha recipe, 129–30; and
knish origins, 83, 92–93, 132–33;
Knyszyn, xi, 113–24, 114, 117, 121,
123; Kovel, 83; lack of Jews in,
93, 99; loss of knishes in, 106–7;
Parisian Jews' origins in, 97;
21st-century knish revival, 126;
Warsaw, 78, 99–108, 105, 121–24
politics and knishes, Lower East
Side, 63, 68–71, 163
potato knishes, 10, 37, 38, 142, 190–91,
233
Proust, Marcel, 78, 91
Próżna Street, Warsaw, 103–4, 105
pushcarts, 29, 56, 58, 63

Queens, NY, 2, 14
Quinlan, Heather, 146–47

Rapillo, Steve, 210, 211–12, 213, 222
Ratner's Lower East Side Dairy
    Restaurant (Delancey Street), 98,
    104, 131, 177, 205
recipe, 233
Redalje, Frume, 10
Redalje/Reidell, Freyda Rifke (Mrs.
    Fritzie Silver), 3–5, 6, 8–12, 11,
    13–14, 206–7
Reles, Abe, 65
religion. *See* Jewish cultural and
    religious traditions
Resnick, Jay, 173, 249n6
Riga, Latvia, 10, 13–14, 214
Riis, Jacob, 65
Rivington Street, 51, 61–64, 126, 216
Roosevelt, Eleanor, 63, 68–71
Roosevelt, Teddy, 65
Rosh Hashanah, 103, 104, 195, 196
Rosten, Leo, 125
Roth, Henry, 153–54
round knishes, 2, 38, 43
Rubinstein, Ada, 187, 191, 192, 192, 196
"Ruby's Knishes" (Abrams, song),
    44–45
Ruby the Knish Man, 41–50, 47, 149
Russia and knish origins, 92, 126
Russian Jewish population, Brighton
    Beach, 18, 22

Sabar, Yona, 134
salt in Jewish tradition, 47–48
sambusek, 79

Schencher, Harris, 171
Schimmel, Rose (Mrs. Joseph
    Berger), 56
Schimmel, Yonah, 55–56, 59–60.
    See also Yonah Schimmel Knish
    Bakery
schmaltz, 87–88, 153, 241n20
schmaltz herring, 74, 93
Schwebel, Abraham, 64, 66
Schwebel, Gussie (née Sussman),
    64–71, 66, 132
SD3 (né Derek Brantley), 157–58
Second Avenue, Manhattan, 61,
    147–48, 148
Sephardic Jews, 79, 88
Shabbat, 82, 84, 104–5
Shaller, Michelle, 188, 193
Shapiro, Yaacov, 154
Shatzkin, Bill, 38
Shatzkin, Mort, 37–39
Shatzkin's, 36–39, 37
Shehecheyanu (prayer for first times),
    175–77, 184
Sherman, Bella, 83–85
shiva, sitting, 13, 53, 82, 235n3
Shoah, 242n32. *See also* Holocaust
shofar, 111, 243n37
shpilkes, 167
Silver, Freyda Rifke "Fritzie" (née
    Redalje), 3–5, 6, 8–12, 11, 13–14,
    206–7
Silver, Laura, 117, 123, 191, 192–93
Silverman, Sarah, 156

Simcha (author's cousin), 80, 89–91
Singer, Isaac Bashevis, 103, 160–61
Singer, Pat, 15–20
Singer Festival of Jewish Culture, Warsaw, 103–6
Smith, Dede, 187, 189, 190, 191, 195
Snyder, Jerome, 63
Spatz, Anna (née Chaneh), 199, 199
Spatz, Sara, 199–200, 203–6, 207, 218
square knishes, 21, 31, 33, 34, 43
Stahl, Fannie (née Goldenberg), 196–208, 199, 203, 215–18, 217, 243n36. *See also* Mrs. Stahl's Knishes
Stasiewicz, Henryk, 116–17
Stohl, Hank, 139–40
St. Paul, MN (Delicious Knishes), 185–96, 191, 192, 195
Streisand, Barbra, 158
stuffed cabbage, 78, 207
stuffed latke vs. knish, 85
suburbs, flight to, and loss of Mrs. Stahl's, 23–24
Superstorm Sandy, 214
Svendlick, Fannie (née Kaufman), 56–57
Sweet, Betty, 188, 190, 196
sweet cheese knish, 10
synagogue, 8–9, 95, 134

Talmud, 88–89, 95
Teitelbaum's Window (Markfield), 161–62
Tel Aviv, Israel, 78–88

television references, 138–45, 140
"Ten Knisch Commandments, The," 62
Thatcher, Kirk, 144
Thomas, Michael Tilson, 205
tiyul shoreshim, 87
Torah, 8, 95–96, 106
triangular knish, 97–98
Trip around the World Is Not a Cruise, A (Williams, album), 154–55

Ukrainian origins (*knysh*), 44, 46, 126–30, 127, 131, 132
Underground Gourmet, The (Glaser and Snyder), 63
United Knish Bakery, 62
Upper West Side, 99, 160, 166, 198, 199–200, 202
Utica Avenue knish man, 149

varenike, 84–85, 96
varnishkes, kasha, 178–79
vatrushka, 97
Vayakhel, 95, 96, 242n29
Vineland, NJ, 209–10
vulgar meaning of knish, 153–57, 246–47n32

Walk on the Moon, A (film), 42
warming methods, 75
Warsaw, Poland, 78, 99–108, 105, 121–24
Weegee (Usher Fellig), 39, 236n24
Weingarten, Susan, 88

Weingast, Morris and Sam, 20–21, *23*
Welcome Back, Kotter (TV show), 141–43
Whatever Works (film), 146
Wildman, Noah, 219–21, *221*
Williams, Pearl, 154–55
Wisdom, Norman, 145–46
Wise, David, 150–52, *151*
Wise Sons, 196–98
Wiśniewski, Tomasz "Tomek," 109, 111, 113, 115, 116
Wolfson, Dede, 187, 189
Wolynetz, Lubow, 127–28, 130–31
Wood, Evan Rachel, 146
Woodbourne, NY, 42
Works Progress Administration (WPA), 58

Yellow Boutique, The (La Boutique Jaune), 91–92, 97
Yiddish language and culture: connection to food, 93, 96; Katz's songs, 152–53; knish in, 94–95, 125–26, 147–49, 152–56, 159–60; Second Avenue establishments, 61; *shpilkes*, 167; in television, 138
Yiddish theater, 61, 147–49, 152–53, 155–56
Yizkor, 243n38
Yom Kippur, 4, 5
Yom Tov, Batya, 86–87
Yonah Schimmel Knish Bakery, 26, 50–61, *57*, 60, 62–63, 149, 205

Zilberman, Jean, 92–94

HBI SERIES ON JEWISH WOMEN

Shulamit Reinharz, General Editor
Sylvia Barack Fishman, Associate Editor

The HBI Series on Jewish Women, created by the Hadassah-Brandeis
Institute, publishes a wide range of books by and about Jewish women
in diverse contexts and time periods. Of interest to scholars and the
educated public, the HBI Series on Jewish Women fills major gaps
in Jewish Studies and in Women and Gender Studies as well as their
intersection.

The HBI Series on Jewish Women is supported by a generous gift from
Dr. Laura S. Schor.

Laura Silver's book is the HBI's second food book that addresses our
interest in public engagement. Enjoy!

For the complete list of books that are available in this series, please see
www.upne.com.